The Jacobites

The Author

Frank McLynn was educated at Wadham College, Oxford and the University of London, where he was awarded a PhD in 1976. He has written widely on the Jacobite movement, and his previous books are *France and the Jacobite Rising of 1745* (1981), *The Jacobite Army in England, 1745* (1983) – which won the 1985 Cheltenham Prize for Literature – and *Invasion: From the Armada to Hitler, 1588-1945* (1987).

The Jacobites

Frank McLynn

Routledge & Kegan Paul
London and New York

First published in 1985
Reprinted as a paperback in 1988 by
Routledge & Kegan Paul Ltd
11 New Fetter Lane, London EC4P 4EE

Published in the USA by
Routledge & Kegan Paul Inc.
in association with Methuen Inc.
29 West 35th Street, New York, NY 10001

Set in Garamond, 11 on 12½ pt
by Columns of Reading
and printed in Great Britain
by Thetford Press Limited,
Thetford, Norfolk.

Library of Congress Cataloging in Publication Data

McLynn, F. J.

The Jacobites.
Bibliography: p.
Includes index.
1. Jacobites. 2. Great Britain – History –
1689-1714. 3. Great Britain – History – George I-II,
1714-1760   I. Title.
DA813.M38   1985   941.07   84-2484-7

British Library CIP Data also available

ISBN 0-415-00267-2

To Jack Lindsay with admiration

Contents

Plates

Credits

Preface

The principal source for any student of Jacobitism must always be the vast collection of Stuart Papers at Windsor Castle, for permission to use which I am grateful to Her Majesty the Queen. All lengthy quotations not attributed to an obvious or identified source, particularly in the chapter dealing with the Old and Young Pretenders, may be presumed to be drawn from the Stuart Papers. Since this is not a book addressed to scholars I have not thought it either appropriate or necessary to identify the exact source of a given quote, though any interested party gaining admission to the Stuart archives would be able to locate it in minutes, since the 500-odd volumes are laid out with admirable chronological precision.

Any work of this kind must lean heavily on the detailed work of scholars working on a narrow canvas. I hope my debt to the work of Eveline Cruickshank and Rupert Jarvis in particular will be evident, but Jacobitism is a subject that has undergone an academic revival in recent years and it would be pointless to mention all the fine work that has been done in this field. A recent article of mine in *History Today* (January 1983) gives some idea of its breadth and scope.

I would like to thank my editor at Routledge & Kegan Paul, Andrew Wheatcroft, for his unfaltering commitment to this project. And, naturally, I am most grateful to my wife, Pauline, for having to endure my hermit-like existence during the writing of this book. This she did with her usual unfailing cheerfulness and supportiveness.

Introduction

The Jacobite who maintains that some Bavarian count is the rightful king of England may well, on his own presuppositions, be saying what is true.

A.J. Ayer, *Metaphysics and Common Sense*

When I was an undergraduate at Balliol before the war, there was another undergraduate there, slightly my senior, who later became a distinguished philosopher; but what was remarkable about him was that he was a Jacobite. That is to say, he maintained, both in private and on occasion by public demonstration, that the rightful king of England was not George the Sixth (so-called) but a certain Bavarian prince, called, so far as I remember (appropriately) Rupert, and the nearest heir to the Stuart kings.

R.M. Hare, *Applications of Moral Philosophy*

There are three entries under 'Jacobite' in the *Oxford English Dictionary*. One refers to the Israelite descendants of Jacob, and was also applied to the seventeenth-century Puritan refugees. Another denotes members of a Monophysite sect, taking its name from one Jacobus Baradaeus, who revived the Eutychian heresy in the sixth century. The third, most familiar, definition, and the subject of this book, relates to the followers of James II (Latin *Jacobus*) after his overthrow in 1688.

So far, so clear. But the question then arises: how to define the Jacobite era? It can be defined either very widely or very narrowly. Obviously, Jacobitism in its manifold manifestations

I

was not something that sprang fully-armed from the head of the exiled James II. At its widest, the Jacobite period might embrace the 200-year period from the commencement of the Scottish Stewart dynasty as the *Stuart* royal house of England in 1603 to the death of Henry, Cardinal York, in 1807. At its narrowest, it would extend from the flight of James II in 1688 to the defeat of Culloden in 1746.

The three most representative books on the Jacobites, those by Petrie, G.H. Jones and Lenman, exemplify the possible permutations. Lenman begins in 1603 and ends in 1746. Jones starts in 1688 and terminates with Culloden. Petrie opts for the widest possible span, commencing in 1603 and ending with Cardinal York's death. My solution is different again. For many reasons 1688 makes the most convenient starting point. There is more difficulty about where to end. 1746 is too soon. There are strong arguments for ending the story in 1759 with Conflans's defeat at Quiberon, or in 1766, on the death of James Francis Edward Stuart, the 'Old Pretender', when the pope refused to accept his son Charles Edward as King Charles III of the United Kingdom. In the end I have decided on 1788, the year of Charles Edward's death, as the most appropriate stopping place. This is not just so as to achieve an exact Jacobite century, though one could argue this case along biographical lines (Old Pretender born in 1688, Young Pretender died in 1788), nor to achieve a certain neatness – after all, it could be argued, if there was a Jesuit century in Japan, why not a Jacobite century in Europe?

But there are more profound and cogent reasons for the periodisation I have adopted. Throughout this study it is argued that there was a peculiar milieu that related to the world of the Jacobites. In the years 1787–89 profound changes were under way that would destroy that world forever. In 1787 the Founding Fathers met in Philadelphia to adopt a federal constitution for what would be the United States of America. In 1789 the French Revolution began, obliterating the *ancien régime* of which Jacobitism was an appanage. And in 1788 a new continent was being colonised in Australia. At the very time Charles Edward Stuart lay dying in Rome, the first settlers were landing at Botany Bay. As clear proof that Jacobitism was still seen by its enemies as a living force, the first governor of the Australian colony, Arthur Philip, had to swear that he would not attempt to restore Charles Edward or his successors to the throne of England. As a final argument for ending the Jacobite period in the 1780s, there is the not insignificant consideration that the annexed estates of the 1745 rising were not restored to the descendants of their former owners until 1784.

We are dealing, then, with a Jacobite century in which Europe was profoundly affected, often in subtle ways, by the descendants of an essentially aristocratic exiled clique. The main problem for the presenter of such a crowded canvas is what to leave out. Each chapter below properly merits a book to itself and in many cases has already received it.

The most striking thing about the Jacobites was that they considered kingship to be indefeasible, a God-given right that could not be taken away by man, whatever the monarch did. The logic of this view produces the conclusion that there have been no true *de jure* sovereigns of the United Kingdom since 1688. Some students of kingship, not unnaturally alarmed about the disloyal or treasonable implications of this position, have argued that, according to the laws of tanistry, when Henry Stuart, Cardinal York, accepted a pension for life from George III in 1800, referred to him in a letter to Lord Minto as 'Your Gracious Sovereign' and left him his personal heirlooms, he was in fact assenting to a transfer of the royal office. Yet Cardinal York continued to his dying day to refer to George III as 'the Elector of Hanover'. From a Jacobite standpoint no alleged laws of tanistry could override the divinely appointed doctrine of a king's indefeasible right. The Jacobite position was similar to that taken by international lawyers when confronted by the South American Drago and Calvo doctrines. These clauses, inserted into agreements with multinational companies, denied them the right, in the case of a dispute with the South American nation-state, of appeal to the International Court of Justice. International lawyers pronounced these clauses worthless on the ground that no one can sign away his pre-existing rights under International Law, *even if he should be willing to do so*. So it is with kingship, said the inveterate Jacobite. Whatever Cardinal York did or did not do could not in any way affect the divine, hereditary and indefeasible right of kings. God's law took precedence over all man-made laws or customs.

I have had two main aims in writing this book, one attainable, the other probably not. In the first place, I have tried to avoid . really well-trodden ground. Consequently I have omitted any detailed treatment of the best-known incidents in the Jacobite saga, such as the events leading up to the marriage of Clementina Sobieska to James Stuart, the five-month flight in the heather of Prince Charles in the summer of 1746, or the duke of Cumberland's bloody retribution in the Highlands after Culloden. Those who wish to read about these stirring events can find exhaustive treatment in the works of, respectively, Peggy Miller, Eric Linklater and John Prebble.

Secondly, I have tried to bridge the gap between the academic scholar of Jacobitism and the general reader attracted by the perennial romance of the subject. I am well aware such an attempt is likely to attract the usual fate of all 'liberal' or 'middle of the road' solutions – to be despised by both sides. But in the sincere belief that the fruits of historical scholarship should be conveyed to a wider audience than that of the specialist, I cheerfully submit to my doom.

Chapter 1

Aftermath of revolution: the struggle on the Celtic fringes, 1689–91

La race des Stuarts a mis 119 ans à s'éteindre après avoir perdu
le trône qu'elle n'a jamais retrouvé. Trois prétendants se sont
transmis dans l'exil l'ombre d'une couronne: ils avaient de
l'intelligence et du courage, que leur a-t-il manqué? La main
de Dieu.

Chateaubriand

Curs'd be the Papists, who withdrew
The King to their persuasion
Curs'd be that covenanting crew,
Who gave the first occasion.
Curs'd be the wretch who seiz'd the throne,
And marr'd our constitution.

And curs'd be they who helped on
That wicked revolution
Curs'd be those traitorous traitors who
By their perfidious knavery
Have brought our nation now into
An everlasting slavery.
Curs'd be the parliament, that day
Who gave their confirmation
And curs'd be every whining Whig
And damn'd be the whole nation.

James Hogg, *The Jacobite Relics of Scotland*

I fought at land, I fought at sea,
At hame I fought my Auntie, O
But I met the devil and Dundee
On the braes o' Killiekrankie, O.

Burns

The Jacobite movement came into being when the 'Glorious Revolution' of 1688 removed James II of England from the thrones of England, Ireland, and Scotland (of which he was James VII). Naturally, to understand Jacobitism completely one cannot simply begin in 1688. The Jacobite risings in Britain were fought over a variety of economic, social and religious issues, some of which had their origin during the English Revolution of the 1640s and others of which, such as church lands, dated back to the Reformation itself. Not for nothing do Lenman, Insh and Sir Charles Petrie in their works on the Jacobite movement begin the story much earlier in the seventeenth century than 1688. Nevertheless, one has to start somewhere, and there are many good reasons for starting Ibsen-like *in medias res*. It is worth recording that the Jacobite sensibility itself would have approved of this approach. The eighteenth century's great hero among classical authors was Horace, who in the *Ars Poetica* praised Homer for plunging the reader into the midst of the story of the *Iliad* instead of tracing it *ab ovo* (from the egg of Leda, from which Helen was born).

The story for our purposes, then, begins with the landing of William of Orange at Torbay on 5 November 1688 in response to the secret invitations of large numbers of the English aristocracy, and the flight of James II to France after a miserable month of vacillation and dithering. One of the great historical coups d'état was thus achieved without any significant bloodshed at the outset.

It is worth asking what the 'Glorious Revolution' really represented. According to the Whig theory of history, fashionable in the nineteenth century, it meant the triumph of liberty over despotism. To others it is the most dramatic chapter in a moral or supernatural tale entitled 'The Ill-Fortune of the Stuarts'. The Stewart dynasty of Scotland had been fabled for its misfortunes even before James VI of Scotland became James I of England in 1603 (and hence, in all but Scottish usage, the Stewarts became the Stuarts). Kings of Scotland since 1371, the Stewarts could record in their annals James I murdered, James II killed by accident, James III murdered, James IV killed at Flodden, and, more famously, Mary Queen of Scots beheaded and Darnley assassinated. Since becoming the Stuarts of England, their luck had not changed. Charles I was beheaded, Charles II defeated at Worcester and driven into exile, while 1688 marked James's *second* period of exile (this time permanent). The saga was to continue: later chapters contained James III's seventy-eighty-year-long exile and Charles Edward Stuart, defeated in the 1745 rising, lurching into a pathetic and drunken old age.

To biographers of James II, 1688 has often been taken to be a contingent, even aleatory, historical event that could have been avoided by a wiser or more resolute monarch. Its contingent nature tends to be stressed by all those critical of James II's propensity towards authoritarianism and arbitrary power. Had he kept a low profile on Catholicism, it is argued, and refrained from promoting Catholics in 1687 – tactless, so soon after his ally Louis XIV's revocation of the Edict of Nantes (1685), since it aroused fears of an anti-Protestant pogrom – had he not pressed for the repeal of the Test Act, he would have escaped the taint of 'popery'. Had he not increased the numbers of the standing army from 5,000 to 15,000, thus bringing to a head fears about royal absolutism that never entirely went away while the Stuarts were on the throne, and accentuating the traditional English dislike of standing armies, he would have escaped the reproach of 'tyranny'. Had he not overestimated the grip he had on the country's loyalties and affections – a natural overestimate, given the ease with which he had put down Monmouth's 1685 rebellion – he might have been more on the alert against the machinations of the violently anti-French William of Orange. Had he been politically more astute, he might have kept his nephew Monmouth in the Tower as a hostage and thus cut the ground from under William's feet.

All true, so far as it goes. But if all that was involved in the Glorious Revolution was the replacement of a somewhat wild-eyed monarch by a more biddable one, it would hardly warrant the amount of historian's ink and type that has been expended on it. The truth is that 1688 teaches us something very important about the nature of revolutions. Its significance can only be truly appreciated if it is regarded as the final consolidation of a process begun in 1642.

All cataclysmic revolutions of the 1642 kind exhibit common features. Initially there is a moderate phase, in which the political struggle is *within* the regime, within an existing consensus of goals, values and ideas shared by both sides in the conflict. Then comes a second phase, where the revolution threatens to advance beyond the merely political to become a genuinely social upheaval in which the struggle is *about* the regime. In this second phase the revolution is either pushed through to its radical conclusions (as in Cuba in 1961 or Russia in October 1917) or, more usually, it is arrested as counter-revolution wins the day. The latter process can be seen in the Thermidorean reaction in the French Revolution and in the Carranza/Obregon reaction in the Mexican Revolution. In the English Revolution it was manifested by Cromwell's use of the army against the left in his own party. But as a result of Cromwell's splintering of his own victorious party, once his personal iron grip on England was removed chaos threatened. The men of property took fright. Their own fortunes were in danger. To arrest what they saw as a tide of anarchy, they summoned the Stuarts back from exile.

Yet the *astrea redux* (as Dryden put it) of Charles II's triumphant return to London on that May afternoon in 1660 concealed an irreconcilable conflict in English society. In Charles's mind, he was to be restored to the *status quo ante* the Civil War. To the English landowning aristocracy he was back from exile on probation. His role was not to emulate his father but to guarantee their estates and prosperity by reinforcing Cromwell's Hobbesian state with the emotional trappings that would keep the mob obedient and deferential. Charles II thought that kingship was his by divine, hereditary and indefeasible right. His restorers took a different view of kingship. A monarch held his power on trust from Parliament; it was not indefeasible, it could be revoked for poor or inadequate performance.

The task of the rising mercantile aristocracy was a difficult one. Having defeated feudal and absolutist principles in a great civil war, providing in ideal-type terms the final triumph of capitalism over the old order, they had to make sure that their initial *political* revolution, providing a transfer of power within the elite, was not pushed on by zealots like the Levellers and Diggers to the point of genuine *social* revolution. To achieve this they were forced in 1660 to use the Stuarts. Yet the Stuarts would not necessarily play their game. Charles II was a shrewd politician and, as he put it, he was 'weary of travelling and resolved to go abroad no more', so to a large extent he implicitly accepted the changed facts of regal life while still cleaving to the official ideology of divine right. His brother James had none of his subtlety, as Charles realised: 'When I am dead and gone I know not what my brother will do: I am much afraid that when he comes to wear the crown he will be obliged to travel again.'

James II was unaware of the contradictions in English society and in his own position as king. He confused the instrumental and the affective, took seriously what was meant to be on paper only, seemed to aspire to the reality of absolute power rather than its symbols, and eventually succeeded in convincing large sections of the aristocracy that the gains they had made in the Civil War were in danger. In religion he united both Anglicans and Nonconformists against him, despite his attempts to conciliate the latter party. In foreign affairs he pursued policies subservient to the economic interests of France. A policy of peace with France meant that the Stuarts did not have to be dependent on taxes voted by Parliament.

Put another way, the Restoration of 1660 to 1688 can be seen as a two-stage process. In the beginning the monarch fulfilled the restorers' best hopes: trade and commerce went through a halcyon period, the king seemed to 'know his place'. But towards the end of Charles II's reign the storm clouds began to gather. The Stuart monarchy came to be seen as a fetter on the inchoate financial and commercial capitalism, especially in its alliance with France, the great trading rival. The Exclusion Crisis and the struggle with Shaftesbury were the first signs that all was not well, that the 'new deal' between Parliament and the Stuarts was not working satisfactorily. What was needed in 1685 was a monarch endowed with great powers of realism and skills as a diplomat – someone like 'James III', the Old Pretender, perhaps. Instead there was the doubly disastrous James II – doubly, because to survive the growing rift between king and kingmaker it was necessary for the monarch to have all of Charles II's political expertise but none of his autocratic tendencies. What the three kingdoms got in James II was the precise opposite.

Put simply, there was a structural element in James's fall as well as a conjunctural one. Hence the brilliance of the plan contrived by the Whigs. To invite William over meant in effect cementing the revolution of the 1640s by a second revolution, achieved through a peaceful transfer of power, which would at the same time turn England round to face the one power with whom she had irreconcilable interests: France. The rights of Parliament were to be secured once and for all but without abolishing the monarchy, which played a useful symbolic role. A two-tier sovereignty meant that even if the politicians were discredited, the regime itself would not be.

But, as often happens in such situations, an initially peaceful transfer of power is paid for later by a bloody backlash. The transfer from Kerensky to Lenin and the Bolsheviks was achieved with minimal loss of life. It was the force of White *counter-revolution* that accounted for the millions of dead. Now while the battle casualties caused by the counter-revolution of 1689–91 were numbered in thousands rather than millions, it was in the *reaction* rather than the initial action that the real struggle took place. William landed unopposed, his fleet unchallenged by the Royal Navy. It must have seemed too good to be true, and it was. Once James II had recovered from the trauma of precipitate flight and loss of nerve, he struck back.

Louis XIV treated him royally in all senses of the word. He drew the line, for the moment, at an outright expedition to England itself and steered James's attention towards Ireland. But even before the exiled Stuart monarch could set the Irish project in motion, his supporters in Scotland had taken a hand. The political situation in Scotland in 1688–89 was of Byzantine complexity, particularly in matters of religion, where the esoteric nuances of seventeenth-century Presbyterianism and Episcopalianism seem as baffling to the modern sensibility as the system of gentes among the Iroquois. Any attempt to give a clear account of the many interlocking and intercutting political, economic, religious and clan rivalries is bound to founder ultimately, but suffice it to say that the two key elements in Scotland at the time of the Glorious Revolution were the Parliament or Convention and the charismatic Jacobite leader John Graham of Claverhouse, Viscount Dundee.

Dundee was James's military leader in Scotland and a far more impressive figure than the earl of Balcarran, James's agent in civil affairs. Dundee has frequently been compared to and with his kinsman Montrose, some rating one more highly as general and politician, some the other. But there can be no doubt that as a military captain Dundee was in a very high class. He was a natural man of action and had been with James in London when the news of the Dutch landing came in. In vain did he urge James to stay and fight. When the king fled and William came to London, Dundee returned to Scotland with the few loyal elements of a 4,000-strong army he had originally brought south to fight for James.

Since Scotland was not at the time part of a 'United Kingdom', the nation had to decide whether to accept the Dutchman as king of Scotland. Now were revealed the catastrophic consequences of James's flight. With no worthwhile military arm of the Stuarts to constrain it, the natural Whiggishness of Convention asserted itself. The natural majority in Convention for William and Mary was further increased by the tone of the blustering ukase James sent to it, commanding its loyalty in peremptory tones. The inevitable decision followed; William and Mary were duly offered the crown of Scotland. In a scene immortalised by Scott, Dundee said goodbye to the 'lords of Convention' and set out to seek a military solution to the affairs of Scotland.

But he had to raise an army of infantry to add to his bedraggled cavalry force. Even Cameron of Lochiel joined him with his clansmen, but most of the rest of the clans were uncertain or racked with internal feuds. The sole reinforcements Dundee received from James were a dismounted detachment of Purcell's dragoons. As on all future occasions, communications between Jacobites in the field in Scotland and the leadership in Europe were non-existent. James commenced his Irish campaign while Dundee was in the middle of his Scottish war. If James had reinforced Dundee *before* crossing into Ireland, William would never have dared follow him there.

By July 1689 Dundee had no more than 1,000 men under arms, mostly Camerons and MacDonalds. He was now experiencing the problem that bedevilled all Jacobite commanders in the risings in Scotland: how to keep an army of clansmen in existence over a sustained period of time and how to get the clans to cooperate. It was the fact that Dundee sent many of his Highlanders back to their glens in July because he could not maintain them that decided the Williamite general Hugh Mackay to attack.

Mackay set out to seize Blair Castle, the key strategic position in the Highlands. Dundee reacted swiftly. The fiery crosses were sent out. But at such short notice he could not summon a large force. Though outnumbered perhaps two to one (2,000 as against Mackay's 4,000), Dundee moved to intercept him. Arriving at Blair Castle on 27 July, he learned that Mackay's troops were already in the pass of Killiekrankie. A council of war was held. As usual, the best advice came from Ewen Cameron of Lochiel: attack at once. The Highlanders got to the summit of the pass before Mackay. There they drew up in typical Highland formation, every clan distinct and unmixed with any other. From right to left there were the Macleans, the Irish, the Clanranald MacDonalds, the Glengarry MacDonells, Dundee's cavalry, the Camerons and the MacDonalds of Sleat. After a desultory exchange of musketry, Dundee gave the order to advance.

It was after seven in the evening and the sun was setting in the ravine. When there was only a small space between the armies, the clansmen threw away their firelocks, drew their broadswords and rushed forward with a frightful yell. Mackay's men broke under the charge. The battle was won in two minutes. In vain did Mackay call on his cavalry to charge the Highlanders. The horsemen had seen enough, and joined in the headlong flight of the foot. But in the dying moments of the battle Dundee himself received a mortal wound from a musket ball. Lochiel had warned him not to place himself in the thick of the fray, but Dundee considered that only by a display of personal courage could he hold together his unwieldy army. Dundee's end had all the epic ingredients of Jacobite romance. 'How goes the day?' he asked. 'Well for King James,' came the answer, 'but I am sorry for your lordship.' 'If it is well for him, it matters the less for me,' were Dundee's last words.

Claverhouse's death at the moment of victory was a catastrophe for the Jacobites. Colonel Cannon, who succeeded to the command, was not remotely in the same class as a captain, as soon became clear when the clansmen advanced to consolidate their victory. Although their numbers increased to 5,000 in the aftermath of Killiekrankie, their assault on Dunkeld on 21 August 1689 was beaten off with heavy losses by the Cameronians. This defeat seriously affected the Highland host. Morale slumped, mutual recriminations between Cannon and the Highlanders began, the spirit of faction that Dundee had papered over broke the surface again. Within weeks the Highland army had simply melted away. So ended the Jacobite resistance in Scotland. Not until 1715 would the clansmen be seen in action again. By that time Jacobite sentiment in Scotland had increased dramatically, prompted by the Massacre of Glencoe, the Darien disaster and, most of all, the highly unpopular 1707 Act of Union. But for the moment the focus of Jacobite hopes shifted to Ireland.

By the end of February 1689 the French had made everything ready for James's descent on Ireland. James took leave of Louis XIV at Versailles and landed at Kinsale at the end of March, linking up in Cork two days later with his Lord Deputy, the duke of Tyrconnel. On paper Ireland should have provided an even more favourable arena for the Jacobite reaction than Scotland, but here too factionalism and the cross-cutting rhythms of different and conflicting interest groups were to bedevil operations. The Irish themselves wanted to make use of their co-religionist James Stuart towards the goal of an independent Ireland. The Anglo-Irish and the English who were with James regarded Ireland merely as a stepping-stone to England. There were Catholics who wanted to retain a loose association with England – something like the later Home Rule proposals. And there were the French, who wished to turn Ireland into a military base for operations against Williamite England and its continental allies.

James quickly entered Dublin and set about bringing the whole of the country under his aegis. It was vital that Ulster be occupied quickly, both to prevent William from landing there and to provide a base from which to reinforce Dundee in Scotland. Unexpectedly, the citizens of Derry resisted, fearing massacre by the Catholics. The result was the siege of Derry, a siege whose echoes have come down through the ages. The actual military operations have become obscured in a mist of propaganda emanating from both sides, but it is clear that the siege was vitiated both by the inadequate numbers of the Jacobite investing forces and by the bloodthirsty tactics of the French Field-Marshal Von Rosen, whose scheme to use women and children as hostages to compel Derry's surrender had to be overruled by James himself. The Williamites then scored a tremendous moral victory when the English fleet sailed up the Foyle at the end of July, broke the harbour boom built by the Jacobites, and relieved the city.

Derry's resistance proved crucial in the Irish campaign, for it gave William a bridgehead in Ulster from which to attempt the reconquest of Leinster, Munster and Connaught, all in Jacobite hands by July 1689. By this time, too, Jacobite resistance in Scotland had collapsed and William was free to bring all his strength to bear on 'John Bull's other island'. And, not for the last time in the story of the Jacobites, the French failed to press home their temporary naval superiority by blockading the Irish coast. On 13 August 1689 William's army of Dutchmen and Danes landed in Northern Ireland and quickly occupied Belfast. The onset of winter allowed both sides to prepare for a final campaign in 1690.

The last months of 1689 and the early ones of 1690 saw both sides girding themselves for action. Louis XIV replaced Von Rosen with the duc de Lauzun and effected a famous swap of the best Irish regiments for 7,000 of his own regulars. William for his part poured thousands of reinforcements into Ulster. In June 1690 he arrived in Ireland in person. He then commenced a march on Dublin. On 30 June he reached the river Boyne, having covered fifty miles in seven days. On the south bank of the river he saw the Jacobite forces drawn up. James had the advantage of a defensive position, but William had the better troops and more of them (33,000–36,000 as against the Jacobites' 21,000–30,000). In addition, there were divided counsels in the Jacobite camp about the wisdom of fighting at the Boyne at all. Possibly as a consequence of this dissension, the fords across the river had not been destroyed, nor had the Jacobite flanks been secured.

That afternoon a cannonade was kept up by both sides. The next day, 1 July, dawned bright, sunny and cloudless. The Battle of the Boyne commenced at first light. William ordered his right, under Schomberg, to cross the river farther upstream and then turn the Jacobite left flank. Schomberg's flanking movement succeeded brilliantly; the Irishmen facing him turned and fled. In shame at their countrymen's action, the Irish cavalry made a valiant effort to drive the Dutch and the Danes back into the stream. As the issue on the southern shore of the river hung in the balance, William crossed with his left. He was enabled to do this by the lacklustre performance of Lauzun. When Schomberg detached his forces for the flank attack, a competent commander would have launched across the river at William's left instead of standing on the defensive. Lauzun went one worse. Having waited idly until Schomberg fell on his left, he moved his crack troops, the French, along the southern bank to meet this threat.

This left William with a two-to-one advantage in the main theatre of battle. When the Dutch Blue Guards crossed the river with William for the second phase of the battle, the raw Jacobite levies, unstiffened now by the French veterans, broke and fled. Once again, as on the Jacobite left, it was the cavalry that gave the best account of itself. James Fitzjames, duke of Berwick, James's natural son, held up the Blue Guards and the Danes by a series of successful charges. But force of numbers made itself felt. William gradually worked round the Jacobite right, which should have been protected by the Drogheda garrison but was not.

By noon the Williamites were victorious on both flanks. Despite his advantage, William showed himself a poor commander by allowing the Jacobites to retreat in good order towards Duleek. By sundown James and his defeated army made an orderly arrival in Dublin. Casualties, like numbers engaged, are disputed in the case of the Battle of the Boyne, but it seems that there were at least 1,500 on the Jacobite side and perhaps in excess of 1,000 in the Williamite ranks.

At Dublin James took the disastrous decision to return to France. His apologists claim that he was influenced by the French naval victory at Beachy Head, which seemed to indicate that there was now a chance for a cross-Channel invasion. His Irish allies did not see it like that. They thought of his return to France as a cowardly flight. They saw his action as desertion in the face of the enemy which effectively left them in the lurch. James II never lived down this blow to his reputation nor the canard of his 'cowardice' that subsequently haunted him. Perhaps this explains the headlong withdrawal of the Jacobites into central Ireland. Panic infected the garrisons in Drogheda, Wexford, Kilkenny and Clonmel. William's progress through Dublin to Waterford assumed the dimensions of a walk-over. Only at Athlone, whither the main Jacobite army withdrew, was there a determined resistance. Colonel Richard Grace's defiance not only persuaded the Dutch to raise the siege of Athlone after a week's pounding, but prevented the crossing of the Shannon and bought valuable time for the main army.

The decision was taken to fall back on Limerick and make a last stand there. Lauzun and Tyrconnel, James's viceroy after his departure from Kinsale, were inclined to throw in the towel there and then, but at this point the iron in the Jacobite soul was provided by Patrick Sarsfield, later earl of Lucan, one of the genuine Jacobite heroes, who was to the campaign in Ireland what Dundee had been in Scotland. Sarsfield's advice was that at all costs Limerick must be held. When William arrived before Limerick on 7 August 1690, he found 20,000 Jacobites dug in and 3,500 cavalry under Berwick intelligently strung out so as to prevent the complete investment of the town.

Even so, the Jacobites would not have been able to hold out indefinitely. It was now that Sarsfield pulled off the stroke that, more than anything else, won him his place in the Jacobite hall of fame. Aware that the capture of Limerick would require a very heavy artillery train, William sent for a park of six 24-pounders, two 18-pounders, five mortars, 153 wagons of artillery, plus boats, pontoons and draught horses. It was this formidable train that Sarsfield aimed to put out of action. The night before reaching Limerick the artillery convoy lay at Ballyneety. With a picked force of 500 horsemen Sarsfield set out to destroy it. The soldiers guarding the siege train were sound asleep when, around midnight, Sarsfield's men burst in among them. The entire artillery park was destroyed and its guards slaughtered almost to a man. The mouths of the heaviest guns were stuffed with gunpowder and the entire ordnance piled onto a bonfire which was then lit. The resulting explosion was said to have blasted William out of his slumbers.

This was a dreadful blow to William. After one final attempt to take Limerick by a frontal assault, which was beaten off with heavy losses, the Dutchman gave up, raised the siege and returned to England. Sarsfield's prestige was at its apogee following the artillery explosion. To the Irish he, not James, was the true cause personified. One of his colonels allegedly declared: 'The king is nothing to me. I obey Sarsfield. Let Sarsfield tell me to stab any man in the whole army and I will do it.' It is perhaps not to be wondered at that in 1691 both Tyrconnel and St-Ruth regarded Sarsfield with apprehensive jealousy.

The Jacobites' euphoria over their successful stand at Limerick did not last long. A sober assessment of their chances resulted in the conclusion that a 1691 campaign would deal the *coup de grâce* to James's army. Both Tyrconnel and Lauzun had had enough, and they departed for France in September, leaving the military administration of Jacobite Ireland in the hands of the twenty-year-old Berwick, the future marshal of France. The irony of the new situation was that none of the principals involved in the decisive period of fighting in 1690 (James, William, Lauzun and Schomberg) was even remotely in the second rank as a commander, but now Berwick, arguably the greatest of the Jacobite marshals, was to be faced in the field by the greatest captain of the Glorious Revolution, the duke of Marlborough. By capturing Cork and Kinsale in quick succession, Marlborough achieved more in twenty-three days than all William's Dutch commanders in the whole of the previous year.

By the end of 1690 Jacobite hopes were slender. Only Connaught and western Munster remained in their hands, and of the ports only Limerick and Galway. To make matters worse they were deprived of their only commander of genius: in January 1691 Tyrconnel replaced Berwick on the latter's recall to France. The 1691 campaigning season opened with the Williamite general Ginkel's capture of Athlone. Both Tyrconnel and Sarsfield wanted to construct defensive lines around Limerick, but the new French commander, General St-Ruth, who had come back with Tyrconnel as Lauzun's replacement, felt the loss of Athlone as a personal slur on his reputation and insisted on fighting a pitched battle. Almost a year after the Boyne, on 12 July 1691, the second great battle of the Irish campaign, Aughrim, was fought.

St-Ruth drew up his army in a strong defensive position on the slope of a hill, around which wound a red bog. Near the edge of the marshy ground he constructed a breastwork. Late on the afternoon of Sunday the 12th Ginkel confronted him. Both armies were of roughly the same size, about 20,000 on each side. With Ginkel was the vanquished general from Killiekrankie, Hugh Mackay. Mackay advised an immediate attack. At five in the evening the battle began. The actual combat was a repeat of the Boyne. The Irish fought stubbornly and the Williamites made little progress across the morass. By seven o'clock, with the night closing in, St-Ruth began to think the day was his. 'We will drive them before us to the walls of Dublin,' he cried exultantly. But Ginkel finally managed to break through on the Jacobite left by laying hurdles over the quagmire. With a firm surface to gallop on, the Williamite cavalry began to turn the Jacobite flank.

This was the moment when the battle hung in the balance, but in fact St-Ruth had already lost it by his jealousy of Sarsfield. Sarsfield had been posted in the left rear with the cavalry reserve, out of sight of the battle, with strict orders that he was not to move without an express command. Rather than summon Sarsfield up to deal with Ginkel's cavalry, St-Ruth tried to meet the new threat with his existing resources. Such hubris was not long in meeting its nemesis. A cannonball fired from the extreme range of 800 yards decapitated him. At such short notice and at such a delicate stage of the battle no one on the Jacobite side could take effective control. Their left flank was turned, and after a fierce rearguard action the Irish broke and fled. The first Sarsfield knew of the course of events was when he saw the gaggle of fugitives streaming back towards him. Quickly he withdrew with his intact squadron while the luckless infantry were hunted down and butchered throughout the night. The scale of casualties was enormous. Macaulay recorded this verdict: 'The number of slain was, in proportion to the number engaged, greater than in any other battle of that age.'

Ginkel followed up his great triumph with the capture of Galway. The Jacobites fell back on Limerick. Desperate messages calling for reinforcements were sent to France. Louis XIV decided to make one final effort. A new fleet was fitted out but it arrived too late. The French, as so often later, were serious in their support for the Jacobites but moved too slowly. Tyrconnel had died in August, and Sarsfield, disillusioned with the French after his treatment by St-Ruth, no longer believed that Louis would send help. A Council of War was held and it was decided to negotiate the surrender of all Jacobite forces in Ireland. The Treaty of Limerick was the result. This was the ratification in February 1692 of the articles of capitulation signed by Ginkel. These articles provided for an Act of Indemnity, the restoration of all Catholics to their estates, freedom of employment, profession and worship for Catholics. Cynically William and Mary ratified the Treaty of Limerick knowing its terms would never be kept.

There were two main consequences of the Treaty of Limerick. One was the flight of the 'Wild Geese' from Ireland. Out of 14,000 Irishmen under arms for James, 11,000 chose to follow Sarsfield into exile in France while 2,000 took demobilisation and returned to their homes. Only about 1,000 exercised the option to join Ginkel's army. The other, in flagrant breach of the treaty itself, was the reintroduction of the old 1641 Penal Laws aimed at the Catholic community in Ireland. As a result, no Catholic could vote or take a seat in Parliament, purchase land or hold a long lease. All Catholics were excluded from a career in the armed services and the important professions, from possessing firearms, owning horses or educating their children. All clergy who refused to take the Oath of Allegiance were expelled from the country. The most vindictive aspect of the Penal Laws was their use in the context of the family. By becoming a Protestant, the eldest son of a Catholic could seize his father's estate entire and avoid the otherwise unavoidable necessity of sharing it with his brothers. Moreover, if the wife of a Catholic renounced the faith, she could defy her husband and be freed of any duties towards him with the full backing of the law.

The effect of the Williamite confiscations was to leave only one-seventh of all land in Ireland in Catholic hands. In addition, the Penal Laws were applied with great subtlety by the new regime. Sometimes they were executed with full vigour; more often the authorities turned a blind eye to their infringement in return for good behaviour by the Catholics. The combination of carrot and stick proved most effective and partly explains the quiescence of Ireland during the two great Jacobite rebellions of 1715 and 1745. Ireland, the cockpit of Jacobite resistance from 1689 to 1691, thereafter faded from the Jacobite story. The period of the Protestant ascendancy had begun. But long-term the legacy of the bitterly fought contest of 1689–91 was handed down the generations. The memory of those years refused to go away. Hatreds kindled then live on today in Ireland. 'King Billy' is second in Irish Catholic demonology only to Cromwell, while on the Orange side 'Remember the Boyne' is still a slogan with a powerful emotional charge, as is the satirical song 'Liliburlero' and the tale of the Derry apprentice boys. To the English these events were soon forgotten but, as Santayana once said, those who forget the lessons of history are condemned to repeat them.

Within three years the Glorious Revolution had established itself, having weathered storms in three kingdoms. The revolution appeared to have been consolidated most securely in England. True, there were those who were deeply apprehensive about the schism in the Church of England resulting from the defiance of the Non-Jurors and who felt that the church itself was in danger. But while there were many prepared to combat Whiggism at an ideological level, few campaigned actively for a Stuart restoration. Paradoxically, it was only after 1715, when the Tory party was in effect proscribed, that basic economic motivation led significant numbers of Tories to harbour 'treasonable' thoughts and conspire for the return of the Pretender.

The economic 'take-off' of the new unbridled financial capitalism got under way remarkably quickly. Within a few years the Bank of England, the South Sea Company and the East India Company were arguably more significant institutions than Parliament itself. When later in the Whig era parliaments became septennial, this tendency was reinforced. The most ingenious Whig manoeuvre of all was the creation of the National Debt, which linked the fortunes of debt bondholders with that of the new regime. This is not to say that all debt holders necessarily had an *ideological* sympathy with the Whigs. As Jeremy Black has well remarked: 'To argue that all holders of Bank of England stock were Hanoverian is as ridiculous as to suppose that Trade Unions whose portfolios include South African investments are supporters of apartheid.' But it did mean that the Jacobites constantly had to reassure Englishmen that they would never cancel the National Debt. The issue of the debt became part of a three-sided economic albatross around the necks of the Stuarts which Whig propaganda never tired of playing up: the issue of former church property or 'Abbey lands'; the issue of the Jacobites' 'French connection' in a context where the French were Britain's major competitor worldwide; and the issue of the National Debt in particular and the financial revolution of 1688 in general.

For all that, the revolution had been accomplished with a minimum of bitterness in England. In Ireland the ferocity of the conflict left a bitter aftertaste which was to survive across the centuries. In Scotland the formidable Jacobite fifth column among the clans was still unbroken. Jacobitism was for the moment beaten but by no means cowed. When bad feeling about the 1707 Act of Union and a rising tide of nationalism coalesced with clan Jacobitism, the heirs of William and Mary would have a real struggle on their hands, for the first time since Sarsfield said farewell to Irish shores.

The international dimension

They now *ring* the bells but they will soon *wring* their hands.

Sir Robert Walpole
(on the declaration of the war with Spain in 1739)

Il ne manqua à l'entreprise que la possibilité.

Voltaire, Précis du *siècle de Louis XV*
(on Richelieu's 1745–46 invasion project)

Here's a health to the mysterious Czar
I hope he'll send us help from far
To end the work begun by Mar.

Hogg, *Jacobite Relics*

All these events in Scotland and Ireland were watched with intense interest from across the Channel. It was reported from Paris that all sections of French society had followed the campaign in Ireland with as much excitement as if they had taken place in France itself. And from 1689 onwards one of the dominant patterns in French foreign policy began to manifest itself: a strong ideological, though intermittent, support for the exiled Stuarts.

After the defeat in Ireland, James II returned to St-Germain-en-Laye and sought consolation for the débâcle in meditation and retreat at the monastery of La Trappe. Louis XIV awarded him an annual pension of 600,000 livres. France now had to decide how far it was prepared to press its support for the Stuarts and how this support should be evinced. At first, Louis XIV, prompted by the royal mistress Madame de Maintenon, was inclined to give serious thought to the idea of military invasion. The king and his advisers were impressed by the strength of Jacobitism in Scotland and believed that the multitudinous and multifarious nature of Protestant sects in the British Isles made revolts and risings endemic. Also, many of the leading figures in British politics, like Marlborough, Godolphin and Admiral Russell, had hedged their bets and entered into secret correspondence with St-Germain. Besides, Louis counted on jealousies between the Maritime Powers. Finally, the French navy, after its famous victory off Beachy Head, was in a new mood of self-confidence and ready to brave the perils of the Channel.

Accordingly, although he felt little more than pity for James II personally and seems almost to have despised him, Louis authorised preparations for a descent on England in 1692. An invasion fleet of transports was prepared, with Admiral Tourville commanding a strong escort squadron. In April 1692 James II travelled to the coast of Normandy. Manifestos announcing his triumphant return to Britain were printed. But now for the first time the 'Protestant winds' of the Channel and English seapower combined to point up the hazards of such a seaborne expedition. This was to be a pattern repeated with depressing regularity for the Jacobites over the next seventy years. Contrary winds prevented Tourville's ships from joining the transport fleet, with its 24,000 troops, in the Cotentin. When Tourville finally did clear from Brest, his forty-four ships of the line collided with a superior force (seventy-nine English and Dutch warships) under Admiral Russell. Obedient to Louis XIV's express orders, Tourville engaged in a six-day running fight between Barfleur and La Hógue, which resulted in a complete defeat for the French.

For the time being this was the end of French invasion projects against Britain. The Sun King turned to diplomacy to win allies for the Stuarts. Mistakenly counting on Catholic solidarity among the powers, he announced that any monarch making peace with him would have to recognise, at least implicitly, the favoured position of the exiled dynasty in his affections. In 1692–93 the Emperor Leopold I of Austria appeared as a doughty champion of James II. He suggested that the young prince James Francis Edward Stuart should be universally recognised as the heir presumptive to William and Mary, that until the Stuart prince's accession his family should be paid a pension by England, and that William III should be obliged to promise complete toleration for English Catholics. He even proposed that France and the Maritime Powers should together conquer Egypt or one of the Barbary states as a kingdom for James II.

All of these diplomatic initiatives on behalf of the Stuarts came to nothing. Austria, Sweden, Denmark and Holland were all involved in negotiations to secure a rapprochement between James II and William III, but neither William nor the Dutch were prepared to accept James Stuart as a legitimate successor on the demise of William and Mary. James II for his part refused to renounce his own rights in favour of his son while he was alive. The French kept James in the dark about their complex diplomacy on his behalf, while he himself suspected that they would ditch him to obtain a favourable European peace. Above all, hopes of persuading the powers that the cause of Catholicism and Jacobitism was one and indivisible were torpedoed by Pope Innocent XII's unsympathetic attitude to the House of Stuart. So by 1695 the pendulum swung back in the direction of military endeavours, especially since the death of the childless Queen Mary in that year seemed to make the question of the succession in England a matter of urgency.

Louis XIV now ordered a major expedition to be made ready in the ports of Dunkirk and Calais, under the command of the marquis d'Harcourt. Sixteen thousand troops were assembled. James's illegitimate son, the duke of Berwick, crossed into England to assess the strength of the English Jacobites. Here too one of the constants in the story of French support for the Stuarts first became apparent: the consistently poor quality of the English Jacobites. As on so many future occasions, the English Jacobites were only prepared to rise in revolt once a substantial French army had landed on English soil; the French for their part would only set sail when the standard of revolt had already been raised in England by a credible Jacobite party. The impossibility of squaring this vicious circle vitiated every single project for a French invasion to restore the Stuarts up to 1759. In addition, in 1695 the English Jacobites revealed another of their endemic characteristics: hopeless incompetence in matters of secrecy or intrigue. A plot to assassinate William in February 1696 at Turnham Green was easily discovered and the conspirators arrested.

Faintheartedness by James II, incompetence by the English Jacobites, contrary winds in the Channel and an unceasing English blockade – all of these factors contributed to the running fiasco of 1696–97, while Louis's troops remained bivouacked round Calais. By 1697 the Jacobites had missed their chance. The French were now deep in peace negotiations with the Dutch. In May a peace congress opened at the palace of Ryswick near The Hague. The stumbling-block to the signing of a treaty was the Stuarts. Louis XIV categorically refused to recognise William III. Meanwhile the attitudes of the two principal contenders were harder than ever. William thought the time was ripe to prise Louis away from the Jacobites and settle the succession on his wife's sister, Anne, and her children. James, on his side, refused to discuss a compromise solution in favour of his son and insisted on his legal right to the English throne. An ingenious solution to the problem, whereby James would be offered the now vacant throne of Poland, was also rejected by James, though Louis urged it on him, since the exiled Stuart feared the French would use this as a pretext to abandon support for his claim to the English crown. Louis grew impatient with his protégé and finally agreed to sign the Treaty of Ryswick in September 1697. Without formaliy undertaking to abandon James II or to expel him from his kingdom, Louis XIV agreed to recognise William as king of England, and to desist from aiding his enemies and those of his successors, either directly or indirectly.

The one concession Louis did secure for the Stuarts at the Peace of Ryswick was to get the English to agree to pay the jointure of James's queen, Mary of Modena, after James's death. William hoped to use his pledge on this point as an entering wedge to force the expulsion of the Stuarts from French territory, but at this point Louis dug in his heels. The Sun King felt he had been pushed to the limit of his religious and political principles by recognising William III and was not prepared to be prodded any further on the Stuart issue. As if to emphasise his determination, when James II and his queen attended the wedding of the duke of Burgundy, the dauphin's eldest son, on 7 December 1697, Louis XIV made a point of having Mary of Modena seated between himself and James at the banqueting table.

Jacobite hopes of restoration rose with the death, in 1700, of Princess Anne's sole surviving heir, the duke of Gloucester. But they immediately plummeted again when the 1701 Act of Settlement named the Hanoverian dynasty as successors to the present incumbents on the ground that the Hanoverians were Protestant. Further problems arose for the Jacobites with the death of James II in September 1701, following a stroke. Louis's ministers advised him to seize this opportunity of breaking with the Stuarts and not to recognise James Francis Edward as the true king of the three kingdoms. Louis, however, used the occasion to demonstrate his belief in 'once a king, always a king'. Besides, Louis was not insensitive to the argument that if James Francis's royal title was refused him, this amounted to a denial of his legitimate birth. Louis had seldom showed his absolutist tendencies more clearly than at this juncture. At the cabinet meeting called to discuss the issue, his ministers were unanimous against recognition. Torcy told him that such a step would alienate the English, would amount to a rejection of the Treaty of Ryswick, and would be an empty gesture. It might even be counter-productive, for the young Stuart prince could then be represented by English propaganda as the French king's puppet.

But Louis's mind was suffused with the reality of the divine right of kings. The influential advocacy of Madame de Maintenon, now a close friend of Mary of Modena, weighed strongly with him. Hearing that James II was on the point of death, he went to St-Germain with great pomp, gathered the Jacobite worthies around the deathbed and declared to the half-conscious James: 'I come to tell your Majesty that, whenever it shall please God to take you from us, I will be to your son what I have been to you, and will acknowledge him as king of England, Scotland and Ireland.' The English, however, took the recognition of the 'Pretender' as both an insult and a breach of the Treaty of Ryswick.

With the outbreak of war between England and France in 1702 (part of the wider War of Spanish Succession), Jacobite hopes rose again. England seemed likely to throw away all that had been gained by diplomacy in 1697. Once again schemes to invade the British Isles or to raise revolts in Scotland and Ireland proliferated. Some of these Louis XIV took seriously, even to the point of sending secret missions to Scotland to sound out opinion there, without bothering to inform St-Germain. In the missions of 1705 and 1707 by Torcy's agent Colonel Nathaniel Hooke lay the origins of the 1708 enterprise, the most substantial entered into by Louis XIV on behalf of the Stuarts. Discontent in Scotland had now built up to a pitch where the French expected to be joined by an army of 25,000 Scottish infantry and 5,000 cavalry once they made landfall. A series of events had brought Scotland to the brink of open rebellion, principally the failure in 1704 of the Darien Company in Panama and the 1707 Act of Union, which inclined even Scottish Presbyterians to the Pretender's side.

Nevertheless, it was clear that only a substantial effort from France could crystallise all the latent discontent. What swung Louis over to making a major commitment was the backing for the Stuart restoration project from his most trusted adviser, the duc de Chevreuse, who urged its acceptance strongly on Minister of Marine Pontchartrain, Foreign Secretary Torcy, and Chamillart, the Minister for War. So it was that at the end of February 1708 6,000 Franco-Jacobite troops were embarked at Dunkirk under the command of General Comte de Gace. Louis's declaration of intent stated: 'The king of France has judged the time ripe to crown his services of nearly twenty years past for the late king of England and for the king, his son, and to revenge the insults suffered by the monarchy from the last revolution in England.' However, it is most significant that Louis declared that 'James III' must remain satisfied with Scotland for the time being. Only on Queen Anne's death should he inherit the three kingdoms.

As with all pro-Jacobite projects, the 1708 endeavour was plagued with bad luck from the very beginning. First, James himself caught measles. Next, the squadron under Admiral Forbin left for Scotland late as a result of bureaucratic delays at the Ministries of War and Marine. When Forbin reached Scotland, he found the English admiral Byng barring the way to the Firth of Forth. Unsure of his reception in south-east Scotland, Forbin hoist sail and returned to Dunkirk. Such was the fiasco of 1708. The following year both Torcy and Marshal Villars joined the Jacobite duke of Berwick in urging an expedition from Brest to the west of Scotland. But once again the circumspection of the British Jacobites and lack of decisiveness at St-Germain proved the Stuarts' undoing. Sensing another débâcle, Torcy advised Louis to call off the 1709 descent on Scotland.

Once more, having failed to find a military solution to the Stuart problem, Louis XIV was forced back into diplomacy.

Inconclusive negotiations with the English Tories dragged on until the problem was subsumed in the general peace signed at Utrecht in 1713. As a precondition for their signature, the Maritime Powers demanded the withdrawal of James from France. He retired to the duchy of Lorraine. In Articles 4 and 5 of the final treaty Louis promised to recognise the Protestant succession, and never to allow James to return to France or help the enemies of the Protestant succession or those of the present queen of England.

Despite the grievous blow to the Jacobites dealt by the Treaty of Utrecht, the imminent death of Queen Anne seemed to offer them some solace. Perhaps the Stuarts could be restored peaceably after her decease. But any chance of this foundered when James III refused to renounce his Catholic faith. At this Louis began to conclude that the Jacobite cause was hopeless and started to distance himself from their aspirations. With Anne's death in 1714, an energetic and able man could have secured a Stuart restoration. Scotland, Ireland and the north and west of England were still strongly pro-Stuart. But James was not a man of the right calibre. Consequently, nothing prevented the Whig commercial classes from welcoming the Elector of Hanover as the new king George I.

Even after George's accession, he was so unpopular, as a dour, boorish German king, that a man of no political genius could have unseated him. Despite the spate of riots that swept through the country in the autumn of 1714, James did not know how to turn events to his own advantage. Louis, now tired of war, continued cautious and did not help the Stuarts. Only with the flight of Bolingbroke to the Pretender's court in 1715 did the Jacobites receive a source of fresh ideas, even if these were inspired purely by Bolingbroke's careerism; his Jacobitism was always spurious. But Bolingbroke was disappointed with the lacklustre personal qualities of James when he finally met him at Commercy. Consequently, it was the duke of Berwick who took part in the tripartite talks of June 1715 between the Jacobites, the French (represented by Torcy) and the Swedes. Although Louis XIV was determined not to break the undertakings he had given at Utrecht, he acknowledged that events were propitious for an expedition to restore the Stuarts. He managed to persuade his grandson Philip V of Spain to contribute 100,000 gold crowns to the Stuart war chest, but was unable to inveigle Sweden.

Although Sparre, the Swedish ambassador, urged on his king the golden opportunity presented by the tripartite scheme to strike back at his ancient enemy, the Elector of Hanover, possibly by landing troops from Gothenburg in Tyneside, Charles XII refused to participate. He feared the entry of British warships into the Baltic.

The failure to embroil Sweden was followed by the flight to France of the Protestant Jacobite duke of Ormonde, who had been preparing a rising in the west of England. The English authorities acted quickly against him before he could coordinate movements with Jacobites on the Continent. So it was that two of the leading pieces crucial to Jacobite success in 1715 (Ormonde and the Swedes) were removed from the board before ever the rebellion of '15 was launched. As ever, the English authorities showed themselves in acumen and enterprise to be far ahead of the Pretender's court.

Louis XIV, now a dying man, watched these developments with a mixture of cynicism and his old ambivalence. On 1 September he died. The French played no part in the '15 rising, which took place in the autumn of that year. The Stuarts' strongest supporter had left the scene by the time of Preston and Sheriffmuir. As Bolingbroke presciently remarked: 'The king was the best friend the Chevalier had. My hopes sank as he declined and died when he expired.'

The death of Louis XIV closed the golden age of French involvement with the Jacobites. For nearly thirty years France pursued a pacific policy towards England, Cardinal Fleury being in this regard the perfect complement to Sir Robert Walpole in England. Not until 1743 did France once again wholeheartedly embrace a scheme for the military restoration of the Stuarts. It is clear, then, that the personal attitude of Louis XIV towards the exiled dynasty was not without significance. There can be no doubting the Sun King's personal affection for the Stuarts. He deeply respected a cause dogged by so much bad luck, which as a Christian king he could interpret as a terrestrial trial sent by God to the exiles, prior to his according them eternal salvation. Even hostile critics had to admire the nobility, even quixotism, of his treatment of James II. This was, of course, a consequence of Louis's conviction that James was, like himself, one of God's annointed. For this reason he was prepared to spend more money on James and the Jacobite exiles than he could really afford. He provided him with lavish food and lodgings, allowed him to wear the fleur-de-lys on his coat of arms, raised no objection when James insisted on retaining his title of Defender of the Faith. He even apologised personally to James after the Treaty of Ryswick, explaining that he had recognised William as the English king purely as a matter of form. Louis continued to ascribe to James II, and to his son 'James III', all the concomitant attributes of majesty, most notably the right to touch for the king's evil (scrofula) then regarded as the very symbol of divine grace. Madame de Sévigné remarked: 'The king's magnanimous soul enjoys playing this grand role. What could be more in keeping with the image of the Almighty than standing by a king who has been expelled, betrayed and abandoned like this one.'

Louis's solicitude for James masked an ideological struggle between England and France after 1688, the conflict of Bossuet and Locke, the divine rights of kings versus the divine right of property. The Jacobite issue coloured the ideological conflict between the two states but was not its real cause. France and England were locked in a combat that would have taken place whatever the fate of the royal house of Stuart. Why, then, was Anglo-French conflict endemic from 1688 to 1715 and beyond? There can be many answers to this question. To some observers, the notion of an ideological clash between feudalism and capitalism until 1789, with French absolutism and British constitutional monarchy providing the respective political expressions, has seemed attractive. Others emphasise that in the early eighteenth century there was a great power vacuum which Britain and France simply filled. Yet another school emphasises a kind of Athens–Sparta culture clash, exacerbated on the English side by psychological fear of a more powerful neighbour, possessing three times the population (at the beginning of the eighteenth century) and a stronger economic base. Nearly all are in agreement that Catholicism played a role only in the world of propaganda, since eighteenth-century states did not conduct policy or go to war for religious reasons. For this reason, persistent Jacobite attempts to make the cause of the Stuarts and the cause of the Catholic church as one always ended in failure.

But beyond these cultural and ideological factors, Britain and France were for the entire Jacobite period engaged in a titanic economic and commercial struggle, waged world-wide. India, North America, Latin America were all cockpits of this unceasing economic battle which the British looked increasingly like winning as the eighteenth century wore on. Jacobitism, then, often provided the focus or immediate form of a struggle whose roots lay deeper. For this reason too much should not be made of Louis XIV's apparently idiosyncratic preference for the Stuarts, and in particular for his determination to recognise 'James III' in 1701. Nancy Mitford in *The Sun King* states: 'It is very improbable that the English with their dislike of continental wars would have implemented it [war], had they not been infuriated by this unlucky step . . . the Pope wrote a letter, congratulating Louis on so singular a proof of his piety. That, and the melancholy smiles of Mary of Modena were the only satisfactions he ever had from this decision.'

But the truth is that in 1701 economic factors undoubtedly counted more with both sides. In that year Louis XIV had purchased from a Portuguese company the unexpired portion of their slave contract – the *asiento*. Moreover, on 6 September of that year a decree was passed prohibiting the entry of English textiles into France. These were the factors that weighed with the dominant Whig mercantile class and made them ready for war. Once again we can see how nations' 'objective interests' can be camouflaged by ideology, so that the issue of the legitimacy of the Pretender, which even Louis's ministers had conceded was a somewhat vacuous matter, could be presented as *the* main source of hostility between these two antagonistic powers. And even if we can demonstrate that the French kings Louis XIV and XV were totally sincere in their wish to restore the Stuarts – and I think we can – it does not follow that this was ever *the* principal or even *a* principal French policy aim. Even an absolute monarch had to consult the farrago of aristocratic pressures that passed in the eighteenth century for the 'national interest'. Accordingly, it is not surprising to find that Anglo-French antagonisms, so far from decreasing with the disappearance of the Jacobite factor in international politics, actually increased.

We cannot even be sure how far the kings of France concurred in the totality of Jacobite ambitions, even when they did sincerely back them. Did Louis XIV, and later Louis XV, aim to restore the Stuarts to all the crowns of England, Scotland and Ireland, to only one of them, or to the two Celtic kingdoms alone? The evidence does not allow us to answer this question decisively, but we *can* say that if ideology alone underlay the

French commitment to the Stuarts, the question could not even be posed meaningfully. Wholehearted commitment to divine, hereditary and indefeasible right would logically entail a wish for restoration to the three kingdoms.

What were the advantages and disadvantages for both sides of the association between France and the Jacobites? Probably, on balance, the Jacobites benefited more. As the dreary years of exile wore on, it became more and more apparent that the only way the Stuarts would return to London was at the point of a French bayonet. As Louis XV's minister the duc de Noailles pointed out to him: 'If your majesty truly wishes to see a Stuart king crowned in London, you will have to send 30,000 French troops as altar boys.' This meant that a policy of war was vital for the Jacobites. On the other hand, their alliance with the French made them vulnerable to skilful Whig propaganda about 'popery' and 'arbitrary government' – the two phrases were invariably used together by Whig ideologues in a kind of inevitable association of ideas.

For the French, the Jacobites represented a legitimate means whereby they could cripple their great rival and take her out of the battle for global hegemony. True, this was to play for very high stakes, and most of the time the French saw only the stake money being paid out with none of the winnings accruing. French public opinion was far from unanimous on the advisability of protecting the Stuarts. Some French observers felt that Louis XIV's protection of James II and 'James III' worsened relations between France and the European Catholic rulers, by ensuring that these remained within a Protestant alliance. This made it more difficult to achieve a lasting peace. From 1689 to 1715 there was a persistent undercurrent of opinion on all sides, even among some English Jacobites, that it would be better for the Stuarts to move to Lorraine, Berne or the Electorate of Cologne. During Louis XIV's reign the papacy continually advocated that the Stuart court should leave France.

Relations between the French and the Jacobites can almost be seen as symphonic in form. The period 1715–40 is best considered as one in which, after the ferocious first movement of Bourbon support for the Stuarts from 1689 to 1713, a slow andante of indifference prevails. Then, from 1740 to 1748 there is a stirring allegro of pro-Jacobitism followed by a short final movement from 1756 to 1759. Certainly Louis XIV's death marked a turning point in French assistance to the Jacobites. For the next twenty-five years they looked in vain for support from Versailles. Louis's nephew, the duc d'Orléans, now regent (Louis XV being five years old in 1715), showed quickly the way he meant to go on. Louis XIV had always had a soft spot for the Stuarts and had consistently seen value in the possibility of civil war in England as a means of keeping the British out of the Low Countries. There was also the principle of divine right at stake. Naturally enough, the regent was not so concerned about the latter point. He took a hard-headed view of French interests. He was prepared to play the Jacobite card if it could be shown to help the French economy or if George I went back on the Treaty of Utrecht, but otherwise he wanted to keep the Stuarts on a tight rein.

There was talk of Orléans providing arms and men for the 1715 rising in return for the marriage of James Stuart to his second daughter, Mademoiselle de Valois – this was supposed to have been arranged by Bolingbroke and was his sole 'contribution' to the '15 – but it came to nothing. Actions spoke louder than words. In response to protests from the earl of Stair, the British ambassador in Paris, that twelve Jacobite ships lay in northern French ports loaded with muskets, swords and powder barrels, Orléans showed himself a master of icy detachment. He did not give the ships up to Admiral Byng, as Stair had demanded, but ordered them unloaded so that they were useless to the rebellion. He then pointed out to Stair with cold correctness that he had taken the action purely and simply out of conformity to the Treaty of Utrecht. Nevertheless, this was a severe blow to James, who had to creep around France dressed as a sailor before he embarked at Dunkirk in December.

Orléans maintained his steely detachment from the Jacobites until his death in 1723. But the approach of Louis XV's majority brought no comfort for the exiles, for a new star appeared at Versailles. This was Cardinal Fleury, who was to be the most powerful voice in French foreign affairs from 1726 to 1743. While the long European peace lasted, Fleury wanted even less to do with the Jacobites than Orléans had. When George I died in 1727, James thought this might be another opportunity for him to present himself to his rightful subjects. He raced through northern Italy to Lorraine, eager to embark once more for the British Isles. But Fleury refused to allow him to set foot on French soil. James was not like his son when it came to defying the French, so he slunk disconsolately back to Rome.

The Jacobites had to wait until 1740, the year of general warfare in Europe for the Austrian succession, before they again received encouragement from France. War always provided the Jacobites with their best opportunities, and even the circumspect Fleury now began to see a use for them. But still Fleury drew back from a full-scale French invasion in favour of the Stuarts. He inclined towards fomenting a diversionary rising in Scotland. This led James to conclude that the French were interested in restoring his dynasty to the throne of Scotland alone. So three years passed in circular and inconsequential negotiations.

But with Fleury's death in January 1743 the Jacobites' hour seemed to have struck at last, especially as James's confidant, Cardinal Tencin, was expected to ascend to the position of First Minister. When Louis XV declared that henceforth he would be his own prime minister, Jacobite hopes seemed to have been dashed once again. But events in Europe nudged Louis towards support for the Stuarts. The war was going badly in Germany. Louis's network of alliances had failed and France itself now seemed in danger of invasion. Reasoning that attack was the best form of defence, Louis planned to invade England without warning and without a declaration of war.

To throw a cloak of legitimacy over the enterprise Louis put out feelers to the Stuart court in Rome. He asked that Charles Edward, the 'Pretender's' elder son, accompany the expedition. The ever-cautious James, fearful that a change in French policies might lead to his son's incarceration, dithered and vacillated but eventually gave his consent, or rather washed his hands of the affair and allowed his son to make the decision. Characteristically, Charles Edward took up the offer with alacrity. Leaving Rome early in January 1744, he made his way to Paris without incident.

Meanwhile bureaucratic delay at Versailles was proving fatal to the French enterprise. On paper their plan was admirable: a diversion under Earl Marischal Keith with 3,000 men in the Highlands and an army of 10,000 veterans under France's greatest soldier, the comte de Saxe, to be landed near London. Admiral de Roquefeuil was meanwhile to stand out from Brest with a squadron of twenty-two ships, and lure the English fleet down to the Isle of Wight, thus allowing Saxe to cross unimpeded. If the French could have crossed the Channel in January, surprise would have been complete. But Roquefeuil disastrously botched his part of the plan and narrowly escaped annihilation by Admiral Sir John Norris. Meanwhile London had learned of Charles Edward's flight from Rome and began to put two and two together. With the issue in the balance the weather, staunchest of all friends of the Glorious Revolution, took a hand. A violent storm at the beginning of March 1744 struck Saxe's transports in Dunkirk Roads. Twelve vessels were lost, seven of them with all hands. While Versailles pondered whether to call off the expedition, a second storm struck five days later and settled the argument once and for all.

Paradoxically, with the expedition abandoned and England safe, France finally issued a formal declaration of war. Charles Edward experienced the first of his many angry disillusionments with Versailles. When pleas and cajolery failed to persuade Louis XV to revive the invasion attempt, the young prince began to toy with the idea of going it alone. With the aid of a Franco-Irish clique based on Nantes and St-Malo – represented by men like Antoine Walsh and Pierre André O'Heguerty – he began to collect arms and money for a voyage to Scotland without the knowledge of the French court. In July 1745 the *Doutelle* (or *Du Teillay*) and the *Elisabeth* sailed from Nantes to western Scotland, carrying the prince, the 'seven men of Moidart' and a small quantity of ammunition. The 1745 rising had begun.

Taken by surprise by the landing of the Stuart prince in Arisaig, the French court, instead of committing itself fully at the outset, vacillated and waited to see how events would turn out. This was a decision that was to have disastrous consequences. When Charles Edward's victory at Prestonpans in late September convinced Louis XV that the '45 was a serious affair, he gradually wore down the opposition of powerful ministers in his Council of State (as ever, the Council was divided on the Jacobite question). A full-scale expedition was then prepared: some 15,000 men under Louis's favourite the duc de Richelieu were to land on the south coast of England, catching the Hanoverian armies between two fires. The expedition was to prepare openly at Dunkirk, making the English think landfall was to be somewhere in the Thames estuary, but at the last moment the troops were to be embarked at Calais and Boulogne ready to cross and secure a bridgehead near Rye.

In London the duke of Newcastle and the other Whig ministers trembled at the prospect of a combined assault from the

Highland army in the north and the French in the south. But alas for the Jacobites, there was no communication between the two forces. Shortage of money forced Charles Edward to march south from Edinburgh and invade England before the French were ready. Richelieu heard about the retreat from Derby while he was still at Boulogne. With his resolve weakened but not yet abandoned, the weather and the Royal Navy did the rest. Admiral Vernon dealt the *coup de grâce* to the French invasion plan by learning of the projected switch of the assault force from Dunkirk to Boulogne and moving in to blockade the latter port. After a month of mental anguish Richelieu threw in the towel and returned to Paris. Thus ended serious French assistance for the '45. Some troops were landed in Scotland, but the French treasure ship bearing vital caches of louis d'or was intercepted and Culloden was the result. The French did, however, retrieve their reputation at the eleventh hour by a sustained and eventually successful attempt to locate Charles Edward and rescue him after his legendary five months in the heather.

The honeymoon with the French did not last long. Charles Edward's monomania about regaining the throne for the Stuarts soured relations with his saviours. At first, on his return to Paris, he was lionised, but when he realised there was no immediate assistance to be got from France, his mood changed and his relations with the French court worsened. Matters came to a head with the signing of the Treaty of Aix-la-Chapelle in 1748, which terminated the War of Austrian Succession. The treaty required the expulsion of Charles Edward from France but the prince, unlike his father after the Treaty of Utrecht, refused to go. No amount of cajolery or promises of pensions could move him. In the end Louis XV had no choice. In December 1748 the Stuart prince was arrested while entering the Paris Opera House, imprisoned briefly at Vincennes and then expelled to Avignon.

So bitter an ending to a once thriving relationship might have seemed the final chapter to all contacts between France and the Jacobites, but there was one act still to play. With the coming of the Seven Years' War the French once more thought of an invasion of England on behalf of the Stuarts. Lally-Tollendal, Stanislaus Leszynski and the duc de Belle-Isle were among those who, as early as 1755, had urged projects for a descent on England on Louis XV. All were aware that another war with England was imminent.

Cardinal de Bernis, the French Foreign Minister, wanted none of it. Not until he was replaced by the duc de Choiseul, in December 1758, did the final French attempt to restore the Stuarts get off the ground. So keen on the idea was Choiseul that Charles Edward allowed himself to be reconciled to Madame de Pompadour and through her to arrange a meeting with Choiseul. The meeting took place in the garden of the Hôtel de Choiseul on 7 February 1759. Although the prince arrived very drunk, Choiseul was able to assure him that Louis XV was even then gathering a mighty fleet to carry him back to England.

The Scottish Jacobites were contacted through Lord Blantyre, who proposed a landing on the west coast of Scotland, a manifesto promising the resumption of Scotland's old laws and customs, and Lord George Murray as military commander. He asked for food and clothes for 20,000 Highlanders and a French force of 8,000 troops. If possible, diversionary landings should be made in Wales and on the east coast of Scotland.

The usual problems of liaison and mutual suspicion between the French and the Jacobites in the British Isles and their agents dogged the preparations. Charles Edward himself complained that Choiseul was keeping him in the dark. Choiseul for his part did not trust the Jacobites' discretion or their security. His main interest in 1759 was in trying to draw the Swedes into a joint Franco-Swedish-Russian naval operation to compel Britain and Prussia to sue for peace. The Swedish leaders drew back at the prospect of such a bold enterprise. Sweden was riven with factionalism, and the Swedes were fearful of getting too deeply embroiled with Prussia, whose Protestantism they respected, and with Britain, on whom they depended for their iron trade. Consequently Swedish diplomats gave Choiseul lukewarm guarantees only. The Russians for their part were reluctant to cooperate with their old Scandinavian enemy on such a scale. For various reasons, too, Spain and Austria were unwilling to participate.

On 14 July 1759 Choiseul informed Louis XV's Council that because of French losses in Canada, Africa and India and the stalemate in Germany he proposed that an army be embarked at Le Havre to make landfall at Portsmouth. A diversionary force would clear from Brest and disembark at Glasgow. The Channel crossing would take place at night to gain the element of surprise and would be on a scale not seen since the Spanish Armada. No less than 337 ships and 48,000 men would be involved. Twelve flat-bottomed Swedish cargo boats would be equipped with cannon and act as floating batteries to protect the fleet. There was little opposition to the plan in the king's Council; the entire discussion turned on how to finance it.

Naval preparations went on on a vast scale at Le Havre, Brest, Toulon and Rochefort, while troops were assembled in Ostend, Dunkirk, St-Omer, Lille and Vannes. To a large extent the Jacobites themselves were kept in the dark about detailed planning. Choiseul and the duc d'Aiguillon, who was to command the Scottish diversion, thought that Charles Edward might not have 'a steady enough head' to play much of a role. Choiseul expected that at the very least the French could wrest Scotland away from the Hanoverians and against this outcome gave d'Aiguillon plenipotentiary powers to negotiate a peace settlement with England.

But by this time the formidable English secret service knew of the plan. The duke of Newcastle, alarmed at the scale of French ambitions, counselled a negotiated peace. Yet Pitt remained calm, confident that British naval supremacy would see her through. He feared Choiseul's overtures to the Swedes and Russians more than his mighty armada.

At this juncture the French Navy Minister Nicolas Berryer took fright at the thought of the unwieldy Swedish flat-bottoms duelling in the Channel with the Royal Navy. Together with the War Minister Marshal d'Estrées he insisted that the expedition could go ahead only if a large squadron of warships escorted the invaders. These wrecking tactics of the French Ministry of Marine were added to by the guns of the Royal Navy. Admiral La Clue left Toulon in August and passed through the Straits of Gibraltar, but his fleet was destroyed by the British off the Portuguese coast. This made the invasion of England impossible, given Berryer's premises. Still, Choiseul clung to the 'special expedition' of d'Aiguillon to Scotland. By this time the Jacobites under Charles Edward were chafing at the delays and warning the French that if there were no simultaneous landing in England, no one in Scotland would rise. Relations between Charles Edward and Choiseul plummeted, especially when the Foreign Minister tried to get the prince to commit himself clearly by signing a declaration in which he formally withdrew from a descent on Scotland alone.

On 25 November 1759 Admiral Hawke destroyed the Brest fleet under the comte de Conflans at Quiberon Bay, south of Belle-Isle. This decisive battle put an end for all time to French attempts to restore the Stuarts. With it too went any hope of saving Canada or India by defeating the English in England. Yet the daring raid by Thurot on Ireland in the same year showed what could have been achieved with the right degree of commitment from all the French ministers. As always with the French, it was too little, too late.

Although Choiseul himself returned to the idea of an invasion of England in 1768, the Jacobites were not involved. The last chance for them had gone at Quiberon and everyone knew it. But even those resigned to the new realities were unprepared for the aggressive anti-Jacobitism of the new king Louis XVI in 1774. 'The Stuarts are an unlucky family; I wish to hear no more of them,' said Louis, thus bringing to an end nearly a hundred years of ideological and dynastic support from France for the 'Pretenders'. So set was Louis XVI against the Jacobites and all their works that he refused to pay the French pension of 40,000 crowns a year to Charles Edward, originally offered to him as the main inducement to marry. Even in financial terms the 'bonnie Prince's' ill-fated marriage to Louise of Stolberg did not get off to a happy start. All Charles Edward's inveterate bitterness towards France seemed vindicated by Louis XVI's attitude. Had Charles lived another year to see the French Revolution or another five to see Louis's execution, there is no reason to think he would have mourned the king's passing. Yet, according to Chateaubriand, the Stuarts' links with the Bourbons could not be shrugged off so easily. Writing in 1807 he gave it as his opinion that 'the fatality attached to the Stuarts dragged with them in the dust other kings, among whom was Louis XVI'.

Even at the zenith of the Jacobite cause, French foreign policy paid a high price for its support of the House of Stuart. Moreover, the intellectual image of France in Europe was tarnished by its association with the Jacobites as the influence of the Enlightenment deepened and Whig propagandists successfully coopted it as being in some way linked with the new currents after the Glorious Revolution. But the relationship was not all loss for France. Jacobite diaspora, particularly after the failure of the 1745 rising, enriched France by the cross-fertilisation of French and English culture, and made an important contribution to the development of French financial, mercantile and industrial capitalism.

Of all the supporters of the Stuart dynasty, the most faithful was the papacy. After 1715 the Jacobite court in exile was always on papal territory. Yet it would be a mistake to think of Vatican policy towards the 'Pretenders' as monolithic. Not only is an awareness of chronology all-important here, since the popes became more lukewarm as the Jacobite cause seemed a lost one, but there is also the fact that different popes had very different attitudes to the Stuarts within the general parameters of token support. There were many pontiffs in the eighteenth century: cardinals were elevated to Peter's throne when they were already at an advanced age; it was expressly intended that their reigns should be short. This was partly to assure a constant mobility in the career ranks of the hierarchy and partly out of the superstition that bad luck would attend any pope who reigned longer than St Peter (whose tenure was said to have lasted six years). As a result James Stuart had to deal with six different popes (Clement XI, 1700–21; Innocent XIII, 1721–24; Benedict XIII, 1724–30; Clement XII, 1730–40; Benedict XIV, 1740–58; and Clement XIII, 1758–69). Apart from his three years with Clement XIII, Charles Edward endured Clement XIV (1769–74) and Pius VI from 1774 on.

Clement XI was a wholehearted supporter of the Stuarts, a personal friend of James II and Mary of Modena from the time of his cardinalate. His relations with James, the 'Old Pretender', were complicated by the latter's attachment to Archbishop Fénelon, for in Clement's bull 'Unigenitus' he explicitly condemned the Jansenists. But at least he was sincerely committed to the Stuarts. His successor, Innocent XIII, was not, though the policy of his predecessor and his holy office compelled him to pay lip-service to their cause. More than that he would not do: when James needed a loan to finance a new Jacobite plot in England, Innocent refused to put up the money without security.

Benedict XIII, a much simpler character than Innocent, was disposed to return to the policies of Clement XI, but the marital rift between James and Clementina Sobieska seriously impaired his relation with the Pretender. The pope rather naively took Clementina's side and suspended the papal pension in order to put pressure on James. This led to his temporary residence in Bologna and the eventual papering over of the huge cracks in the marriage.

With Clement XII's accession in 1730, the pro-Clementina policy was put into reverse. James was a personal friend of the pope's nephew, and the Corsinis in general (the pope's family) had close contacts with him. Clement finally resolved Clementina's absurd vendetta over Lord and Lady Inverness by ordering her to obey her husband's wishes. This pope always followed a policy of deference to royal authority: the most notorious instance was his agreement that the seven-year-old son of Elizabeth Farnese, queen of Spain, could become a cardinal.

Benedict XIV too, greatest of the eighteenth-century popes, was personally close to James. It was with him that the Pretender planned and carried out the elevation of his son Henry to the cardinalate. His successor, Clement XIII, was also fond of James but far too beset by political problems to be willing to indulge in sentimental gestures. He refused to recognise Charles Edward as King Charles III of England. He was not willing to give gratuitous offence to England at the very time he was engaged in a life-and-death struggle throughout Europe in defence of the Jesuits and against Catholic monarchs at that, a struggle that may have cost him his own life, by poisoning, in 1769.

Clement XIV was elected on a brief that included the suppression of the Jesuits and the necessity for prelates to bow to kings and temporal rulers. This prescription, however, did not extend to *de jure* monarchs. When Charles Edward made overtures to the pope for the formal recognition of himself and his wife as king and queen of England, he received the same treatment as from the previous Clement: polite refusal. Pius VI completed the tale of Jacobite woe by recognising George III as king of England.

Since the popes had no standing army, the most the Jacobites could look for from the papacy was diplomatic support and financial aid. For actual military assistance they had to look elsewhere. After France, the most likely source of support was Spain. In all the Jacobite risings and all the projects for a descent on England Spain was always hovering in the background, and on one occasion, in 1719, she occupied the foreground. In 1715 an offensive and defensive alliance was concluded between Spain and the Jacobites, providing financial but no military assistance, although in fact no Spanish help of any kind ever reached Scotland in 1715. In 1719 Spain, under Alberoni, was the prime mover in the Jacobite rising that year. But in 1745–46 Philip V dragged his feet, procrastinating over the supply of arms and money for Charles Edward and only deciding to send major reinforcements to Scotland when such help was already too late.

Still, Spain continued to figure in Jacobite hopes and aspirations. In 1747 Charles Edward himself visited the Spanish court in a major attempt to get support for another rising. This mission was a lamentable failure. In 1759 Spain was asked to participate in Choiseul's mighty expedition against England. This time the Jacobites should have been well placed, for the chief minister and Secretary of State for Foreign Affairs in Madrid was Ricardo Wall, an Irish Jacobite. Yet his personal loyalties to the Stuarts, such as they were, took second place to the interests of Spain. He used the inexperience of the new king of Spain as an excuse to take no action.

Next to France and Spain, the Jacobites reposed most hopes of military assistance in Sweden, then a first-rank European power. In 1714 the duke of Berwick made a major attempt to interest Charles XII, the Swedish warrior-king, in an invasion of England. The plan was that 8,000 Swedish troops be embarked at Gothenburg and landed at Newcastle. James Stuart would put up 50,000 crowns to finance the venture. But Charles XII was at that time involved in the siege of Stralsund. With Russians, Poles and Saxons as enemies already, he decided he did not dare risk adding England and Hanover to the list. Berwick felt that the Swedes were being lamentably shortsighted. With the House of Stuart securely established in Britain, Charles XII would have had access to the men, money and ships to fulfil all his most ambitious plans.

Certainly Charles had a better opportunity in 1714 than three years later when he finally did decide to commit himself seriously to the Jacobites. By 1717 the alliance of the Danes with Hanover was irking him. An invasion scheme was hatched between General Arthur Dillon, James's representative in Paris, Count Gyllenborg, Swedish ambassador in London, and Baron Gortz, Sweden's minister at The Hague. The Swedes offered 12,000 infantry and 2,000 horse as an invasion force if the Jacobites would put up one million livres. That sort of money was beyond James's reach, but Dillon obtained the sum on promissory notes from Parisian bankers, payable in twelve months. When the Triple Alliance of England, Austria and the United Provinces objected to the Spanish annexation of Sardinia, Alberoni in return sent James a million livres. All was now set for the Swedish invasion.

But as negotiations reached their final point, incriminating correspondence between Gyllenborg in London and the Swedish Baron Spaar in the Netherlands was intercepted by George I's secret agents, who were no respecters of the immunity of the diplomatic bag. The Swedes were caught *in flagrante*. Gortz was arrested and the entire invasion project collapsed like a house of cards.

After Charles XII's death his sister, now queen of Sweden, turned her back on the Jacobites, refusing even to return the money James had sent to Sweden to finance the abortive 1717 venture. Sensing the way the wind was blowing in Sweden, George II agreed to pay a subsidy of £50,000 a year to keep the Swedish pawn off the Jacobite board. Only in 1745–46 did Sweden once again figure in plans for an invasion of England. The French Foreign Secretary, the marquis d'Argenson, tried to revive the 1717 idea of a Swedish landing, this time in concert with France's own expedition. A Royal Swedish regiment was actually raised for service under Charles Edward but never left for Scotland. D'Argenson's Swedish project eventually foundered on the reef of intense factionalism between the Swedish political parties, the Caps and the Hats. In 1759 Choiseul returned to the d'Argenson plan for a joint Franco-Swedish descent on England, but once again Swedish timidity ruined everything. So great a blow was Swedish defection to Choiseul's overall strategy in 1759 that he kept it from his colleagues on the king's council.

Another possible military backer of the Jacobites was the emerging power of Russia, whose expansion into eastern Europe in the early eighteenth century so alarmed English ministers. It was the abiding dream of Jacobite statesmen, as Nordmann has shown, to construct an anti-British axis consisting of Spain, Sweden and Russia. In 1718 a major Jacobite deputation was at the court of Peter the Great, headed by the duke of Ormonde. Their aim was twofold: to secure the hand of the Czar's daughter for James and to bring Sweden and Russia together in an alliance with Spain against the British Quadruple Alliance (England, France, Austria and the United Provinces). Both aims were frustrated. Peter the Great decided that a king without a country was not a suitable bridegroom for his daughter; and the Swedish alliance project collapsed with Charles XII's death at the siege of Friedrichshall in December 1718.

Yet James did not give up. Throughout 1723 and 1724 his

representatives were lobbying tirelessly at the Russian court. The English ministers were sufficiently alarmed by this activity to suspect a planned Russian landing at Newcastle. But in 1725 Peter the Great died, and Jacobite hopes of Russian support died with him. For all that, the Russian spectre did not entirely go away. In 1745 there was a wild rumour that the Czarina would send troops to help Charles Edward, and in 1747 the prince discussed with his father a far-fetched plan that he should marry the Czarina and receive as his marriage gift a 20,000-man invasion force destined for England.

These were the only European powers remotely likely to help the exiled Stuarts. For most of the Jacobite period the Austrian Empire was firmly in the British camp, anchored there by lavish subsidies. Some progress was made in the 1720s when Bishop Atterbury and the duke of Wharton persuaded the Emperor in Vienna to defend the Ostend Company against the English. Here the Jacobites had a double aim: to cause economic difficulties for England, thus provoking the kind of discontent that might favour a Stuart restoration; and to convince Austria that her commercial interests were opposed to those of Britain in Hanover and therefore that only a change of dynasty could save the Ostend Company from the Anglo-Dutch onslaught. For a while the Ostend Company was a hive of Jacobitism. But eventually Jacobite intrigues in Vienna backfired. Austria committed itself fully to the Georges in England. In 1727 the privileges of the company were suppressed and it was eventually abolished by the Second Treaty of Vienna in 1731.

Prussia's one and only foray into Jacobite intrigues came very late in the day, with the Elibank plot of 1752–53. This plot called for a rising in the Highlands simultaneously with a coup d'état in London, to be signalled by the assassination of the Hanoverian royal family. Earl Marischal Keith was Prussia's ambassador to Louis XV at the time and was privy to the conspiracy. Louis XV was secretly informed of the plan in its outlines, though not the assassination part. Frederick the Great encouraged Marischal to tempt the Jacobites to go ahead with the plot with half-promises of Prussian aid. But Frederick was not in earnest. He was irritated at the British attitude to him and wished to show them what a powerful enemy he could be if he chose. Thanks to the efforts of Pickle the Spy, the conspiracy was punctured. When Archibald Cameron was arrested in March 1753 the rest of the plotters lost heart. At the same time Charles Edward came to realise that Frederick was merely playing with him.

For more than seventy years the Jacobites were a thorn in the flesh of British diplomacy. The existence of the exiled Stuarts provided a card that nations hostile to England could play with minimal risk to themselves. Yet precisely because the Jacobites were used by their putative allies as political levers or pressure points, all the schemes to restore the Stuarts were in vain. Not all their supporters were insincere – Louis XV genuinely had a soft spot for the 'Pretenders' and would have liked to see them on the throne of the United Kingdom – but restoration of the exiles required a unique concatenation of contingent circumstances and a one hundred per cent commitment from a major power like France which never materialised. The spin of the wheel that would bring the one-in-a-hundred chance, the never-to-be-repeated opportunity when for a brief moment all favourable factors were with them was never likely to happen to a royal house as unfortunate as the Stuarts.

Chapter 3

Life and times in a Scottish clan

In truth it was precisely because Montrose and Dundee were not Highlanders that they were able to lead armies composed of Highland clans.

Macaulay, *History of England*

Look at the poetry of Scotland, the heroic part, founded almost entirely on the villainous deeds of the Scotch nation; cow-stealing for example, which is very little better than drabbing baulor; whilst the softer part is mostly about the slips of its females among the broom.

George Borrow, *The Romany Rye*

It is the story of a mountebank and his zany.

Horace Walpole (on Dr Johnson's tour of the Hebrides)

If France was the external key to success for the Jacobites, the internal one lay in Scotland, especially in the Highlands. Only here could an indigenous army of irregulars be raised. The reason for this was the system of heritable jurisdictions, that curious excrescence of *caudillismo* in the glens whereby local government, administration and law making in northern Scotland was left to powerful local magnates by the central government in London. This reflected a situation in which it was too expensive to maintain a centralised bureaucracy and the concomitant enforcement power in geographically remote areas. In Scotland clan leaders had *de jure* as well as *de facto* control over their followers; under the system of wardholding the clansmen had a duty to bear arms for their chief. In Scotland during the Jacobite era a clan leader like Cameron of Lochiel could raise close to 1,000 fighting men at almost a moment's notice.

English Jacobites had no such advantages. There was no tradition of armed feudal or familial followers in England during the Jacobite period. Cromwell's New Model Army had ended any prospect of country gentlemen being able to arm their tenants, to the point where it was a regular complaint in England in 1745 that the use and practice of arms outside the regular army was unknown. And even if English Jacobite squires had had the weaponry with which to arm their tenants, it was doubtful whether they could command their allegiance. As the eighteenth century wore on, English tenants were increasingly disinclined to follow their 'masters' at elections, let alone in military operations. Moreover, the geographical remoteness of the Scottish Highlands and the distinctive culture there based on kinship gave Highland Jacobitism a hermetically sealed quality that contrasted sharply with the situation in England, where government spies were only richly rewarded for reporting Jacobite disaffection. So it was that Jacobite risings were viable in Scotland without foreign support, at least in the short run, but in England a rebellion could not get off the ground unless a substantial foreign army was landed (and invariably that meant a French army).

The population of the Highlands in the early eighteenth century was around 600,000. In theory an army of at least 50,000 well-armed men could be raised. Even leaving aside non-Jacobite clans like the Campbells, this meant that on a 'best case' scenario 30,000 clansmen could enter the field on behalf of the exiled Stuarts. If such a host had ever come together at one time, it would have been unstoppable. Charles Edward got as far as Derby in 1745 with one-sixth of that number. Inter-clan factionalism, government influence through patronage and bribery, plus poor Jacobite leadership, all played their part in seeing that such a mighty army never came into being.

What was the social reality among these clans, so important for Jacobite hopes? The Highlanders proper lived in the mountainous country north-west of the Tay, spoke the Irish or Gaelic language, and retained a distinctive culture based on the notion of kinship and obedience to one's chieftain. They were physically hardy and brought up from an early age to the use of arms. Although the Highlanders were despised by Lowland Scots and the English as barbarians, they in turn considered themselves superior to anyone 'in the plain'.

A Highland clan was a society of men based on what anthropologists call the *gens* system of kinship. That is to say, they believed themselves to be related to each other and descended from a common ancestor. The peculiar Highland twist to the notion of a gens – familiar from the tribes of ancient Athens – was that all men in the same clan bore the same surname. A clan could be a small, simple structure, or there could be subordinate or cadet branches of a single clan, dependent on an immediate war-leader but owing ultimate allegiance to the supreme clan chief. Clan Chattan, or 'the clan of cats', was an ancient confederation of many small clans. It was originally composed of Mackintoshes, Davidsons, MacPhersons, Mac-Gillivrays and MacBeans, and was added to later by the Farquharsons and others.

For the most part the rights of a clan chief to a land title were not established by a written document but by custom and habit. The conflict between legal title by charter and actual occupation simmered away beneath the surface of Highland society in the Jacobite period. But until the failure of the '45 rising it was considered impracticable or too dangerous to make the writ of London run in the mountains. The arrest of a clansman in clan territory by government officials would have been a suicidal action. The heritable jurisdictions whereby sheriffships and other offices were put in the hands of powerful families in the Highlands was a recognition of necessity. No law is more despised than the one that can be disregarded. The clan chiefs could at least implement whatever laws they decided on.

The result of this was that the Highland chieftains exercised greater power over their subjects than the king did over his in London. The chief had the powers of monarch, landlord, judge and lawmaker all in one. As such he might have seemed the most absolute of absolute rulers. Certainly his subjects did not contest his power. All English observers reported, fascinated, that virtue in the Highlands was defined as loving a chief with blind obedience, even though his actions ran against law, government or even God's law itself. But there were subtle customary limits on the power of the chief. He had to prove himself a mighty warrior, he had to provide for the welfare of his clansmen, and this set a limit on his freedom of action. In a word, he was limited by the kind of customary *quid pro quo* of rights and duties that distinguished feudal society and was to disappear under capitalism, when the rights of the powerful remained but their duties vanished. In addition, some clans had tribal councils, where the chief would be advised by leading members of his immediate family and of the clan in general.

The way of life in the Highlands was largely determined by the hard, unyielding geography. It was overwhelmingly pastoral. The clansmen raised black cattle, sheep and goats. Raiding the cattle of a neighbouring clan was as natural an occurrence as a raid of this nature by Matabele on Zulu a century later. Deerhunting and fishing supplemented the diet. Yet destitution was common, largely because the Highlands were overpopulated. Lands were minutely subdivided to increase a chief's military following, but the harsh land could not sustain them. Lands were divided and subdivided up to and beyond basic subsistence level. Every inch of arable land was cultivated to the limit of available skills and technology. One estimate reckoned that even when the land had been remorselessly subdivided, it could still only support half the population. In desperation some clansmen went into the Lowlands at harvest time to earn wages.

Even when the screws were tightened on the tenant until he could be squeezed no more, a clansman rarely left his land for good. The telluric bond tying him to the soil was too strong. Hence the absurdity of the English judicial system in 1746 when it refused to accept the defence pleas that rankers in the Highland army had been 'forced out', on the specious grounds that since they were not guarded night and day they could have run away. The simple answer to this is, where to? Most Highlanders would not have wanted to leave their own patch of earth even if there had been a realistic alternative, which there was not.

The scions of the clan aristocracy could sell their services abroad as fighters or could turn to commerce as Lochiel's brother Fassifern did. But there was no such exit for the ordinary clansman. Frequently he and his family hovered on the edge of starvation. True, there were the occasional clan feasts, and the *tinchal*, or great hunt, where the clansmen acted as beaters to their chiefs, forming an enormous circle and working in towards a suitable glen. The chiefs would then dispatch the game driven past them, with gunshot, spear or sword. Often the *tinchal* was used as a cover for gathering the clans during a rising, as happened with the earl of Mar in 1715. There is a famous description of such a *tinchal* in Scott's *Waverley*.

But most of the time there was no venison to supplement the meagre diet. Certain clans living near the coast were said to live on a regime of shellfish from March to August. There were stories of Highlanders bleeding their cows in winter and mixing the blood with oatmeal, and of cattle so weakened by the process that they were unable to rise from the ground in the morning. Edward Burt, the Englishman on Wade's staff in the 1720s who left an invaluable memoir of everyday life in the Highlands, attributed the homely looks and poor complexions of the ordinary clansmen to their execrable diet. This destitution, incidentally, extended to the properly feudal tenants of the north-east. When his people were hiding Lord Pitsligo after the '45, they were unable to afford salt for his porridge.

The practice of 'uplifting' a neighbour's cattle which so horrified the 'civilised' inhabitants of Enlightenment England was an inevitable result of this destitution. So was blackmail – the old Scots tradition of demanding tribute at the end of a sword. 'Mail' was the old Scottish word for rent or tribute and 'black' referred to the colour of the cattle, the usual form of the tribute. Blackmail was the first but by no means the last 'protection racket' legitimised by a primitive society that regarded such activity as honourable. This propensity to robbery in the hills and glens was evidently of ancient provenance. 'The Highlanders are great thieves,' wrote the Roman historian Dio Cassius in the third century AD.

Military service in the clans was thus both cause and effect of blackmail. One clan chief was said to employ half his men in recovering lost cattle and the other half in stealing more. The greater the levy of armed men the chief required, the more pressure his officers, the tacksmen, exerted, subletting farms in greater numbers than could be sustained on the land and at a much higher rent than the tenants could pay. To find the wherewithal to meet their rents, the tenants had to have recourse to theft and robbery, principally of cattle. So large was the Highland population relative to resources that clansmen were actually discouraged from marrying. A young Highland male made himself an eligible marriage prospect by 'thigging' – begging for corn, sheep and seedcorn among friends.

Yet for the most part destitution in the Highlands did not

breed social discontent between chiefs and their followers. Although Highland chieftains attended the finest universities in Europe and might be waited on at dinner by five or six servants, they often dined on food not much superior to that of their men: pickled herrings or oatmeal tricked out in various ways. Some of the lairds' houses were built of stone and lime, but many of them were simply glorified versions of the clansmen's huts. It was related of one of the Glengarry chiefs that he dwelt in a hut while his castle was being let to an English gentleman. It was said that the only way one could distinguish a chief's or a tacksman's children from other dirty and half-naked Highland urchins was from their being able to speak English. But although the gulf between leaders and led in the Highlands was not great it was significant, as even incremental improvements in living standard will be at the margin. Herring and game, after all, provide a better diet than shellfish, nettles and cows' blood.

Undoubtedly another factor contributing to the rarity of social hatred in the Highlands was the fiction that every man in a clan was a blood relation – for in reality the blood tie *was* largely a fiction. This can be established both indirectly from the fact that before the seventeenth century clansmen did not bear their chief's surname and directly from an examination of the surnames of those who served in clan regiments during the '45. It is clear that kinship as an objective reality was most important in the relations between clan chiefs and clan gentry (tacksmen) and that rank-and-file clansmen commonly changed their surname for another one on change of abode or allegiance. But to establish this is not to deny the *perception* of kinship as a reality among clan members. Here as elsewhere in human behaviour, myth and collective image are far more important than documented 'fact'. Without the average clansman's perception of a network of rights and duties deriving from membership of the extended family of the gens, it is hard to see how the chieftains could ever have exerted their undoubted charismatic hold over their followers.

Incontestably, the key to all unrest in the Highlands was the issue of land. At one time held by the gens in common, by the eighteenth century it had become the chief's by sasine or sometimes by no more than the approval of the clan. This was the situation regarding *ownership*. As far as *use* was concerned, there were three main categories. 'Mensal' land was the chief's preserve. Other land was deeded by gift to families of clan officials like the bard, harper or piper. But the most important species of land was that held by tenants under leases or 'tacks'. The 'tacksmen' or clan gentry were the next stage down in the clan hierarchy after the chief. These tacksmen would cultivate part of the 'tack' themselves. The rest they would sublet to various categories of tenants or cotters. Sometimes the tacksman allowed part of his own tillage to the crofter; sometimes a separate croft was laid off for him. The tacksman was a man of great importance in tribal society. In wartime tacksmen provided the officer class for the clan regiments. If a clansman showed himself reluctant to 'come out' when the chief ordered military mobilisation, it was the tacksmen's job to force him out, usually by burning the roof of his hut over his head.

Relations between tacksmen and subtenants were notoriously uneasy. If a subtenant improved his land by enclosures or other means of productivity, invariably the tacksman would respond by putting up his rent or altering the terms of the lease so that the improved farm was further subdivided to feed more mouths. Towards the end of the Jacobite period, as the impact of the market made its insidious way northwards, some of the more prosperous tacksmen turned themselves into merchants and began to exploit their tenants. For the items they supplied their ignorant 'blood brothers' they levied an exorbitant price. The tenants had no idea what the market price of goods would be in Glasgow or Edinburgh and paid for these transactions in cattle (usually in May). The surplus value extracted in this way could be paid for only by more cattle raids. From this it can be clearly seen that the clan system was in decline even before the '45.

But the more normal situation would be one where a tacksman possessed, say, five or six very poor tenants. In summer they might live on a diet of milk and whey without bread, sleeping as much as their starved bodies would allow them, saving the little butter or cheese they could make until winter. The women did most of the work, drying barley on a large wicker machine over the fire, burning the straw and grinding corn upon querns or handmills. During the winter their diet would improve, with some meat, butter and cheese, but always there was a scarcity of bread. Only in spring was bread plentiful; this was the crucial season when all the serious work was done. Technology was primitive. Even when 'improving' chieftains like Lochiel introduced the water mill, the resistance to change endemic in the traditional Highland culture meant that such innovations were largely disregarded.

All visitors to the Highlands were instantly struck by the poverty and wretchedness of most of the inhabitants. Burt described their cottages as like so many heaps of mud when seen from a distance. Made of sod, heather and stone, containing one room only, divided by a wicker curtain, these bothies provided inadequate protection against the elements. One of Cumberland's men in the Highlands in 1747 described a bothy in the Great Glen full of children suffering from smallpox and lying in dirt and rain, the hut so inadequately roofed that although he walked up and down trying to find a dry patch, the rain followed him wherever he went.

In the middle of the room in such a bothy there would be a great fire, toped by an iron cooking pot. The hut was dark and dank. A dim light was provided by the burning of resinous fir. Here, when they were not working, the inhabitants would sit scorching, close up to the firelight, recounting and listening to ancient tales of clan battles or learning the mystic meaning of the sprigs of plant worn in a warrior's bonnet. Belief in witchcraft, fairies and the second sight was unquestioning and was reflected in the sagas and ballads told to the accompaniment of pipe and song, in which giants and stones that talked played a greater role than the nominal Christianity the clans embraced.

A Highland village would be a collection of such bothies. At one end would be strips of stony earth which the clansmen ploughed with wooden ploughs. On all sides would graze large herds of black cattle: the shaggy brown Highland cattle of our own century are a nineteenth-century cross-breed. Such ponies as could be seen were the property of the tacksmen. The poorly clad clansman would have been amazed at the outsider's interest in his garb, but it is a fact that the Highlander's dress has always attracted the intrigued wonderment of the outsider. The long plaid, pleated into a kilt or draped over the shoulders like a shawl, was the poor man's only clothing. On a winter campaign he would wrap his plaid round him and sleep in it on the snow. Those who believe that trousers are the inevitable sign of social superiority would find confirmation in Highland culture. Since the chief would usually not march but ride a pony, he would wear trews of skin-tight tartan rather than the kilt.

Such was everyday life under the tacksman. Tenants got little

enough in return for their leases. The only return for their labour
and services was likely to be a house (if the rude huts can be
dignified with such a name), grass for a cow or two, and as much
land 'as will sow a boll of oats' – rocky ground at that, requiring
heavy, backbreaking digging. Like much else in the Highlands,
tacks long worked on the hereditary principle. The first dent in
this system was not made until Duncan Forbes of Culloden's
1737 reforms. Of course, after the '45, tacksmen were dispos-
sessed along with cotters, crofters, and the rest of the old society.

Apart from tacksmen and their subtenants, certain small
tenants held their land directly from the chief on a basis of
communal ownership. One man might hold a fourth share of a
farm, another a fifteenth, and so on. These crofts were mainly of
the arable variety. Yet another system of landholding was the
wadset. Here a chief pawned a farm to one of his leading
clansman – Glengarry, say, to Lochgarry – for a certain period at
an agreed sum. When he repaid the money, he recovered the
farm. Here again the wadsetter could sublet at higher rents than
those the owner charged and so make a profit on the deal. After
the '45 the wadset was one of the first of the old customs to die.
The wadsetters either became tenants at increased rents or
emigrated.

It was not surprising that a people on the brink of starvation
and subject to the increasing rapacity of the tacksmen should have
been eager volunteers for a rebellion on behalf of their true king.
A rising at the very least provided opportunities for plunder and
feasting. The more perceptive observers of the clans, like Duncan
Forbes of Culloden, saw that if discontent could be assuaged in
the Highlands, clan leaders would be less inclined to 'come out'
for a Stuart pretender. He spoke of the 'tyranny and unmerciful
exactions' of the tacksmen on the duke of Argyll's lands in
Morven, Mull and Tyree.

In 1737, therefore, Forbes suggested granting tenants
nineteen-year leases if they would 'offer frankly for their farms
such rent as fairly and honestly they could bear'. Tacks of farms
were offered in open competition; rents were raised but the
former labour services of tenants to tacksmen were abolished. In
Forbes's mind these measures were designed to attack the clan
system by curbing the power of the tacksmen. The subtenant
gained freedom from the tacksman and freedom from all services
except those explicitly stated in the nineteen-year lease; these

were to do with mending highways, repairing harbours, paying the cess and the salaries of ministers and schoolmasters.

But the real shrewdness in Forbes's scheme lay elsewhere. One of the services deliberately *not* mentioned in the lease was military service. This meant that a tenant could no longer lose his holding if his tacksman ordered him out during a Jacobite rising and he refused. Here Forbes was attempting to tap one of the most deep-seated sources of discontent in the clans. The most controversial aspect of landholding in the Highlands was the system of services in kind owed to a landlord. Only in this sense is it correct to align the Scottish patrimonial system of chieftains with feudalism proper. According to some authorities, the Scottish equivalent of the *corvée* was much more deeply resented than the payment of money rents. This was one reason why certain tenants – those of Lochiel and Ardshiel, for example – found no difficulty after 1745 in paying double money rents, one to the new laird implanted by the Commissioners for Forfeited Estates, and another to their rightful lords in exile in France. To get the burden of services, particularly military service, off their backs was considered well worth the payment of a double money rent.

On the other hand, tenants failed to appreciate that the duty laid on them to perform military service was a two-edged broadsword. When eviction became, after the '45, simply a function of money, rents and the market, nothing stayed the hands of rapacious landlords. But before 1745 evicting a tenant meant depriving the clan of one less claymore. Chiefs and tacksmen thought long and hard before expelling a crofter and did so if at all for social rather than economic reasons.

If anything Forbes's measures exacerbated tensions in the Highlands, especially since his reforms came a year after the enactment of punitive laws against Episcopalians. Some subtenants and some tacksmen did accept his offers, but the conservatism of the people, the interests of the majority of tacksmen, and above all the need to maintain the chieftains' military rolls worked against him. Moreover, his reforms alarmed the clan leaders by bringing the money economy and cash nexus closer to the Highlands. Argyll began to abandon his position as clan chief in favour of becoming a mere landowner. This went beyond anything hitherto experienced; the rentier ethos for the first time began to harm members of Clan Campbell itself. Rents on the

Argyll estates were raised and tacks went to the highest bidder, regardless of clan or family.

The dominant figure in the authoritarian, patriarchal society of the Highlands was necessarily the chief. Enlightenment thinkers, fascinated by the concept of the 'noble savage', found in the Highland chief one who had gone one better. He had all the violence and martial valour of a savage yet outdid many 'civilised' men in learning, wisdom and breadth of experience. A clan chief would normally speak both English and Gaelic as well as French, Latin and Greek. He and his sons might have been educated in Paris or Rome or, at least, Edinburgh or Glasgow. His wife was regarded as a lady and always referred to as such. The peacock-like clan chieftain would cut a splendid figure amid the general squalor of the bothies. His hair would be powdered and beribboned, his bonnet trimmed with the eagle feather denoting his rank, and his tartan jacket and waistcoat would be set off by different-coloured stockings. Sometimes a chief would choose to wear a kilt rather than trews. The plaid would be held at his left shoulder with a silver brooch, there would be a silver and leather sporran around his waist, and his calves would be covered to the knees with tartan hose. Highland culture answered to unwritten sumptuary laws. With each item of clothing a different colour, the chief would coruscate in green, yellow, blue and scarlet, like a South American parakeet.

An expert swordsman and dancer, a connoisseur of claret and fine paintings, this cultivated laird held the power of life and death over his subjects. Sometimes he exercised it. There is the story of the Clanranald chieftain whose judgment was Polynesian rather than Solomonic (and thus presumably he qualified twice over as a noble savage). A woman had been accused of stealing from him. Clanranald ordered her tied to the rocks by seaweed, there to remain until the Atlantic swept in and drowned her. Such absolute power was never questioned. We hear of clans cursing their chiefs but never rebelling against them. Offenders against the social laws of the glens were evicted or, in extreme cases, sold to sea captains plying to the Americas.

But though the source of a chief's authority was traditional, its exercise depended on charismatic powers. If a chief showed himself too bookish, he might forfeit the right to lead out the clan in time of war. The clansmen might make a younger brother *de facto* war chief. In modern parlance, an unmartial chief would 'lack credibility'. The model leader was one who hunted the stag and the wild cat in the hills, was quick to defend his honour and never let an insult to the clan go unavenged. As in many primitive societies, the concept of 'honour' was all-important.

The clan's honour was symbolised by its slogan, a savage motto of mayhem or a reminder of the past. This was always cried in battle or in times of alarm or emergency. The clan's identity was further reinforced by the badge of heather, oak or myrtle a man wore in his bonnet. The commitment to 'honour', whatever its less pleasant consequences in the form of blood feuds, was taken very seriously indeed and provided the social cement of the Highlands. No police force was needed in a context where a clansman took a sacred oath of loyalty and obedience on his drawn dirk, which he kissed solemnly and asked to be stabbed with if he were guilty of perjury. This oath, taken on the 'holy iron', had all the combined power of religion and legal compulsion. This was why travellers in the Highlands time and again commented on the absence of individual theft as opposed to the collective 'uplifting' of cattle by the clan. Indeed, forays against the herds of neighbours were themselves an affair of honour. Nothing better illustrates the gulf in comprehension between the English and the Highlanders than the eighteenth-century dictum 'Show me a Highlander and I will show you a thief' – a saying that could only ever be verified in the peculiar context of cattle.

As was to be expected, a chief's prestige among his peers depended, not on his wealth or income, but on the number of fighting men he could enlist. With 4,000 broadswords at his command, the chief of a combined Clan Campbell would have an indisputable superiority. MacDonald of Glencoe with no more than 150 claymores at his call would rank somewhat lower. That was why in Jacobite terms Lochiel with his 1,000 fighting men was so important.

The great drawback about clan society from the military point of view was the reluctance of chieftains to cooperate. One of the most interesting facts about Highland history, which Macaulay long ago pointed out, was that none of the clans' great exploits was performed under a *clan* leader. Neither Montrose nor Dundee was a clan chief. Nor was the military genius of the '45, Lord George Murray: as Duncan Forbes of Culloden pointed out, 'the Murrays is no clan family'. The reason for this was that no clansman would obey the orders of another clan leader. A Jacobite commander had perforce to be a non-clan laird, and possessed of superlative diplomatic and political skills. Despite his genius as a captain, Montrose could not keep his motley alliance in being. Unintentionally, he alienated the Gordons, who imagined that he favoured the MacDonalds against them. Even Lord George Murray, who performed wonders in dampening down clan feuds during the '45, finally fell victim to jealousy and factionalism of this sort. He narrowly staved off a mutiny among the Glengarry men in January 1746. But it is no exaggeration to say that the less than brilliant performance of the MacDonald regiments at Culloden was caused by their pique that Lord George and the Athollmen had been given the place of honour on the right.

The ultimate absurdity in this process of clan jealousy took place in 1689. The Camerons had raided the territory of the Grants and killed a number of them. Among the slain was a former Glengarry MacDonell who had renounced his clan allegiance in order to become a Grant. But, declaring that blood was thicker than water, the Glengarry MacDonells in Dundee's army claimed that the Camerons had no right to have killed him; they should have handed him over to the chief's justice. Dundee tried to mediate, pointing out the absurdity of Glengarry wounded pride in this matter. But the chief of Glengarry stormed out of the meeting, vowing vengeance against Lochiel and the Camerons. When it was pointed out that he was outnumbered two to one, he exclaimed: 'One MacDonald is worth two Camerons.' Had Ewen Cameron of Lochiel been of a similarly choleric disposition, civil war would have broken out in Dundee's army. But Lochiel was a statesman, refused to rise to Glengarry's taunts, and so the affair was eventually smoothed over. The outcome of these clan feuds was not always so favourable to the exiled dynasty. The Stuart papers at Windsor make it clear that clan loyalty and the desire to pursue a vendetta against an ancient enemy usually overrode the clans' nominally supreme duty to the House of Stuart.

The symbolic and actual importance of a clan chief received its visible manifestation in the form of the 'tail', the retinue of clan functionaries who followed the chieftain on his journeys in time of peace: the personal bodyguard, bard, piper, bladier and gillie, walking in that order. The bard was of particular importance in a culture that depended on oral tradition. The history and legend of each clan was his to record, embroider or invent. The piper's function was to urge on the clansmen in time of war and to soothe them in time of peace. The bladier was something like the Mafia's *consigliere*, a Highland lawyer chosen for his position by the possession of debating skills of great subtlety. The gillie (or gillies, depending on the importance of the clan) carried the chief's broadsword, buckler, brogues, bridle and baggage. In peacetime wherever a chief's tail went it would be housed and fed. Laws of hospitality were sacred in the Highlands. Early eighteenth-century sources speak of armies of tramps being supported by the generosity of the destitute clansmen. Lowland beggars were drawn north by the open-handed generosity in the hills and glens.

Such was the Highland society of the Jacobite period. In its peculiar mixture of civilisation and barbarism it mirrored the wider society of the century but outdid it in extremes. This peculiar symbiosis of culture and savagery is well illustrated in the case of MacDonell of Barisdale. A scholar and a gentleman, he had engraved on his broadsword the well-known lines from Virgil:

Hae tibi erunt artes, pacique imponere morem,
parcere subjectis et debellare superbos.

Coll MacDonell of Barisdale, the man who subscribed to such lofty sentiments, was in fact the most feared and hated man in Charles Edward's army in 1745–46. A cousin of Glengarry, he was a powerful, muscular man, six feet four inches tall. But he was also both an accomplished cattle thief and a thieftaker. He routinely exacted a tithe of one-fifth of the catch from all local fishermen. While he thus played both ends against the middle, he constructed a torture chamber, in which were not only the usual stocks but an instrument which came to be known as 'the Barisdale'. This was an iron machine where rings were clamped onto the hands, feet and neck of a victim. Thus held fast, the luckless thief or fisherman would have a large weight placed on the back of his neck and a large spike set under his chin, so that if he yielded to the weight on his neck he would spear himself through the chin.

But above all, the society of the Highlands was a military society, geared to irregular warfare and cattle raiding. It is this military aspect which aligns the patrimonial society of the clans before the '45 most closely with feudalism proper. Every male old enough to carry arms was automatically a soldier in the clan regiment. The social hierarchy of chief, chief's brothers, tacksmen, subtenants. was mirrored in the military formation of the regiment, with the added refinement that the most important families within a given clan occupied the front rank in line of battle. The ordinary clansmen would be armed with musket or pistol, Lochaber axe or claymore – not the original weapon properly so called, but the basket-hilted broadsword. Their tactics when fighting against Williamite or Hanoverian armies were to advance within shot of the enemy and then discharge their muskets and pistols. As soon as fire was returned they fell to the ground to minimise casualties. While the enemy was reloading, the clansmen would jump to their feet and charge with the claymore and targe (Highland shield). Often, too, pistols and muskets would be used as clubs for close-order fighting. The shock effect of this charge was tremendous. The Whig soldier plucked from the stews of London by a press-gang cannot have relished confronting this charge delivered at great speed, accompanied by the yelling of the clan motto.

The chief's armament was similar to that of his men, except that his equipment was more lavish. His bull-hide targe or target would be studded with silver bosses. He would be armed with the Highland dags – claw-handled steel pistols. The double-edged, basket-hilted broadsword, a yard long and two inches wide, which he carried at the hip would be complemented by a silver dirk and a tiny black knife tucked into the top of his hose.

In wartime the clans were raised by the fiery cross – two burnt or burning sticks to which was tied a strip of blood-stained linen. The cross was carried across country by relays of runners like an Olympic torch. In 1745 it was related that Lord Glenorchy of the Breadalbane Campbells rallied his people against the Jacobites in this way and that the cross travelled thirty-two miles across Loch Tay in three hours.

Clan armies were formidable adversaries when they fought on terrain of their own choosing, as their record in the Jacobite risings shows. Historians have sometimes been seduced by the defeat of Culloden to dismiss the clan army as a paper tiger, citing the fact that well-served field artillery could fire a field-piece once every fifteen seconds by 1746. They forget that Culloden was a special case, fought on a field tailor-made for regular armies and unsuited to clan warfare. Even with the invention of the ring bayonet around 1700, which made every musketeer his own pikeman as well, the average English infantryman was, man for man, no match for the clansman. Charles Edward went so far as to say that each Highlander was worth ten government troops, and until Culloden, where the outcome owed nothing to the Highlanders' lack of valour, he was proved right. Charles's mistake, which contributed greatly to his psychological disorientation after Culloden, was to infer from their previous form that his men were truly *invincible*.

Many military myths have arisen from the Highlanders' defeat at Culloden. Cumberland's special bayonet drill, and his grape and case shot field-pieces, are usually cited as demonstrating the technological superiority of his army and the anachronistic quality of the Highland charge. The military facts of Culloden need closer examination. Charles Edward's army was tired and hungry; it was fighting on a badly chosen field; it was outnumbered two to one; some of its crack regiments like the MacPhersons were not present on the day of battle; the MacDonalds on the Jacobite left took no part in the battle; and so on. Culloden stands out as an aberration in a campaign where not only the previous three major engagements but all the minor encounters save one had ended in Jacobite victory. It was little short of miraculous that the Jacobite right ever got to close quarters with Cumberland's army. The theory was that no enemy would continue to advance over its own dead when it lay four deep on the ground before a British regiment in line, directing sustained fire at the oncomers. Yet that is precisely what the clan regiments did on that fatal April afternoon on Drummossie Moor. The failure of the '45 was a failure of resources, supplies, quartermastering, ammunition, money, communications, nerve, even perhaps intelligence in all senses; but it was never a foregone conclusion in military terms, whatever the 'know-best' of modern historians say.

But if there was nothing wrong with the Highland army in 1745 that a regular supply of money, men and reinforcements from France could not have put right, it has to be admitted that Highland society was, for other reasons, in deep decay before the last rebellion dealt the *coup de grâce*. The main cause was the encroachment of a money economy. Even before 1745 the

Campbell leaders were converting themselves from clan leaders with duties into mere landlords. The disastrous impact of the infamous Loch Arkaig treasure of 1746 on clan loyalties and behaviour fittingly symbolised this. The irruption of gold into a society where specie was scarce had a corrupting influence that is the stuff of moral tales. Where money and the market entered the glens, Jacobitism declined. Money, the root of all evil, was both cause and effect of the Jacobite twilight in Scotland. Why, we may ask, did the formerly Jacobite clans of the Macleods and the MacDonalds of Sleat not 'come out' in 1745? Thereby hangs a grisly tale.

Norman Macleod of Dunvegan and Sir Alexander MacDonald of Sleat were at once the two most powerful chiefs of Skye and the most important Jacobite apostates. Although it has often been alleged that these two failed to join the prince because he brought no certain guarantees of aid from France, or because their lands were exposed to retaliatory raids from the Royal Navy, the real reason for their defection from the Stuart cause is altogether more sinister. In 1739 Macleod and his kinsman Sir Alexander MacDonald devised a scheme for deporting some of their tenants to North America, to be sold as drudges for the Southern plantations. Details of the plot were divulged to the authorities and it was discovered that none of the tenants earmarked for this fate, together with their wives and children, had committed crimes punishable by transportation.

In the ensuing scandal both Macleod and MacDonald were threatened with prosecution. Macleod appealed to Duncan Forbes, the Lord President. He promised loyal support for Forbes's anti-Jacobite measures in the Highlands if Forbes in return would quash the actions pending against himself and MacDonald. No proceedings were brought against them, and in 1745 Macleod and MacDonald amply repaid their debt. Macleod kept Duncan Forbes informed of all developments in the Jacobite clans and, despite protestations of loyalty to the Prince, which even managed to fool the old fox Lord Lovat, he managed to prevaricate until the end of December 1745 when, learning of the retreat from Derby, he openly revealed his hand and raised a force for Forbes (which was, however, ignominiously routed at Inverury on 23 December). The failure of Macleod and MacDonald of Sleat to rally to the prince's standard was a heavy blow to the Jacobites. With the Skye clans in his army, Charles

Edward would have been able to invade England without meeting Cope at Prestonpans or, more significantly, he could have entered England with a force as large as the one that confronted Hawley at Falkirk. The consequences of the Skye chiefs' treachery were momentous.

This, then, was the society from which the Jacobites recruited their manpower. Enough has been said to indicate why the clans formed a powerful fighting machine. It remains to be explained why this fighting machine could be enlisted on behalf of the House of Stuart, and why in Scotland in general powerful Jacobite sentiment survived until 1745.

The mosaic of Scottish Jacobitism

We never had any Tories in Scotland according to the proper signification of the word and the division of parties in this country was really into Whigs and Jacobites.

David Hume, 'Of the Parties of Great Britain'

The oldest Celtic laws which have been preserved show the gens still fully alive. In Ireland, after being forcibly broken up by the English, it still lives today in the consciousness of the people, as an instinct at any rate. In Scotland it was still in full strength in the middle of the eighteenth century, and here again it succumbed only to the weapons, laws and courts of the English.

Engels, *The Origin of the Family, Private Property and the State*

> Our Darien can witness bear
> And so can our Glencoe, sir
> Our South Sea it can make appear
> What to our kings we owe, sir.
> We have been murder'd, starv'd and robbed
> By those your king's and knav'ry
> And all our treasure is stock-jobb'd
> While we groan under slavr'y.

Hogg, *Jacobite Relics*

Jacobitism in Scotland was a mixture of religious conviction, nationalism and anti-Argyll sentiment among the clans. In all cases it was a defensive reaction to forces unleashed by the

Glorious Revolution. There is also the obvious but not negligible consideration that the Stuarts (or Stewarts) were a *Scottish* royal house. So whereas in England Jacobitism tended to be a negative phenomenon – a cause for those who disliked the existing system of politics but had little positive to recommend as an alternative – in Scotland Jacobitism was a truly positive political dispensation.

Easiest to deal with, perhaps, is the Jacobitism of the north-east. Here Episcopalianism reigned supreme, and the claim of the Stuarts through hereditary, indefeasible right was an article of faith. Since in the properly feudal system of the north-east the laird could raise recruits on his lands, such ideological conviction could easily be translated into action, though in practice in the Jacobite risings the feudal tenantry often had to be 'forced out' by the Highlanders.

The connection between episcopacy and the Scottish nobility can be dated from the Restoration. Before 1660 the anti-royalism of the Scottish nobles had attracted the Presbyterians, but in the reign of Charles II there was a strong swing to episcopacy among the Scottish aristocracy. After 1688 this meant Jacobitism, and when that creed became increasingly identified with Scottish nationalism after 1707, Episcopalianism itself became more fashionable. Jacobitism, then, was endemic in the north-east for purely religious reasons. In a word, the area was Jacobite because it wanted an Episcopal church and was denied it under the regime of the Glorious Revolution. There was also a significant pocket of Catholics there, forming part of the Lowland vicariate. Because the north-east was richer, more populous and politically more important than the Highlands, its support for Charles Edward in 1745 was invaluable.

Episcopalianism continued to thrive in the north-east, since church appointments depended on the will of territorial magnates. Although, as part of the Revolution settlement, lay patronage in the kirk had been abolished (1690), this provision remained a dead letter. The lairds and nobles of the north-east were determined that their will would be done in their own territories, and regarded these provisions of the Revolution settlement as unwarranted interference. They were prepared to keep their own appointees in place, by force if necessary, simply issuing commands to their tenants accordingly. And even within the terms of the 1690 'reform', the right to appoint ministers to vacant livings was merely transferred from the old patron to the elders and heritors, or principal landowners, of the parish. But in many parishes the old patron and new heritor were one and the same.

Another reason for Whig failure to break down the traditional system in the north-east was their general reluctance to provide money for patronage or reform in Scotland. The official Presbyterian appointments could not be implanted against the wishes of the local magnates unless the incumbent Episcopalian retired gracefully. Naturally he would not do this unless adequately pensioned off. Since the Whig establishment would not provide the money for this, the incumbent Episcopalians faithfully echoed their temporal lords' political views from their pulpits. Even if a Presbyterian minister *were* settled, he could be refused recognition by a High Sheriff (and territorial magnates could usually secure this office), refused admission to kirk or manse, refused payment for his office, or generally find his life made impossible for him. Yet another reason for difficulty in replacing anti-Revolution ministers was that the new ministers would have to be trained in universities which were themselves strongly Jacobite.

Put simply, Episcopalianism was the 'natural' religion of Jacobitism in Scotland – far more than Catholicism – and Presbyterianism was the religion of the Whigs. Only among the clans did this correlation break down. Catholic clans aside, only the Camerons, Appin Stewarts and MacDonalds of Glencoe were Episcopalian; the rest were Presbyterian. But among the clans other factors making for Jacobitism were at work.

The Jacobitism of the Highland clans presents a complex picture. Not all the clans were Jacobite. The most powerful of all, the Campbells, was staunchly Whig. Moreover, even among the Jacobite clans not all could be relied on to rise if the Stuart standard were set up in Scotland. Many of the clans that did 'come out' were divided, brother against brother, demonstrating that, in Scotland at least, the risings of 1715 and 1745 were true civil wars. Few clans or families were committed in their entirety to one side or the other in the struggle.

In theory most of the clans supported the Stuarts. In fact they seldom did so wholeheartedly. Even where families were not divided by principle, they tended to divide *themselves* for prudential motives. In 1745 Angus, chief of the Mackintoshes, was on the Whig side, in the service of Lord Loudoun, but in his

absence his young wife, Anne, raised the clan for Charles
Edward. Even the Chisholms, a nominally Catholic clan, were
divided in loyalties, so that there were few of them on the field of
Culloden. A favourite tactic was for the clan chiefs to remain at
home, officially loyal to the government, while a son brought out
the clan for the Stuarts. Another was for a family to send one son
to fight with the Hanoverians and another with the Jacobites (this
ploy is familiar from Stevenson's *Master of Ballantrae*). So in
1745 we find, for example, the earl of Airlie sending out his
second son, Lord Ogilvy, to head the feudal tenants of Airlie, and
Lord Lewis Gordon, second son of Alexander, duke of Gordon,
fulfilling much the same role, both in Charles Edward's army.
The manoeuvre was common to Lowland feudal laird and
Highland clan chief.

Of the clans proper, only the Munroes, Mackays and
Campbells were unequivocally Whig. The staunchest Jacobites
were the Camerons, MacDonalds (Clanranald, Keppoch and
Glencoe), MacDonells of Glengarry, MacPhersons, Stewarts of
Appin, Chisholms, Drummonds, Farquharsons, Frasers,
Gordons, Grants, MacBeans, MacGillivrays, Macleans,
Mackintoshes, McKinnons, MacLachlans and Menzies. Officially
Jacobite clans, with patchy records of support for their true king,
were the Macleods, MacDonalds of Sleat, Macraes, Mackenzies,
MacDougalls, MacGregors and Sinclairs. The Rosses and Suther-
lands tended to incline to the Whig side in an actual rising.

The attachment to the Stuarts among the clans has puzzled
some observers, since such support was not in evidence in the
1680s, and has led the more unwary to suggest that the Jacobite
risings were from the clan viewpoint simply large-scale plunder-
ing expeditions. Such an explanation is completely unconvincing,
since looting could be carried out with relative impunity by the
clansmen at any time without the risk of pitched battles. To solve
the riddle, at least one historian has been led to postulate a
profound intrinsic sympathy between the reigning Stuart
dynasty's patriarchal view of the role of kingship and the social
and intellectual world of the Gaelic Highlands. According to this
view, Stuart authoritarianism before 1688 is seen as analogous to
the authoritarian family structure of the clans, and in particular
James II is argued to be the Gael's best friend. It is clear,
however, that James II had no especial love for Scotland or
matters Celtic, nor is clan attachment to the Stuarts discernible in

the early 1680s. On the other hand, the motivation to rebel in 1689 does appear to stem from a genuine attachment to James II, so the puzzle remains. Other writers have concentrated on the contingent aspects of the '45 and have stressed the revenge element in the clansmen's incursion into England – the clans had a score to settle with the English because of the execution of the mutineers in the Highland regiments in 1743.

As precipitants towards the rising all these alleged motives fail to convince. Much more plausible is the idea of pressure on the means of subsistence because of the overpopulation of the Highlands. The population of the Scottish Highlands was estimated as 652,000 out of a total for Scotland of 1,265,380 in 1755, and it must have been higher in 1745 before the death toll in the rising and the transportations afterwards. Such a pressure, however, merely triggered the forces already in existence which impelled the clans to rise in 1745, and it is these which we must now consider. Principal among them was the predominance in the Highlands of Clan Campbell, which because of its pro-Whig stance pushed most other clans into opposition to the regime.

It is generally agreed that the dynamic element in the history of the Highlands in the sixteenth and seventeenth centuries was the expansion of three great clans, the Campbells, Gordons and Mackenzies. The other powerful dynasty in the Highlands, the Atholl and Tullibardine family, played relatively little part. The Campbells had expanded in the south-western Highlands, mainly at the expense of the Macleans and MacGregors. In the north the Mackenzies had encroached on the lands of the Macleods, while in the Central Highlands the Gordons were for most of the seventeenth century locked in combat with Clan Chattan – a confederation of smaller clans from Lochaber to Badenoch, comprising the MacPhersons, MacGillivrays, Macleans, MacBeans and others, under the nominal leadership of Mackintosh of Mackintosh. By the eighteenth century many of these struggles had been resolved or had subsided. By 1715 the conflict between the Gordons and Clan Chattan was largely a thing of the past. In 1745 the relevance of most inter-clan disputes to Jacobite or Whig affiliation was extremely tenuous. During the 1715 rising both the Macleods and the Mackenzies were uniformly Jacobite – indeed, the greatest element of Highland support for the Old Pretender came from the Mackenzies in the Grampians. But in 1745 the Mackenzies took no part in the rebellion, nor did the majority of the Macleods, who stayed home in obedience to their chief. New disputes had supplanted the old, and most of them did not concern the major powers in the Highlands and were disputes between Jacobite clans. The Camerons were locked in a dispute with the Mackintoshes over conflicting charter rights to their territory, and a similar quarrel made bitter enemies of the Mackintoshes and the Keppoch MacDonalds. The Frasers were feuding with the MacDonalds. Even within a single clan there were problems. Within the Catholic Glengarry clan Coll MacDonell, Young Barisdale, an influential supporter of the Prince, who later raised a second scratch regiment for Charles Edward, greatly disliked the commander of the Glengarry men, Lochgarry. The one dynamic factor which had increased in importance since the seventeenth century was the dominance of Clan Campbell.

In more than one hundred years of rivalry with Clan Campbell, the other major clans of the Highlands, like the Camerons and the MacDonalds, had seen the balance of power swing ever more strongly in the direction of the dukes of Argyll, and for them the landing of Charles Edward Stuart in 1745 provided a last desperate chance to destroy the ancient enemy. As Macaulay put it: 'The MacDonalds had once possessed, in the Hebrides and throughout the mountain country of Argyleshire and Invernessshire, an ascendancy similar to that which the House of Austria had once possessed in Christendom. But the ascendancy of the MacDonalds had, like the ascendancy of the House of Austria, passed away; and the Campbells, the children of Diarmid, had become in the Highlands what the Bourbons had become in Europe.'

The existence of Clan Campbell in the eighteenth century was basically irreconcilable with that of other traditional clans because the dukes of Argyll had set relations with their tenants on a legalistic, feudal footing which bade fair to extirpate the customary traditions of the gens or clan. Fundamentally, in the eighteenth-century Highlands a feudal system of land tenure, with rights clearly vested in the person owning the land, was being superimposed on an older, patriarchal social system, in which personal status and hereditary familial relationships were the supreme characteristics. A feudal superior was not necessarily the patriarchal chief, and feudal charters granting land ownership were not accepted by clansmen whose entire way of life inculcated a belief in the rights of kinship rather than of legal ownership. In short, the conflict between the traditional clans and the Campbells underlined the famous contrast between patrimonialism and feudalism drawn by Max Weber, where the direct structure of authority under the patrimonial system (as in the case of the clans) was in contradistinction to the indirect feudal structure. The 'mediate' superiority of a feudal landowner disturbed the readily comprehensible pattern of a hereditary monarch as the natural superior of a clan leader. To quote Macaulay again: 'The feudal system had, some centuries before, been introduced into the hill country, but had neither destroyed the patriarchal system nor amalgamated completely with it. In general he who was lord in the Norman polity was also chief in the Celtic polity; and when this was the case, there was no conflict. But when the two characters were separated, all the willing and loyal obedience was reserved for the chief. The lord had only what he could get and hold by force.' The conflict in the Highlands was thus between the dukes of Argyll, who accepted the 1688 revolution and embraced the new regime with its clearly formulated land titles, and those clans, like the Camerons and MacDonalds, who wished to preserve the old way of life.

This clash between the traditional clan system and the feudal system introduced by the Campbells, who aimed to integrate the Highlands under their hegemony, had the effect of swinging the clans behind the Stuarts, almost as a reflex action to the pro-Hanoverianism of the House of Argyll. There is no doubt that by 1745 the Jacobite clans were engaged in a desperate struggle to preserve a traditional way of life. Clansmen were often in the position of owing allegiance to their clan chief while having to recognise the duke of Argyll as a landlord; many rapidly anti-Campbell clansmen were settled on land held in the titular sense by the Campbells simply because these lands were so extensive that they could not be farmed by Campbells. The best-known example of a clan chieftain with an armed following but no title to land was Alexander MacDonald of Keppoch, who was killed in action at Culloden, even though his dispute was mainly with the Mackintoshes, who had aped the Campbells' method of acquiring charter rights. Less well known but even more significant for the issue of the Campbells was the plight of Clan Cameron. The Cameron leaders had pared down their territorial ambitions and tried to hang on to their possessions, compensating for their lack of a clear title to jurisdiction with the loyalty of their tenantry.

The struggle between Campbells and Jacobite clans were not waged merely over nominal superiority. By 1745 there was a clear pattern of indebtedness to the Campbells by the lesser clans; these debts would be liquidated in the event of a Stuart restoration. Some idea of the extent of anti-Campbell feeling in the Highlands can be gauged from a mere rehearsal of all those clans who in 1745 had scores (often literally) to settle with Clan Campbell. The MacGregors had been feuding with the Campbells since time out of mind. The Stewarts of Appin felt peculiarly vulnerable, pressed against the western sea by their mighty neighbour. The Macleans had been constantly invaded and harried in their territory by the race of Diarmid, and would be again during the '45. The Camerons felt the weight of the territorial incursions by the dukes of Argyll. The MacDonalds were animated by ancient rivalries and present apprehensions. For all that, it cannot be claimed that the Campbells were outstanding supporters of the Whigs in a crisis. The Munroes were the only clan actually to join Sir John Cope on his march to Inverness in August 1745. The sons of Diarmid did not make a dramatic appearance on the side of the Hanoverian dynasty until the very day of Culloden, when it was already obvious who was going to win the civil war. Nevertheless, this does not affect the main point and, all in all, it is safe to hazard the generalisation that the Highland clans were motivated in their Jacobitism more by hatred of the Campbells than by love of the Stuarts.

It *is* possible to overdo the Campbell factor and to exaggerate the ferocity of the struggle between Camerons and Campbells. In 1745, for instance, the Cameron clan's chief enemies were Huntly and the Mackintoshes. Moreover, the ambivalence of Rob Roy during the '15 shows that not even the MacGregors were motivated by single-minded hatred of the Campbells. Nor can the presence of most of the MacDonald clans, in arms for the Stuarts in both risings, be construed as part of an anti-Campbell crusade or an attempt to re-create the Lordship of the Isles. There is also the fact that Clan Campbell was frequently split into two factions: one section under the leadership of the dukes of Argyll, the other under the earls of Breadalbane. During the '15 the Campbells in the Breadalbane branch joined the Jacobite earl of Mar under Campbell of Glenlyon.

But at a more profound level, to deny the ultimate importance of the Campbell factor in explaining clan Jacobitism is to fail to appreciate the extent to which the interests of the Campbells and their rivals were irreconcilable and to imagine that the Jacobite chiefs were incapable of seeing this. In particular, given that the traditional clans were threatened not only in the short term by the feudal system proper introduced into the Highlands by the Campbells, but also in the long term by the capitalist system of the Glorious Revolution, a perceptive observer could appreciate the threat to the authority of the clan leaders only too well. As Weber pointed out, feudalism, unlike patrimonialism, opens the door ultimately to the substitution of legal-rational forms of authority for traditional ones. An intelligent chieftain could, by the early eighteenth century, sense the ultimate withering away of his patriarchal position if drastic action were not taken.

Yet another point entered into the deliberations of thoughtful clan leaders like the Camerons of Lochiel. The hereditary kings (the Stuarts) appealed strongly to the clan leaders since their own authority rested on hereditary jurisdiction and customary and traditional rights. This authority was being challenged by the same legal or constitutional (i.e. deriving from statute rather than custom) system which had unseated a king in 1688. The issue was well summed up by the author of the 1745 'Calm Address'; either the law was supreme – and the law and constitution had declared in 1689 that William was the true king – or the true source of legitimacy was not legalistic and was logically prior to anything Parliament might decide. In the case of the clan chiefs the latter argument would carry the implication that their rights over their clan transcended the requirements and entailments of land ownership as decided by the law. It is true that in the early eighteenth century there seemed no alternative to the heritable jurisdictions – the chief source of a clan chieftain's power – because the Scottish crown lacked the financial resources for a legal bureaucracy. But how long would such a state of affairs last? Could it long survive the social change which seemed to be portended by the construction of General Wade's roads in the Highlands?

Before 1745 the Campbells did not have the power to topple the other clans once and for all. The Whig system of government which they had embraced was inoperable in the Highlands, chiefly because of the lack of patronage available to offer wavering chieftains or doubtful Jacobites. The third duke of

Argyll tried to attract Highlanders to him by patronage, but was in the end reduced to more draconian measures, such as making political loyalty a prerequisite for tenancy on his estates. Moreover, the very system of heritable or hereditary jurisdiction of the clans worked against the Campbells. Hereditary jurisdiction was held in the form of the 'regality' such as the House of Atholl and the House of Argyll itself possessed. The regality was a *de facto* independent kingdom where the king's writ in theory ran only in cases of high treason. In addition, hardly any justices of the peace could be appointed because of the refusal of Jacobite leaders to take the Oath of Allegiance. Moreover, the hereditary system posed the old conundrum of *quis custodiet ipsos custodes*. The earl of Cromarty, whose conversion to Jacobitism was belated and motivated purely by self-interest, on being bankrupted retreated to the Highlands to escape his creditors. There, no action could be taken against him except with the help of the sheriff, and he was himself the hereditary sheriff!

There are many features of the Jacobite movement which tell against its being *purely* a movement of nostalgic reaction. Historians have not liked the simplistic view which sees the Jacobite risings as some kind of cultural clash between the Celtic Highlands and north-east and the Anglo-Saxon remainder. But if for 'clash of cultures' we substitute socio-economic conflict, the idea of a collision of irreconcilable interests (between Highland clans and Episcopalian north-eastern landowners on one hand and urban Scotland, the harbinger of a capitalist revolution emanating from England, on the other) looks distinctly more appealing. The clash between the clan system proper and the feudal system of the Campbells was but the opening shot in a battle that would ultimately engulf the feudal system itself and bring all Scotland under the aegis of market forces.

For beyond the threat to the Jacobite clans from the Campbells lay the much more serious onslaught from the capitalist system itself. The Campbell leaders had already demonstrated that they were prepared, when the time was ripe, to convert from being feudal landowners with quasi-familial obligations to being landlords obeying the remorseless dictates of the market. It was only a matter of time before it was deemed expedient in London to take Scotland under the wing of the Whig supremacy by the provision of patronage. It is no mere rhetorical question, then, to ask how long the system of heritable jurisdictions could have survived, even if there had been no rising in 1745.

The most serious objection to the view which denies any significance to the Jacobitism of the clans beyond the contingent fact that certain clan leaders were in fact adherents of the House of Stuart by conviction, is that we are left with no credible motivation either for their rebellion or their Jacobitism itself. It is a supreme irony that some modern economic and social historians by their elimination of all other possibilities should bring us back to the great romantic myth of sentimental Jacobitism – what George Borrow once scathingly called 'Charlie o'er the Water-ism'. It is frequently stated in the literature on the subject that it was ultimately loyalty to the House of Stuart that brought the clans out, that in 1745 the chiefs were shamed into supporting a rebellion to which they did not subscribe, that Lochiel, whose adherence to the prince truly launched the '45, was convinced by the sober plausibility of Charles Edward and his assurances of aid from France. Yet it is surely a devastating riposte to this to point out that not one single clan chief risked everything in the rising for the House of Stuart. The units from the Mackintosh clan which fought on the prince's side were raised in defiance of the clan chief by his wife, Lady Mackintosh. Most of the clan chiefs took no part in the rising, but sent sons or kinsmen to head the clan regiments: Alexander MacDonell of Barisdale sent his son Coll to head their contingent; Ranald MacDonald of Clanranald's stayed at home and sent out his son Ranald; John MacDonell, chief of Glengarry's, did not come out but sent his second son, Angus, to lead the clan regiment; Dugald Stewart, chieftain of the Stewarts of Appin, gave his command to his kinsman Charles Stewart of Ardshiel. In this way the chiefs could claim, if the rebellion failed, that their kinsmen or clansmen had refused to obey their orders. The three clan chieftains who commanded their own clan regiments, Lochiel, Cluny MacPherson and Alexander MacDonald of Keppoch, all had special reasons for apparently venturing all in the Stuart cause. Keppoch had no clear title to territories and seemed on the point of being overwhelmed by the Mackintoshes; Cluny MacPherson only joined the prince on being given security for his lands; while even the 'Gentle Lochiel' of Jacobite legend did not raise the standard until he too had been given security for his estate – his reward in the form of a French regiment after the '45 was financially more profitable than his lands.

None of this looks like striking loyalty to the House of Stuart. Yet the current orthodoxy would apparently have us believe both that the clan chiefs had no profound underlying motivation to rebel against the Whig supremacy and that they were *a priori* loyal to the exiled dynasty. The considerable ambivalence displayed by the chiefs argues rather for the notion that they had very compelling reasons to rise, for their own survival and for a threatened way of life, but that they had serious misgivings about the likely outcome.

Behind the immediate threat to the way of life of the Jacobite clans posed by the Campbells was a second wave of menace – the spreading capitalist revolution of Edinburgh, Glasgow and the Lowlands. General Wade's Highland roads, constructed in the 1720s, in themselves constituted as great a danger to the clan system as the railways were to do to many peasant societies in the nineteenth century. But the real breakthrough for capitalism in Scotland came with the Act of Union in 1707, which gradually began to swing south and central Scotland behind the Hanoverian regime. Naturally the effects of this took time: in the '15 the Whigs had overwhelming support only in the south-west of Scotland and in Glasgow, but by 1745 they were beginning to tighten their grip on the whole of Scotland south of Aberdeen and the Highlands.

The economic genesis of the Act of Union can be sought in the late seventeenth century. Protectionism had been tried under the 1681 Act for the encouragement of Trade and Manufacture but this experiment failed. With the collapse of the Darien scheme at the turn of the century, demands grew in Scotland for access to colonial markets; this was in fact the chief motivation for acceptance of the Act of Union in 1707. Because of the economic recession of the 1690s any government in power after the Glorious Revolution was bound to be unpopular. The four-year famine from 1695 to 1699 was interpreted by some as a sign of God's wrath at the impiety of dethroning an anointed king. Along with government unpopularity went a growing feeling that, as a result of the Union of Crowns in 1603, England would invariably prevail in any clash of interests with Scotland. All these economic discontents were subsumed in a more general opposition to the Act of Union.

The year 1707, then, saw an increasing polarisation of opinion between supporters and opponents of the United Kingdom. The effects of the Act of Union were several. Adam Smith alleged that it enabled the new United Kingdom to outstrip France by creating the largest free trade area in the world. On the Scottish side compensation of £40,000 to the shareholders of the Company of Scotland brought much-needed capital into business life and provide a great stimulus to the Scottish economy. The opening of the colonial and plantation trade was to make Glasgow the chief tobacco port of the realm by the 1720s; Scottish trade in corn and cattle to England prospered; English capital was invested in Scotland and encouragement was given to the Scottish linen industry, especially with the establishment of the Board of Trustees for Fisheries and Manufacturers in 1707.

But there were also many drawbacks to the Act of Union. In the first place, the expected advantages did not materialise overnight. The immediate consequences seemed to be increased taxation and a loss of French trade. In addition, the Scottish clothing industry was now badly affected. For the ordinary person the imposition of the malt tax and excise duties seemed an unsatisfactory *quid pro quo* for the access to colonial markets enjoyed by a minority of capitalists. The malt tax involved a levy of equal duty on malt in Scotland and England. This enraged Scots for three reasons. In the first place, the Treaty of Union expressly exempted Scotland from contributing to the costs of war in which England was engaged, yet the malt tax was specifically designed to meet those costs. Secondly, the Act explicitly exempted Scots from a malt tax during the War of Spanish succession, and in 1707 this war was still six years from its end. Thirdly, the Act of Union specified that future taxes were to be fairly apportioned between the two countries but, given that the annual value of the Scottish barley crop was a tiny fraction of the value of the English one, an equal tax was manifestly unjust. The new Malt Tax Act passed after the Treaty of Utrecht was not implemented in Scotland, but in 1725 Walpole proposed to introduce it there at half the English rate of sixpence a bushel so as to yield £20,000 annually. This provoked a serious Malt Tax riot in Glasgow in 1725 and helped to fuel Scottish Jacobitism, even though not all opponents of the tax by any means were Jacobites.

The Act of Union also introduced an unwonted Customs and Excise system which shocked Scotland by its authoritarian bureaucracy. The new fiscal system in effect prevented the Scots from exchanging their agricultural and fisheries products for the manufactures of the Continent. The wool trade was curtailed in Scotland as it had been in Ireland to deny raw material to England's foreign rivals. This ban on the export of wool led inevitably to a sharp decline in Scottish wool prices. On the import side, the Scots now had either to engage in contraband or buy English manufactures at a cost higher than that on the Continent. Scotland, in a word, paid the price for a policy of protectionism designed to help England alone. As Scottish exports of wool were cut back (mainly to deprive the infant Swedish textile industry of raw material) smuggling arose to take their place. Clashes between smugglers and government officials grew more frequent, reaching their bloody climax in the Edinburgh Porteous riots. Smuggling tended to correlate increasingly with Jacobitism, since Scottish grievances against the Hanoverian regime were overdetermined, having both an economic and a political genesis. Economically the Malt Tax and excise duties harmed Scotland in the ways mentioned; politically their implementation by an army of excise officers seemed to portend an increasing Westminster authoritarianism and the infraction of traditional local autonomy.

Yet another consequence of the Act of Union was that the Presbyterian brand of Scottish nationalism sank without trace; union effectively handed over the leadership in the quest for a specifically Scottish identity to the Jacobites. It was widely considered that union meant an abandonment of a uniquely Scottish destiny and personality in return for being tied to an unacceptable English foreign policy. The Jacobites made the most of their role as standard bearers for Scottish nationalism. After 1707 enthusiasm for the House of Stuart became closely identified with nationalism and a nostalgia for the Scottish past. The cultural revival of the early eighteenth century owed much to Jacobitism. Nearly all printers and booksellers were Jacobite sympathisers; the cultural life of Edinburgh was sustained by gentlemen's clubs, many of whose members were politically disaffected. Almost all members of the legal profession were crypto-Jacobites, and even Lord Kames, who in 1745 produced a forthright attack on the doctrine of the hereditary and indefeasible right of kings, was friendly with Lord Lovat and sympathised with the Jacobite attempt to preserve a distinctive set of cultural values and a unique way of life. There were of course those who were unsympathetic to Stuart aspirations *per se* but longed for Scottish independence, preferably in the form of a republic. This Scottish republicanism coloured the thoughts of many who were prepared to use the Stuarts as a Trojan horse, and some of these were at the very centre of the Jacobite movement. The most notable was perhaps George Keith, the hereditary Earl Marischal of Scotland, who later (after his abandonment of the Stuarts) revealed to Rousseau his essential republicanism.

Jacobitism, then, against the odds survived the long period of peace nurtured by Walpole from the Treaty of Utrecht in 1713 to the war with Spain in 1739. Until the outbreak of war, the Jacobite movement in Scotland can be said to have achieved mixed success. It failed to harness fully the widespread disaffection in the Lowlands towards the government in London but survived as an ideology among the gentry and among Episcopalian and Roman Catholic clergy. As an intellectual force it was far from moribund, having many links with the Enlightenment in Europe, and as an engine of Scottish nationalism it had many favourable structural elements to draw strength from. When it is remembered that a few minutes' hard fighting at Prestonpans in 1745 was enough to deliver the whole of Scotland into Charles Edward's hands, something of the strength of Scottish Jacobitism can be appreciated. In Scotland, at least, the '45 was no 'rash adventure'.

Chapter 5

Who were the Jacobites?

To make the wrong appear the right,
And keep our rulers in;
In Walpole's time, 'twas Jacobite,
In Pitt's, 'tis Jacobin!

Edward Coxe (1805)

May you, may Cam, and Isis, preach it long,
the Right Divine of Kings to govern wrong.

Pope, An Essay on Criticism

I shall do for the Welsh Jacobites what they did for me: I shall
drink their health.

Prince Charles Edward Stuart

Any treatment of the Jacobites must sooner or later address itself
to the question: who exactly were the Jacobites, and what did it
mean to be a Jacobite? Much pointless discussion has taken place
among scholars as to whether such and such a group was 'really'
Jacobite. Historians concerned to minimise the importance of
Jacobitism have argued that few people actually believed in
divine, hereditary and indefeasible right, and that in any case
people are seldom motivated by ideology as opposed to interest.
But this is to overlook the fact that a real or pretended attachment
to the House of Stuart could legitimate all kinds of behaviour that
might otherwise be dubbed deviant.

Country squires objecting to the army of government officials
about to be released on the shires, village labourers rioting over

enclosures or the construction of a turnpike road, the poor protesting about the Salt Act, the Edinburgh proletariat who joined in the Porteous riots or in vocal opposition to the Malt Tax – these were all groups who could hallow their opposition to the Whig supremacy by appealing to the allegedly superior authority *de jure* of the 'king over the water'. A man who hoped for a Scottish republic or an Ireland freed from the English yoke might well decide to use Jacobitism as a Trojan horse for such an ulterior purpose. The Earl Marischal would fit well into this category if Rousseau's recollections of his confidences are correct.

It can be objected that this makes Jacobitism a catch-all. Yet all influential political doctrines have this feature. If a man opposes the capitalist system because he feels it to be inherently unjust or because he feels he would do better under socialism, is it then correct to say that he has no sympathy for Marxism simply because the grounds of his opposition to capitalism are not those of theories of praxis, alienation, surplus value, commodity fetishism or the 'class for itself'? Many people are attracted to alternative political ideologies because of a merely negative dislike of the *status quo* and a feeling of being 'agin' the government'.

It is the confusion of Jacobitism in this sense with ideological Jacobitism proper that has enabled historians to label the defeat of the Jacobite risings 'inevitable' and to argue that in the eighteenth century the cause of the Stuarts was an 'anachronism'. The *status quo* always enjoys an advantage when people are politically apathetic, simply through inertia. Real attachment to the Hanoverian regime is not shown by a failure to rally to the Stuart standard. What matters is how many people were prepared actively to rally to the Hanoverians' *defence*. Put like this, there can be only one answer to the counter-question, how many people were pro-Hanoverian?: very few. A genius at political mobilisation could, in another era, have welded together an overwhelming anti-regime coalition from the disparate 'out' groups who were prepared to see the 'Pretender' back on the throne, but the capacity for forming mass movements did not appear in European history until the French Revolution. It would be truly anachronistic to look for such a capability during the Jacobite century.

Nevertheless, when we speak of Jacobites it is best to refer specifically to the group of people who, for reasons of ideology or self-interest, attached themselves to the cause of the House of Stuart for a sustained period of time rather than on an *ad hoc* basis. We have already analysed the reasons why Scots of all varieties should have been attracted to Jacobitism. In general, the sober conclusion would be that the most ideologically motivated Scots – and also those who lost most in the Jacobite risings – were the properly feudal lairds (mainly Episcopalian) of the north-east and the Lowlands. The clan leaders can be seen in almost every case to have been motivated by hard-headed calculations of interest.

Another group that might be thought likely to produce substantial quantities of 'real' Jacobites turns out to be a disappointing source: the Catholics of the British Isles. The English Catholics of Lancashire and Tyneside did, it is true, make some sort of showing in the 1715 rising. But by 1745 they were conspicuous in Charles Edward's army only by their absence. In Scotland, too, Catholicism was insignificant alongside Episcopalianism and even Presbyterianism in the Jacobites' religious profile. The equation Catholic = Jacobite always made good Whig propaganda but was never a serious proposition. Even in Catholic Ireland, where draconian penal laws against 'Popery' were on the statute book, a 'softly softly' approach by the authorities towards Catholicism yielded hefty dividends. There was scarcely a peep out of Ireland during the two great Jacobite risings, and successive lords-lieutenant felt confident enough about local security to divert large parts of their standing army for use in England.

In so far as there is any identifiable religious connection with Jacobitism in the eighteenth century, it must be sought not among Catholics but among Scottish Episcopalians and English non-jurors – those members of the Anglican church who had refused to take the Oath of Allegiance in 1689 or the Abjuring Oath of 1701, and whose allegiance to the principles of divine, hereditary and indefeasible right was likened by Macaulay to the ancient Egyptian worship of cats.

It is generally assumed that, as the years wore on and the chances of a Stuart restoration appeared more slender, support for the Jacobites decreased, at least in England. But in one case it can be demonstrated that, if anything, precisely the opposite happened. The price of the years of rock-solid Whig hegemony from 1715 to 1761 was the proscription of the opposition party, the Tories. The first two Georges proscribed the Tory party because they listened to Whig propaganda describing the Tories as crypto-Jacobites. But the effect of turning a major political party into a sect of untouchables was to create a self-fulfilling prophecy. In desperation at the prospect of generations in the political wilderness, many Tories actually *did* turn to Jacobitism and repose all their hopes for a political future in the restoration of the House of Stuart. By 1745 there was a powerful Tory 'fifth column' in England, which suffered, however, from the grave defect that it could not make itself viable as a rebel military force.

Until the rebellion of 1745 Jacobitism was a limb of Toryism itself. Although the extent of Jacobite sentiment within the Tory party in the early eighteenth century has long been disputed, it may safely be asserted that the Jacobites within the Tory party stood to the rump of the party much as a socialist faction would stand to the Labour party today. Unfortunately, however, an analysis of the social composition of Jacobitism within Tory ranks does not take us closer to an understanding of Jacobitism as a social phenomenon. Jacobites of whatever kidney, whether motivated by principle or interest, cannot be said to form any readily identifiable social grouping. An examination of members of Parliament during the years 1715–54 produces no clear pattern. Supporters of the House of Stuart can be found among both long-serving members and those who entered Parliament for the first time in 1741; among army officers, though rarely among naval officers; among industrialists, and above all among lawyers. But the same classifications also provide some of the most committed Whigs.

Although the Jacobite and the Tory ideology were at many points close, what really made the Jacobite element in the Tory party so strong in the thirty years 1715–45 was the political proscription of the Tories in the reign of the first two Georges, a situation which drove them to desperate expedients. After 1715 the Tory gentry could no longer provide for younger sons in the expected manner, since traditional places in the army, civil service and church were denied them. Tory army officers lost commissions, often without compensation, Tory lawyers could no longer aspire to posts as judges or KCs. The predominantly Tory lower clergy could not rise to episcopal office; Tory merchants could no longer obtain government contracts or directorships of the Bank of England and other great public companies. Many of the Tory gentry could no longer afford to stand for Parliament, once deprived of office-holding, and were deprived of their traditional political base in the counties through being excluded from the county lieutenancy. As Bolingbroke expressed it: 'If milder measures had been pursued, certain it is that the Tories had never universally embraced Jacobitism. The violence of the Whigs forced them into the arms of the Pretender.'

It was only to be expected that prospects of political power weighed heavily with supporters of the House of Stuart. Almost as persuasive was the prospect for debtors of having their debts wiped out by a root and branch dismantling of the old regime. The relationship between debtors and creditors was a key political issue in the eighteenth century. The 1787 Philadelphia Convention which drew up the United States constitution devoted more of its time to discussing whether debts should be liquidated under the new regime than to considering all the nuances of federalism – some would say with fatal later results.

Bankruptcy as a motive for Jacobitism ran deep and wide, across the social spectrum of Jacobite support. Three of the members of the prince's council in 1745 were bankrupts: the earls of Kilmarnock and Cromarty and the prince's secretary, John Murray of Broughton. Kilmarnock, who went to the block for his part in the rebellion, made no bones about this. 'For the two kings and their rights I cared not a farthing which prevailed; but I was starving, and, by God, if Mahommed had set up his standard in the Highlands, I had been a good Muslim for bread and stuck close to the party, for I must eat.'

Murray, Kilmarnock and Cromarty were only the most famous bankrupts attached to the Stuart cause. Many more were to be found in the Jacobite movement in general and in the Highland army in 1745. In the '15 many northern Catholics found their loyalty to the Stuarts overdetermined as financial ruin oppressed them. Economic depression, such as the slump in the north-eastern coal trade after 1693, coincided with the imposition of a new land tax to pay for war. Among the northern gentry it was particularly the Catholics who were hurt by these developments, since the penal laws cut off the possible financial escape route afforded to others in the form of government office-holding; before 1715 there was scarcely a single Catholic gentleman in Northumberland whose estates were not heavily mortgaged, but whereas in 1715 the northern Catholic gentry had 'come out' mainly because of their parlous financial state, by 1745 this social group had virtually disappeared. No real connection can be found between Catholicism and bankruptcy in the '45. Nevertheless a whole new class of ruined men had arisen. A string of bankruptcies occurring among the lesser gentry in the years after 1730, mainly caused by agricultural depression, led men to Jacobitism in the way that desperate situations often lead to desperate expedients.

The Jacobite movement was full of men actuated by bankruptcy. The correlation between financial insolvency and Jacobite politics can be well observed in the career of the duke of Wharton. Even more notorious is the case of Charles Caesar (MP for Hertfordshire), whose financial Jacobitism was miraculously transformed into zeal for the Protestant succession when Walpole agreed to write off his debts. There was a huge class of actual or potential Jacobites among men who had nothing to gain from the new regime of 1688, had lost their place in society since then, or stood to make enormous gains from the overthrow of the Whig supremacy. Many of these actually took up arms in the '45: government records frequently speak of Jacobite prisoners known to be bankrupts. In one 1746 indictment for rebellion alone we find the following list of bankrupts: Sir John Wedderburn of Blankness, David Fotheringham of Powrie (who acted as Jacobite governor of Dundee), James Lindsay of Glenquist, James Hepburn of Keith, Patrick Walland of Abertrothock and David Carmichael of Balmeddie (all members of the Scottish gentry).

This 'economic Jacobitism' was well appreciated at the time. Creditors realised with trepidation, and debtors with joy, that debts would be liquidated if the Hanoverian regime was overthrown in the Jacobite risings. It was a common jibe in Ireland in 1745 that Catholic debtors had suspended payment to their creditors until they could see the outcome of the rebellion. There were of course many other manifestations of Jacobitism by reason of pecuniary advantage. One obvious category of such Jacobites through interest comprised all those who stood to regain lands forfeited in earlier risings or, as in the case of the Irish Catholics, expropriated in the Cromwellian and Williamite conquests.

Perhaps the most fascinating group of 'economic Jacobites' were the smugglers of the south coast. Contraband in the Channel had become big business by the early eighteenth century. Organised crime syndicates took over the smuggling operations and, Mafia-like, added extortion, bribery, highway robbery and murder to their activities. Many of the senior customs officials were themselves clients of the smuggling rings.

Revenue officials fought a losing battle with these smugglers. 1733 was a high-water mark for Walpole's officials. In the very year his notorious Excise Act was being bitterly contested in the Commons, his customs officers seized an estimated 10 per cent of the year's total contraband cargo, including 54,000 pounds of tea and 123,000 gallons of brandy. The scale of profits possible to a smuggling syndicate can be imagined when it is realised that tea bought in Holland at 3½ pence a pound sold in England at anything from 17 pence to 25 pence, and that French brandy bought for £1 a keg retailed at £4 in Britain. So great was the power of the smuggling syndicates that some of them, like the Hawkhurst gang, were capable of assembling a small army, some 300 strong, to recover cargoes impounded by the Customs. It is related that in 1747 this gang marched from Kent to Dorset in pursuit of a cargo of tea, stormed the Poole customs house and marched back to Kent with their booty.

These men, like other marginal groups, supported the Jacobites because they were the most famous political group 'agin' the government. The theory that the Hanoverians were an illegitimate and possibly also an 'illegal' dynasty was obviously popular with men who daily defied its laws. While in most cases the 'Jacobitism' of the smugglers simply amounted to finding a pretext of legitimacy for their illicit trading, sometimes it went beyond that into active support. When the French were preparing their invasion of England in late 1745 at Calais and Boulogne, they received invaluable information from traffickers in cross-Channel contraband about Admiral Vernon's movements. Whether the smugglers' attachment to the House of Stuart would have survived its advent to power is another matter.

It is already clear, then, that Jacobite sentiment was in most cases peppered with ambivalence. This was especially true of international Jacobitism. The Jacobites in France are a good example. Some, like Lord Clare, clearly put their own career in the French service first and the cause of the Stuarts second. Others, like Thomas Lally Tollendal, though regimental commanders in the Irish Brigade in the pay of Louis XV, were prepared to exert themselves to the maximum in the hope of a

Stuart restoration. For another group, the Stuarts were the Trojan horse towards the ultimate aim of republicanism. Piere André O'Heguerty, the leading thinker in the Franco-Irish shipowning Jacobite clique, wanted an Irish republic, and argued to the French court that Ireland's true long-term interests would not be served if the Stuarts were restored to the three kingdoms. The Earl Marischal wanted a Scots Republic but could see no way to dispense with the Stuarts in the short term. His nationalistic aims received unexpected support after the '45 in the shape of the returned French envoy, the marquis d'Eguilles, whose experiences in Charles Edward's army had convinced him that a republic in Scotland most closely matched French interests. Yet another group of Irish exiles, typified by Lord Clancarty, wanted the return of their attainted or expropriated estates, and supported the Stuarts for this reason.

The strong streak of ambivalence running through so many Jacobites in Britain was visible in France as well. There is something of a mystery about the Jacobite provenance and the eventual fate of so many of these figures who served Charles Edward in France; the best-known such shadowy figure was the prince's envoy to the French court in 1745, Sir James Stewart of Goodless, Lord Elcho's brother-in-law. The ambiguous stance of Marischal, Clare and O'Heguerty is also worthy of examination. Of course, in the case of O'Heguerty, like that of the other Franco-Irish shipowners, Antoine Walsh and Walter Ruttledge, other motives were at work. Their principal occupation was privateering, and a Jacobite rising in Scotland would compel the Royal Navy to withdraw ships from convoy and patrol duties in the English sea lanes in order to blockade Scotland; this would then open up the Channel to the French privateers.

Since the overwhelming majority of Jacobites in France were Irishmen in the service of France, either informally, like Walsh and O'Heguerty, or officially, like Lally and Clare, through being regimental commanders in the Irish Brigade, the Irish dimension of Jacobitism received a good deal of attention during the '45. Particular bitterness arose within Charles Edward's army over this issue. The Scots felt that the prince favoured the coterie of Irishmen ranged around John William O'Sullivan, the army quarter-master. Scottish officers were unable to gain an introduction to Charles Edward, while the most worthless individuals with O'Sullivan's recommendation secured rank and favour (one

Irish deserter from the British dragoons received a commission, when his sole motive for joining the prince was that he had murdered his regimental sergeant). The baneful influence of such as Strickland and O'Sullivan on Charles Edward led to bitter resentment and recrimination from the more hot-tempered Scottish commanders like Lords Elcho, Ogilvy and George Murray, who regarded the military pretensions of the Irish favourites with utter contempt. The privilege bestowed on Irishmen infuriated all those Scots gentlemen who had enlisted in the Jacobite army at their own expense, especially when it was considered that the Irish officers risked nothing if captured; their French commissions would enable them to secure the status of ordinary prisoners of war, while the Scots were likely to suffer the fate prescribed for 'traitors and rebels'. Although Lord George Murray scathingly remarked that their military know-ledge did not extend beyond an ability to mount guard, many who held the lowly rank of captain in the French service were promoted to colonel to ensure higher pay on return to France. Captain Brown of Lally's was promoted colonel simply for conveying the news of the battle of Falkirk to the French court. When Charles Edward proposed giving command of the Manchester regiment to the Irish officer Sir Francis Geoghan, a near-mutiny of his colonels resulted in the command's being given to Towneley.

Perhaps the most spectacular example of an Irishman 'on the make' was provided by Richard Augustus Warren. At the beginning of 1745 Warren was a bankrupt merchant from Marseilles, grubbing a precarious living as a volunteer in the French army. After six months with Charles Edward in Scotland, in which time he never saw military action, Warren was sent to Versailles to exaggerate the significance of the trivial skirmish in which the duke of Perth dispersed the forces of Lord Loudoun (the so-called 'Rout of Moy'). As a reward for this 'exploit' Charles Edward bestowed a colonelcy on Warren, and Louis XV supplemented this at his interview with the prince's aide-de-camp by making him a Knight of the Order of St Louis. Truly an opportunistic Jacobite could, with luck, rise high and fast in the eighteenth century.

Yet it would be a gross oversimplification to suggest that there were *no* committed Jacobites. Jacobite ideology certainly had its attractions. Apart from its function as an ideology of

86

Scottish nationalism, Jacobite doctrine contained three main strands. There was the quietism of Fénelon, so beloved by James, and given a new coat of ideological paint by the Chevalier Ramsay and the Jacobite mystics of north-east Scotland. The principal element in this was the acceptance of God's providence. Lord Pitsligo's writings, with their strongly devotional and pietistic flavour, give one a good idea of this type of Jacobite ideology. Then there was the theory of kingship by divine, hereditary and indefeasible right, taken over from the seventeenth-century theorists Bossuet and Filmer, and advocated by brilliant Jacobite essayists like Charles Leslie and Bishop Atterbury. The 'divine right of kings' had a long history before the Jacobite period and was a doctrine particularly associated with the Stuarts. The idea that a king's authority came directly from God, to whom alone the monarch was responsible for his actions, was acceptable to a wide range of people. So too was the hereditary principle, which avoided disputes about the succession. What stuck in most eighteenth-century throats was the idea of an *indefeasible* divine right. This meant that whoever had the right to be king could not lose it, *whatever* he did. Obviously this made the Glorious Revolution of 1688 an act of sacrilege against God. To counter this dogma, Whigs stressed that kingship was in trust, held only by the will of Parliament, which could be revoked.

The third strand in Jacobite ideology was what is sometimes referred to as the 'Country' position. This meant opposition to 'corruption' – a term used in the eighteenth century in a technical sense to denote the existence of the National Debt, excise and other high taxation, placemen, pensions and, above all, a 'standing army'. Good government, according to 'Country' ideology, meant adherence to an 'ancient constitution', located in a golden age in the past, the separation of powers, annual parliaments, and the militia principle. This 'Country' ideology was of great importance in the series of Jacobite manifestos drawn up prior to attempted French invasions (such as that of 1743–44) by James Stuart himself. The National Debt was a particular target for these manifestos, as Charles Edward's series of proclamations from Edinburgh in October 1745 shows. As late as 1753 Charles Edward wrote a memorandum, incorporating proposals for an annual parliament, abolition of placemen and the standing army, plus other features of the 'Country' programme, in the event of his restoration.

How great a part ideology played in the motivation of Jacobites in general it is difficult to tell. Some of them ignored it completely, some used it as rationalisation for economic interests, but others undoubtedly took it seriously and genuinely believed in it. Among ideological Jacobites in Charles Edward's army in 1745 we can clearly identify, at the top level, Lord George Murray, Lord Pitsligo and Lord Balmerino.

Lord Pitsligo was singled out by Dr William King in his *Anecdotes* as the one truly saintly man of the eighteenth century. When he set out from Aberdeen with his cavalry troop of Banffshire gentlemen, Pitsligo demonstrated his utter unconcern for worldly advantage with these words: 'O Lord, Thou knowest that our cause is just. March, gentlemen.' Another epitome of the ideologically committed Episcopalian north-east was Arthur Elphinstone, Lord Balmerino. In his pre-execution speech in 1746 Balmerino showed absolutely no signs of recanting. Instead he made the following prayer: 'O Almighty God, I humbly beseech thee to bless the king, the Prince of Wales and the Duke of York, and all the dutiful branches of the Royal Family.' Lord George Murray's account of his motives was less fulsome but just as concise: 'I am satisfied there is much greater need of a Revolution now to secure our liberties and save Britain from utter destruction than there was at the last, even if the king's rights were not in question.'

At a lower level in Prince Charles's army the influence of ideology can be seen too. The fanatical pro-Stuart Laurence Oliphant of Gask, second-in-command in Kilmarnock's cavalry, said simply: 'God sent our rightful Prince among us and I followed him.' And this is John Daniel, of Perth's regiment, explaining why he joined the Jacobite army in England: 'The first time I saw this loyal army was betwixt Lancaster and Garstang; the brave prince marching on foot at their head like a Cyrus or Trojan hero, drawing admiration and love from all who beheld him, raising their long-dejected hearts, and solacing their minds with the happy prospect of another golden age.'

Even within the sphere of doctrine it is doubtful if Jacobite ideology can be described as 'anachronistic' in, say, 1745, unless we restrict the said ideology narrowly to a belief in divine, hereditary and indefeasible right. Yet, even so, we are confronted by a puzzling feature about the human imagination to which historians of ideas have not paid sufficient attention. The rejection of the hereditary principle in politics by the Whigs and advocates of Glorious Revolution ideology was not followed by its rejection in economics. Rather the reverse, since the overthrow of the divine right of kings was followed by the enthronement of the divine right of property. Not even Locke, who based his entire political philosophy on the 'natural' rights of property, could explain how such 'natural rights' included the right of bequest. The question was too difficult, so he ignored it.

Now it does seem that contemporary historians, in placing so much emphasis on the 'anachronistic' nature of the theory of the divine right of kings in the eighteenth century, are themselves unconsciously underlining the deep springs of irrationality in human discourse. As the Chevalier Ramsay pointed out on behalf of the Jacobites, why should there be this differential treatment of economic and political power? Why is it 'absurd' to expect political power to be transmitted across the generations but 'natural' for a man to be able to leave property to his children? Historians who employ terms like 'anachronistic' to describe the Jacobite movement in the eighteenth century, on the grounds that there was something unenlightened about divine right, are in effect smuggling in a hidden premise that people are overwhelmingly influenced by rationality. Yet the twentieth-century attachment to 'divine right' in the bequeathing of hereditary property shows conclusively that this cannot be so. When the conceptual skeins are unravelled, what 'anachronistic' seems to mean, in statements like 'the cause of the Stuarts was anachronistic', is simply 'had been devastated by successful propaganda' – a quite different matter.

It should be clear enough that the motives even of sustained and enduring Jacobites, as opposed to the *ad hoc* variety, were always very mixed. It would be pleasant to conclude that virtue was its own reward and that believers in providence fared better than the cynics, the devious and the calculating. An analysis of the fate of those who were 'out' in the Jacobite risings shows that this was not so. The axe and the gibbet were visited on ideologue, debtor and self-server alike. The one exception was perhaps the most deserving case. Lord Pitsligo's saintliness was a byword even among the Whigs; possibly for this reason the search for him in the north-east after Culloden was not pressed whole-heartedly. Scott rightly claims that a great prince (which George II was not) would immediately have pardoned Pitsligo and set his 'treason' down as misplaced idealism.

Mention of Pitsligo leads to a final point about the Jacobites and their motives. It is hard not to see them as being, in the round, of a marked *moral* superiority to their enemies. The Whig supremacy was symbolised by Walpole, the very avatar of the god of corruption. The Hanoverian Tories were exemplified in Bolingbroke, the archetype of political trimmer. The Jacobites were represented by men like Bishop Atterbury and the duke of Ormonde. In the '45 itself the singularly unpleasant George II stood in contrast to the attractive but ineffectual James Stuart. While the Whigs were represented by princes of cynicism, duplicity, corruption and machiavellianism like the duke of Newcastle, Henry Pelham, Lord Hardwicke, Lord Chesterfield and the duke of Cumberland, the Jacobites could boast Lord Pitsligo, Lord Balmerino, Lochiel, Lord George Murray and even (at this stage in his career) Charles Edward himself. It is not disputed that the majority of Jacobites were motivated by obvious self-interest. But the best of them far outshone the best of the Whigs. It is no mere rhetorical question to ask whether there can be found on the Whig side a single figure who can be identified as ideologically committed, beyond all suggestions of material interest, to the much-vaunted Protestant supremacy. To conclude thus is to be open to charges of violent pro-Jacobite partisanship. But the accusation is largely pharisaical. Such judgments are the staple of history. Even the most unregenerate revisionist would not claim that the Nazi leadership had the stature of Churchill, Roosevelt or de Gaulle. It is a tribute to the power of the Namierites in historiography that the Whig spades have not often been called the spades they were.

Chapter 6

The first wave: the Jacobite risings of 1708, 1715 and 1719

The wind and the waves are always on the side of the best navigators.

Gibbon

The Tories in England long imagined that they were enthusiastic about monarchy, the church and the beauties of the old English Constitution, until the day of danger wrung from them the confession that they are enthusiastic only about ground rent.

Marx, The Eighteenth Brumaire of Louis Bonaparte

> There's some say that we wan
> And some say that they wan
> And some say that none at's wan;
> But one thing I'm sure,
> That at Sherramuir,
> A battle there was, that I saw, man.

Hogg, Jacobite Relics

The struggle between Revolution principles and Jacobitism had a momentum of its own, unaffected by changes of leadership. William III died in 1702, to be succeeded by James II's daughter Anne. James himself had died the year before, when the thirteen-year-old James Francis became James III *de jure*. But these changes of monarch seemed almost incidental to the real conflict, which was waged with increasing ferocity in the early years of the eighteenth century. The Whigs responded to Louis XIV's recognition of 'James III' by introducing an oath, to be taken by all ecclesiastics, university and school teachers, abjuring the 'Pretender'. James himself was attainted for high treason, and it was made a treasonable offence for anyone in England to correspond with him or send him money. When Dr Sacheverell preached the virtues of passive obedience (criticising the 1688 revolution) in 1709, he was brought to trial in a *cause célèbre*. It was in this context of ever-augmenting bitterness that the Jacobite risings took place. The contested succession was the occasion for all the last battles fought on British soil. Apart from Killie-krankie, the Boyne and Aughrim in 1689–91, the Jacobite risings proper saw six further full-scale engagements: Sheriffmuir and Preston in 1715, Glenshiel in 1719, and Prestonpans, Falkirk and Culloden in 1745–46.

The Jacobite risings are a historical curiosity in more ways than one. Perhaps their most curious aspect was that as the objective conditions favouring a Stuart restoration worsened, so they came closer to success. On paper the '08 attempt should have been something of a walkover, given the fury in Scotland over the 1707 Act of Union. Yet it was the Jacobites' most ignominious failure. The 1715 rising fared better, even though the fact of a European peace and French non-involvement worked against its likely success. But the rising which came closest to military success was the '45, undertaken in the least promising of all historical contexts, when on paper the rebellion should never have got off the ground. This raises interesting problems of historical structure versus conjuncture as primary causal motors, as also the role of subjective conditions versus objective conditions. It also prompts crucial questions about the nature of revolutionary leadership.

Properly speaking, there were only three Jacobite risings involving military engagements on British soil: those of 1715, 1719 and 1745. For some reason historians have chosen to include the French attempt to land troops in 1708 as a 'Jacobite rising', though by this logic the 1759 expedition ought presumably to count too (unless a Jacobite rising includes occasions when a Stuart pretender got sight of Britain). For the sake of completeness, however, we shall devote a few lines to the fiasco of 1708. For although the Jacobite attempt to foment rebellion in Scotland in 1708 cannot properly be called a 'rising' – since nobody actually rose – it is of great interest since it illustrates many of the recurring themes of the Jacobite risings.

First, there was half-heartedness by the French. Louis XIV gave the order for 6,000 men to assemble in Dunkirk because he was smarting under Marlborough's victories and wished to strike back at his tormentor. It was a reflex action of *ancien régime* France to toy with ideas of an invasion of Britain when a continental war was going badly. But the keen edge of Louis XIV's enterprise was blunted by factionalism between Minister of War Chamillart and Minister of Marine Pontchartrain. The choice of naval commander was also a disaster. Admiral Forbin was half-hearted about the enterprise, and express orders had to be sent from Versailles even to get him to put to sea. Nevertheless, Louis XIV's seriousness cannot be doubted. Six thousand men were assembled at Dunkirk to be transported in converted men o'war and privateers, accompanied by five warships. Louis wished the twenty-year-old James godspeed and informed his diplomatic representatives in Rome, Geneva and other neutral cities about the impending restoration bid.

Next, there was the combination of Channel weather and the Royal Navy. The invasion fleet was blockaded in Dunkirk during March 1708 by Admiral Byng's squadron. When contrary winds forced the British away towards Brittany, Forbin at last put to sea. Having survived dreadful gales, the fleet arrived outside the Firth of Forth to find a Royal Navy flotilla waiting for them. A running fight developed until, outnumbered, Forbin stood away for Aberdeen and Dundee. James begged to be put ashore with just a few men; he had a plan for capturing Edinburgh Castle. Since there was no sign of a rising in Scotland to welcome him, Forbin and the army commander, the comte de Gace, concurred in finding this idea quixotic and refused to disembark him. There was to be no heroic exploit like that of his son thirty-seven years later for the young James.

Since Forbin would neither risk a single ship in attempting to put troops ashore on the Forth nor allow James himself to land, it was obvious that he had from the very start been a disastrous choice as admiral of the expedition. But the fact that there was no coordination between Jacobites in France and their partisans in Scotland helped his defeatist cause. With little protest from Gace, Forbin put about and headed for Dunkirk. One lesson, though, was learned from the débâcle, and was used by Charles Edward thirty-seven years later: that a descent on Scotland was better attempted from the west coast.

Undoubtedly Forbin missed a great opportunity in 1708. Even if he had put James ashore alone, great things might have been achieved. Scotland was denuded of troops, and ten battalions of battle-fatigued, seasick troops, hastily withdrawn from Flanders by the government in London, would not have provided a major obstacle to a general uprising in Scotland, maddened as the country then was by the Act of Union. Resentment at English highhandedness was at its apogee in Scotland in 1708 following the desperately unpopular incorporating union of 1707. Queen Anne might have been prepared to come to some arrangement with James at this juncture rather than risk a bloody civil war. But it was not to be.

As always throughout the Jacobite risings, luck was against the Stuarts and their supporters. James, a born loser if ever there was one, had to endure heavy seas all the way back to France into the bargain. The only one to gain from the '08 was the comte de Gace, who received the baton of a marshal of France for his part in this fiasco!

Another feature of the '08 which prefigured the circumstances of later, more serious descents on Scotland was the ferocity with which the London government pursued those who were so much as suspected of Jacobite sympathies. The duke of Gordon and Lords Seaforth, Errol, Murray, Marischal and Traquair were imprisoned in Edinburgh Castle. The duke of Atholl, who pleaded 'illness', had an unfriendly troop of soldiers quartered on him in his castle.

Once again, too, it can be observed how a Jacobite diversion in wartime affected military movements in Europe. Marlborough's victory at Oudenarde in July 1708 was made possible by Forbin's pusillanimous actions. Without the ten battalions detached to Scotland, he would not have dared bring Marshal Vendôme to a pitched battle. With their return he was able to win his third great victory. This was a signal reversal of fortunes, for usually the French stood to gain something at least from every Jacobite attempt.

The seven-year gap between the débâcle of 1708 and the Jacobite rising of 1715 can be partly explained in terms of enhanced Jacobite hopes of a peaceful Stuart restoration. In 1710 the Tories, widely held to be favourable to the 'Pretender', came to power. The new government included Robert Harley, earl of Oxford; Henry St John, Viscount Bolingbroke; and the duke of

Ormonde. Much was expected of these three at the Stuart court in St-Germain-en-Laye. But such hopes were soon dashed. It was this government which signed the Treaty of Utrecht, among whose provisions was the expulsion of James from France. Thenceforth, until the '15, James took up residence in Lorraine.

The death of Queen Anne found both the English Tories and the Continental Jacobites in confusion and disarray. A few days before Anne's death a blazing row had taken place between Oxford and Bolingbroke, which led to Oxford's dismissal. Bolingbroke had spent the last hours of the queen's reign dealing with a personal rival when he should have been bending his energies to opposing the Whig duke of Shrewsbury, the new Lord Treasurer. An enterprising man might have planned to appear on English soil the moment Anne died and declare himself king, but this was not James's way. George I was proclaimed king and emissaries sent to Hanover to bring him to London with all speed. In June 1714 a price of £5,000 was put on James's head. This was raised to £100,000 in September.

George I landed at Greenwich in September 1714, but it was a year before the expected Jacobite backlash took shape. Why was this? The primary cause was France. When the Elector of Hanover was proclaimed king, James hurried to Paris, only to be informed by the French minister Torcy that Louis XIV required him to leave French territory immediately, in accordance with the terms of the Treaty of Utrecht. This time France put the maintenance of the peace ahead of Stuart ambitions, and refused to get involved.

The secondary cause was lack of a military commander. It had been thought that with Marlborough's rapid fall from grace in England he might be available as a Stuart captain, but the first of the Churchills never committed himself openly to anything less than a cast-iron certainty. Wisely, he kept his head down and took himself off on a European tour. The duke of Ormonde had fled with Bolingbroke to France in March 1715 to avoid being impeached for Jacobite activities, but he was not a man of sufficient calibre to mastermind a military operation on the grand scale. His role was restricted to the minor one of putative commander of the rising in the south-west of England. That left Berwick, James's half-brother, as the obvious choice.

Berwick was already a military hero of the War of Spanish Succession and a marshal of France. But he found himself pulled in two directions at once. On the one hand, he was a member of the Stuart family. On the other, he was a naturalised French subject whose first loyalty lay with France. It was inconceivable that one who was a peer of the realm, a provincial governor and a marshal of France could disobey the king and leave the country to attack a nation with which France was at peace. Yet when he pointed this out to James, the 'Pretender' flew into a towering rage.

Bolingbroke was no soldier, Berwick refused the commission and Marlborough was out of the reckoning. This was the background against which the earl of Mar insinuated himself as *de facto* Jacobite commander. Nevertheless, preparations were pushed ahead for a rising. Jacobite spies alerted the clan chieftains as to what was in the wind, and letters and arms were transported from France to the Highlands. Money for the future use of Scottish Jacobites was conveyed to Drummond Castle; arms were hidden near Fort William. Even more encouragingly, money began to flow into the Jacobite coffers. The king of Spain sent 428,520 French livres, and was later to send 200,000 crowns on an ill-fated treasure ship. A wealthy French banker gave 50,000 écus in return for a title when James was restored. The duke of Lorraine contributed 25,000 golden louis. The pope provided £20,000 in the years 1714–16. Even Marlborough secretly donated £2,000 as an insurance policy.

Initially the Jacobite rising of 1715 was planned as a three-pronged affair. The south-west of England was to be the main area of operations. Here James was to land in company with Ormonde. The risings in the Highlands and the border counties were originally designed as subsidiary affairs. The rebels in the south-west were to march on London, and those in the Highlands on Edinburgh and Glasgow. But it was a fatal flaw in the initial planning that no definite objective was ever laid down for the border uprising. This was to have catastrophic consequences.

Even before the imbroglio on the border revealed itself, things started to go badly wrong. The rebellion in the south-west was betrayed by spies and nipped in the bud in September 1715. This brings us to another recurrent motif in the Jacobite risings: lack of liaison between Jacobites in Britain and those on the Continent. Long after the rising in south-west England was scotched, James arrived at St-Malo, preparing to cross to

Plymouth. Having travelled to the coast from Bar in Lorraine in disguise, James waited at St-Malo from 8 November 1715, gloomily watching the high seas and Channel storms. Not until 2 December did he learn that all was lost in south-west England. Then, disguised as a sailor, he proceeded along the coast to Dunkirk, intending to make the Scottish part of the campaign the nodal point of the rebellion.

But meanwhile disaster had struck in both England and Scotland. The débâcle in England had already been prefigured in the lack of a specific objective for the Jacobites of the border country. That in Scotland was largely due to the lacklustre performance of the earl of Mar. John Erskine, eleventh earl of Mar, scion of one of the oldest houses in Scotland, was a notorious trimmer – hence his nickname of 'Bobbing John'. He had been disposed to accept the Glorious Revolution and the Act of Union, but a snub from George I in September 1714 decided him to make overtures to the Pretender. A second, directly personal snub by George I at a royal levee in August 1715 made Mar's mind up for him.

The next day he sailed for Scotland, organised a *tynchal*, or great hunt, on his estates in Aberdeenshire, and on 6 September raised the blue and gold standard of the House of Stuart at Braemar. Although Ormonde was still officially captain-general of James's armies in Britain, Mar was now the *de facto* commander. But, as Berwick had predicted, Mar was not the man for the job. On paper everything was in his favour. He had begun his campaign in a friendly country, and was supported by a large number of the nobility of Scotland and many of the clan chiefs. Against him the Whig commander-in-chief, the duke of Argyll, could muster initially no more than 1,500 men. Even his own clan, the Campbells, was split, with many following the pro-Jacobite Breadalbane faction. Yet Mar vacillated and delayed. Fabian tactics are fine for the commander who has the support of an entrenched political and social system, but they were disastrous for the revolutionary leader. By his inactivity Mar threw away the most favourable military odds the Jacobites ever enjoyed.

At first Mar's lack of ability was masked by the easy initial successes he enjoyed. An abortive Jacobite attempt to seize Edinburgh Castle seemed more than compensated for by Mar's taking of Perth, which gave him command of all Scotland north of the Tay. But when he still took no decisive action in October, doubts began to surface. By the end of the first week in October the Glengarry men, Clanranalds and Mackintoshes had joined the army, as also the proscribed MacGregors under the legendary but villainous Rob Roy. The total muster produced 10,500 foot and 1,500 horse. Against this Argyll had as yet barely 2,000.

It was more than ever essential for Mar to take decisive action now that things had fizzled out in the south-west of England. Later he was to plead two constraints: lack of information about James's movements, and lack of money. The second was certainly a more cogent consideration, since the collection of public monies (excise and cess) did not produce enough revenue to support the army. Mar had to issue a proclamation, ordering all landlords in his army to raise money from their estates by forcing their tenants to pay a levy of twenty shillings on every hundred pounds Scots of valued rent. Yet money should not have provided an insuperable barrier to a successful campaign. After all, there were rich pickings just to the south, in Edinburgh and Glasgow.

Realising that he would have to take *some* action, Mar did the worst possible thing in the circumstances: he split his forces. Mackintosh (or 'Old Borlum', as he was generally known during the rising) was detached to cross the Firth of Forth. Mackintosh's contingent should have marched immediately south to bring the borderers back north so as to catch Argyll between two fires, but instead it marched towards Edinburgh, captured the town of Leith, and wasted time beating back skirmishing parties from Argyll's army before finally heading for the border.

Mar meanwhile continued to let the initiative slip away from him, waiting for the last dribble of reinforcements to come in. Finally, when he had almost made up the numbers lost by the dispatch of the Mackintosh party and once again had more than 9,000 men under arms, he held a council of war in Perth, on 9 November. It was decided to cross the Forth above Stirling and sweep down on Argyll, who was in Edinburgh. Hearing of this plan from his spies, Argyll marched north to meet the Jacobites with an army of just over 3,000.

On Sunday 13 November 1715 the two armies met in battle at Sheriffmuir, north of Stirling. On the right wing the Jacobites carried all before them. The dreaded Highland charge crumpled up Argyll's left wing with ease. But the Jacobite left itself was defeated through lack of a cavalry screen. Finally, at about 4 p.m., the two victorious elements wheeled around to confront each other, Mar with 4,000 men, Argyll with 1,000. This was Mar's greatest chance for a decisive victory. But in the gathering gloom he hesitated to press home his advantage. Darkness came on, leaving both sides to claim a victory. Argyll had lost 663 dead and wounded against Mar's casualties of 232, but there was no doubt that he was the moral victor. The famous Rob Roy watched the battle with his MacGregors from a vantage point a mile away, waiting to see which side would be victorious. Of Mar he is reported to have said: 'If he cannot win without me, then he will not win with me.'

Sunday 13 November 1715 was truly the unlucky thirteenth for the Jacobites. Apart from Sheriffmuir, there was the loss of Inverness to the Whigs in the north, and in England the conclusion of the battle of Preston. For in the English theatre of war the campaign had taken on many of the features of *opéra bouffe*. The desperate plight of the debt-ridden or bankrupt northern English gentry provided the tinder which hamfisted attempts to arrest the two leading lights of northern Jacobitism flared into flame. James Radcliffe, 3rd earl of Derwentwater and Thomas Forster, MP for Northumberland, were thenceforth to be the driving force in the English rebellion. The leadership was given to Forster, a Protestant, rather than Derwentwater, whose Catholicism was thought likely to alienate the English.

Volunteers started to come in in significant numbers. The English Jacobites made their initial base at Warkworth, south of Alnwick, in early October, then set out on a march through Alnwick and Morpeth to Hexham. Meanwhile the Jacobite Lord Kenmuir raised the Stuarts' supporters in south-west Scotland (Dumfriesshire, Kircudbright and Wigtownshire). Forster's men marched north to meet them, and a junction of the two forces was effected at Rothbury on 19 October. This augmented force in turn linked up with Borlum's Mackintoshes at Kelso on 22 October, making an army of about 1,500 in all.

While the Whig general Carpenter marched north from Newcastle with a force of 1,000 men to meet them, the Jacobite army of England met in a council of war at Kelso to decide what to do next. None of the three contingents had definite news or instructions from Mar. The council of war degenerated into an unseemly wrangle. The Scots wanted to march on Glasgow. The English Jacobites did not want to penetrate farther into Scotland.

The English for their part wanted to march on Lancashire to link up with the Jacobites there, but the Scots did not want to cross into England. A compromise decision was taken to deal with Carpenter first. This might have been the correct decision in the short term, but the obvious strategy was to outflank Argyll by moving into Scotland. In the event the only truly unsound idea, the march on Lancashire, was opted for.

The march towards Carpenter quickly turned into farce. Kelso, Jedburgh, Hawick, Langholm: up and down the border they trekked, Scots and English both suspicious of one another, neither willing to fight in the other's country. They lacked the resolution either to close with Carpenter or to besiege Dumfries. Eventually Forster sold Borlum and Kenmuir the idea of a march to Lancashire with the promise of loot.

The Jacobite itinerary took them from Langholm through Longtown, Brampton, Penrith, Appleby, Kendal and Kirby Lonsdale into Lancashire. From Lancaster they proceeded south to Preston, where they arrived on 10 November. Instead of closing the trap on Argyll in Scotland, Forster had put his own head on the block. As the Jacobites moved south, Carpenter swung across the Pennines to cut off their retreat, while a second Whig army under General Wills came up from Manchester.

Caught in a vice, Forster decided to barricade Preston and defend it to the death. It was decided not to make a stand at Ribble Bridge on the grounds that the river Ribble was fordable and the defenders could be cut off. On Saturday 12 November Wills's forces arrived outside the town and the battle of Preston began. From their defensive position behind the barricades in Preston, the Jacobites beat off Wills's forces with heavy losses, losing forty-two killed and wounded to the Hanoverians' seventy-six. But on Sunday morning General Carpenter arrived on the scene with three regiments of dragoons. Previously the road to Liverpool had been open, but now Carpenter blocked this exit. The Jacobite army was completely surrounded.

At this point Forster decided to throw in the sponge. There were furious scenes between the Scots and the English when it was known that Forster contemplated surrender. But eventually the inevitable was accepted. No decent surrender terms could be had, so the Jacobites gave themselves up under the ominous rubric 'at discretion'. This was on Monday 14 November 1715. Nearly 1,500 prisoners were taken.

The Jacobite star was sinking fast. The desertion rate after Sheriffmuir reached epidemic proportions. In the north Simon Fraser, later Lord Lovat, consolidated the position of the Frasers by turning his coat and declaring for the Whigs once he saw which way the chill winds were blowing. While Mar contemplated putting out feelers to Argyll over possible ceasefire terms, the ground was cut from under him by the sudden arrival of James in Scotland, on 23 December. The 'Pretender' landed at Peterhead when all was virtually over, having once again sailed through mountainous seas from Dunkirk. It was not the least of Jacobite misfortunes that their most promising military campaigns always seemed to take place in winter.

If the Jacobites hoped that the coming of their king would revive flagging morale in the army, they were doomed to disappointment. James arrived with no new ideas or plans, nor any promises of further help from foreign powers, and seemed genuinely perplexed at what he found. Instead of the 16,000 men he expected, Mar had but 5,000. It was soon easy to pierce the veils of deception and learn the truth about Sheriffmuir and Preston. Far from giving a lead at this crucial moment, James's health cracked under the strain. When he recovered, early in January 1716, it was to discover that technical difficulties stood in the way of his proposed coronation at Scone. The coronation, originally scheduled for 23 January 1716, was shelved. Proceeding from Dundee via Scone to Perth, on 8 January James had a disastrous meeting with the Huntly and Seaforth Highlanders. Where a born leader like his son would have enthused and inspired them, James succeeded only in depressing and demoralising them.

Worse was to come. The ill-luck that always dogged the Stuarts struck again. The ship bearing the Spanish gold that alone could keep the Jacobite army in being ran aground on the Dundee sandbanks and was stranded. This disaster was an uncanny pre-echo of the loss of the treasure ship *Le Prince Charles* thirty years later during the '45. In both cases the demise of their treasure ships sounded the death-knell for the Jacobite rising. By mid-January Argyll started to advance towards them with an army three times as numerous. The odds were now as firmly stacked in his favour as they had been in Mar's at Sheriffmuir.

Despondency provoked desperate measures. The Jacobites

tried to deny Argyll supplies by creating a 'scorched earth' belt of land between Dunblane and Perth. This action merely had the effect of further alienating the Scots of Perth from the Pretender. At a council of war held in Perth on 29–30 January the decision was finally taken to retreat into the Highlands and abandon the rebellion as a lost cause. While Argyll advanced from Stirling to Perth, the tattered remnants of the Jacobite army retreated to Montrose via Dundee. There, on 4 February, James embarked for France on the *Marie Thérèse*. His precipitate departure caused bad feeling among the Highlanders but, given that he had no heir at the time, his departure was inevitable and probably saved the Highlands from the ravages of a hue and cry. General Gordon was left behind as nominal commander-in-chief to supervise the dispersal of the clans in mid-February at Ruthven. Mar embarked with James. He at least was lucky. In England Kenmuir and Derwentwater, taken prisoner at Preston, were to pay for rebellion with their heads.

With France in alliance with England and hopes of Swedish assistance dashed in 1717, it seemed there could never again be a Jacobite rising after the 1715 attempt. Yet help for the Stuarts came from an unexpected quarter. Elizabeth Farnese, Philip V of Spain's second wife, was the niece of the duke of Parma and introduced an Italian dimension into Spanish expansionism. In 1717 and 1718 Spain seized Sardinia and Sicily and seemed poised for an assault on the kingdom of Naples. Both the Austrian Habsburgs and the British took fright at this new development. War was declared on Spain. Admiral Byng destroyed a Spanish fleet off Cape Passaro on the Sicilian coast. Spain was reeling.

Cardinal Alberoni, Spain's first minister and the confidant to Elizabeth Farnese, decided to take a leaf out of Louis XIV's book and strike back at the tormentor in his home base. A Jacobite invasion was the perfect instrument for Alberoni's policy. An embassy from James, consisting of Ormonde and the two Keith brothers (the Earl Marischal and his brother James, the future Prussian field-marshal), went to Madrid to confer with Alberoni. An invasion plan was drawn up. There were to be two landings: one in England under Ormonde, the other in Scotland under the Keith brothers. Ormonde pressed for an army of 10,000 but was promised 5,000. In addition, he would have 1,000 cavalry, ten cannon and arms enough for 15,000 men – such were the numbers expected to rally to the Stuart standard in England.

Marischal's descent on Scotland, designed as a diversion, was to be a more modest affair: just six companies of Spanish troops and 2,000 weapons. Ten men o'war and nineteen frigates would transport Ormonde's expedition to Coruña. Three frigates were to suffice for Marischal, who would embark at San Sebastian. James himself would accompany Ormonde.

Ormonde's invasion fleet was assembled at Cadiz in March 1719. It was to call at Coruña to pick up the commander-in-chief. The fleet duly put to sea, but before it could put in at Coruña it had been shattered off Cape Finisterre by storms of unusual ferocity. Many of the ships were sunk or damaged, some were scattered into the bay of Biscay; only a few limped into Coruña.

It has often been observed that whenever James the Old Pretender set foot on a ship bound for the reconquest of his kingdoms the weather took a hand. 1719 was no exception. The weather that destroyed Ormonde's armada in the Atlantïc gave James such a buffeting in the Mediterranean that it took him a month to get from Italy to Catalonia. It then took him another month to get to Coruña via Madrid, where he arrived in time to hear of the maritime débâcle from Ormonde.

But as so often in the Jacobite risings, fate, while torpedoing the main expedition, allowed the diversionary one to proceed. On 11 March the Earl Marischal cleared from San Sebastian with his small force of Spanish troops. He called at Le Havre to pick up other Jacobite leaders; with him now were James Keith, General Gordon and Lords Tullibardine, Seaforth and Lord George Murray, veterans of the '15.

All three of Marischal's ships were at the rendezvous at Stornoway in the Isle of Lewis. But then the dissension began. The Jacobites split into two camps, one following Marischal, the other Tullibardine. Marischal was for landing on the mainland in Mackenzie country and pressing on to Inverness with Seaforth's clansmen. Tullibardine argued that they should remain on Lewis until they heard from Ormonde. Majority opinion favoured Marischal, but Tullibardine then trumped his ace by producing a commission James had given him in 1717, giving him command of all troops in Scotland.

Marischal bowed to this document but retained his command of the Spanish frigates. There were now two warring commanders supervising an amphibious operation. Marischal, with the Spanish under his thumb, eventually got his way. The Jacobites moved to the mainland and made their headquarters at the castle of Eilean Donan at the head of Loch Alsh opposite the Isle of Skye. Here they learned of the fate of Ormonde's invasion fleet. Tullibardine now wanted to return to Spain, but the Keith brothers spiked his guns by sending the Spanish frigates home.

On 9 May 1719 events took an ugly turn. A British squadron sailed into Loch Alsh, overwhelmed the forty-five-strong Spanish garrison, blew up Eilean Donan Castle, captured its store of munitions and burned the stores. With few provisions, an acute shortage of ammunition and no means of retreat, Marischal had to withdraw inland. No doubt it was his intention to reach Inverness, but the Hanoverian General Wightman advanced down the Great Glen and cornered the Jacobite army at Glenshiel. Although Seaforth's Mackenzies had risen and a handful of MacGregors under Rob Roy, Marischal's force numbered no more than 1,000. Wightman had no great advantage in numbers but he had a formidable battery of cohorn mortars, which tore holes in the Jacobite ranks. The Highlanders melted away into the hills, but the Spaniards were forced to surrender. All the Jacobite commanders made good their escape. Such was the fiasco of the '19.

The triumph of Walpole's diplomacy in the 1720s and 1730s ended any further hopes of a Jacobite rising during James's young years. In the three risings he had been involved in, James had seen disaster pile on disaster. In the first one he had sighted the Scottish coast without landing. In the second he had spent an unhappy month in Scotland when the rising was practically over. In the third he never got closer to the British Isles than the northern coast of Spain. It was to be twenty-six years before the clans 'came out' again. When they did, James was already an old man, and the centre of the Jacobite stage was held by an individual of much sterner stuff, his son Charles Edward, the 'bonnie Prince' of legend.

Chapter 7

The last wave: the Jacobite rising of 1745

In the year 1745 the throne and the constitution were attacked by a rebellion which does not reflect much honour on the national spirit: since the English friends of the Pretender wanted courage to join his standard, and his enemies (the bulk of the people) allowed him to advance into the heart of the kingdom.

Gibbon

It is probable, indeed, that the Jacobites of the day were incapable of considering that the very small scale on which the effort was made was in one great measure the cause of its unexpected success.

Scott, *Redgauntlet*

What has your family done, sir, thus to draw down the vengeance of heaven on every branch of it, through so many years?

William King, *Political and Literary Anecdotes of His Own Time*

The Jacobite rising of 1745 has always excited the popular imagination, and rightly so. Novels, songs and poems celebrate this event, which has almost become the 'matter of Scotland', a kind of mystical paean to Scottish nationalism. And it is true that history records few examples of an apparently quixotic adventure coming so close to success, against all the odds. For if 1715 was the Jacobites' Battle of Midway when, like the Japanese in 1942, they held all the military cards, 1745 was their Leyte Gulf.

Against all factors of probability, indices of economic stability, and so on, Charles Edward Stuart came close to a military triumph that would have echoed down the ages. Why did he nearly achieve the military upset of the century and why did he ultimately fail?

In the first place, Charles Edward had that indispensable asset of all successful revolutionaries, a powerful intuition of the true weakness of his foe, which may yet be masked by an appearance of invincibility. The 'Country' ideologues had not been crying wolf when they pointed to the corruption endemic in Hanoverian England. Walpole's poison had done its work only too well. The older tradition of civic virtue and martial responsibility was almost dead. The Whig grandees, driven by stark pecuniary interest, had, by their proscription of the Tories, alienated the powerful squirearchy. The mass of the people remained apathetic to the outcome of the dynastic struggle. In other words, the social base of Whig prosperity was not broad enough. Not enough people had benefited from the era of the moneyed interest and the National Debt to make it worthwhile for them to lose their lives. As an anonymous pamphleteer put it in an appeal to the 'lower sort of people': 'It well deserves your thought whether it is worth your while to beggar yourselves and your families that the man's name upon the throne be James instead of George.' For this reason the defence of England against the Highland invasion in November–December 1745, the very crux of the rising, was a farce. All the much-vaunted second and third tiers of national defence, the militia and the subscription and volunteer regiments, simply melted away like summer snow in face of the Jacobite threat.

The second aspect of Charles Edward's acumen is more controversial. The perception of the prince as a 'rash adventurer' or Polish blockhead has perhaps now taken root too deeply to be dislodged, but to set against it there is this. After 1744 it was clear to all that the French would never again seek to invade the British Isles on behalf of the Jacobites unless very powerful inducements indeed were put before them. Charles Edward realised that to remain in France, lobbying ineffectually, was a waste of time. He had to take his own destiny in hand and set the match to the combustible combination of circumstances that he sensed in the British Isles. Had the prince been successful, as he came within an ace of being, we would surely nowadays hear less of the 'rash adventurer'. If the key to Jacobite success or failure was ultimately the French, and they could only be energised after the 1744 débâcle by a pre-existing rising in Britain in favour of the Stuarts, wherein can Charles Edward be faulted? It must be remembered that the French in 1744–45 were playing dog in the manger. They would neither launch another expedition across the Channel nor allow any encouragement of any kind at Court.

In addition to his strategic gifts – Sir Alexander MacDonald of Sleat, no friend of the prince, called him the best captain in his army – Charles Edward had the good fortune to enlist as his lieutenant-general a man of tactical genius, Lord George Murray, who served him well in the campaign. But since such good fortune seldom comes unmixed, the Jacobite cause thereafter suffered from the fatal defect that the prince and his commander were like chalk and cheese, separated by a great chasm of misunderstanding and incompatibility, where each man seemed profoundly irritated, almost viscerally, by the other's presence.

As for Charles Edward's ultimate failure, once again we must seek the French connection. The French were sincere in their desire to aid the prince – and none more so than Louis XV himself – but their effort in turn was stymied in a number of ways. They left their bid too late, and then abandoned their expedition too early without making the necessary adjustments for a different kind of operation. The force that the duc de Richelieu had poised at Boulogne at the end of December should have been ready a month earlier to be truly effective. Even so, its destination should then have been switched from England to Scotland. Louis XV had wasted time finding out how serious the rebellion in Scotland was before deciding to commit himself. His Ministers of State were lukewarm towards the idea of a French invasion, and their bitter rivalries reduced the effectiveness of the invasion plans when they were implemented. By the time Richelieu's force was ready, Charles Edward was already retreating from Derby. It then needed only the discovery of his invasion plans and a few bruising encounters with the Royal Navy to make Richelieu call off the project.

Finally, we must allow a large role in the '45 to the play of the contingent and the aleatory – in a word, to luck. If Charles Edward was lucky up to the moment of Derby, he scarcely had a day's good fortune thereafter. The most spectacular blow of fate was the loss of the French treasure ship *Le Prince Charles* in late

March 1746, which meant that, bankrupt of funds, the prince had to seek an early engagement on unfavourable terms with the duke of Cumberland at Culloden.

One is tempted to present the first phase of the rising as a triumph of zeal, commitment and willpower over complacency, arrogance and incompetence, but this is too simple. The first Scottish campaign, from August to October 1745, was an affair of small numbers, in which the prince had the advantage of the superior mobility of an army of irregulars, and the government the advantage of command of the seas. In this way it was possible for the two armies who had missed each other in the Highlands to confront each other outside Edinburgh, at Prestonpans, since Sir John Cope, the government commander-in-chief in Scotland, re-embarked his army in the north-east and put it ashore south of Edinburgh. Above all, though, the prince had the advantage of a first-rate captain in Lord George Murray and the not inconsiderable benefit of being able to harness Scottish nationalism to his cause. One has only to imagine the motivation of the clansmen, fighting for clan, nation and hereditary king, as compared with that of Cope's troops, fighting for subsistence pay and to avoid the lash, to grasp this point.

Ominously, not only was the prince opposed in Scotland by his traditional enemies, like the Campbells, but many of the officially pro-Jacobite clans who were 'out' in the '15 did not appear in the field this time. This seriously affected the prince's numbers. Insufficient numbers in the Jacobite army meant two things: Charles Edward's army had to await Cope and fight him, in the hope of persuading others to join them; and there was no possibility of pressing straight into England after the capture of Edinburgh. So it was that the Prestonpans campaign, which Cope saw initially as a race to the Lowlands, was nothing of the kind. Moreover, even after the victory at Prestonpans, the prince lacked a big enough army to invade England immediately. The month's sojourn in Scotland after the battle wasted precious time, but Charles Edward had no choice, since even when he did descend into England, he possessed an exiguous army that lacked credibility. Barely 5,000 clansmen crossed the border with him.

Charles Edward Stuart arrived on Scottish soil (the Isle of Eriskay) on 23 July (Old Style) and on the Scottish mainland two days later. The story of how he talked round a reluctant Lochiel (chief of the Clan Cameron) and Clanranald (an important

MacDonald chieftain) has become the stuff of romance, but, as has been made clear in the context of the '15 and will be again later in this chapter, they did not need as much prompting as is commonly supposed. On 19 August the Stuart standard was raised at Glenfinnan, at the north end of Loch Shiel, over a tiny army of some 1,300 clansmen. Numbers were truly the key to the first Scottish campaign, as the government commander Sir John Cope had little more than 3,000 troops at his disposal in the entire country. Thus did the impact of the battle of Fontenoy – fought in May 1745, where Cumberland was defeated by the great comte de Saxe – register on the Celtic fringes, and so it was that a tiny force that in normal circumstances would have presented a risible spectacle was able to pose a credible threat to King George's army.

The Jacobites proceeded to seize the Corryarack Pass, on the road to Fort Augustus, hoping to ambush Cope as he came north from Stirling. Cope was forewarned, but instead of retreating to Stirling he pressed on to Inverness, in hopes of keeping the northern clans loyal to the House of Hanover by his presence. This manoeuvre left the heartland of Scotland open to the Jacobites. Moving down to Perth, where the prince was joined by his two future lieutenant-generals, the duke of Perth and Lord George Murray, the clansmen defied Cope to race them to the Lowlands, while they prepared for the advance on Edinburgh. Cope embarked his forces and landed them at Dunbar, but in the meantime Edinburgh had fallen, except for the garrison in the castle, which held out until relieved in November. The stage was now set for the first trial of arms between government and Jacobite forces. Both armies at this stage contained little more than 2,000 men.

Thanks to Robert Burns and others, 'Johnnie' Cope has passed into legend as a hopeless military incompetent, but the truth is different. Advancing to the relief of Edinburgh, Cope selected a very strong field for battle at Gladsmuir or Prestonpans, with the sea acting as a natural defence to the north. Had the Highlanders chosen to make a frontal attack from the south or west, they would almost certainly have been defeated, given the powerful artillery Cope had at his disposal. There was one weak spot in the Whig army's defences, and it was Lord George Murray with his tactical 'green fingers' who spotted it. On the eastern side of Cope's forces was a seemingly impenetrable morass. Murray proposed marching round it and falling on the enemy flank, but as it turned out an even better opportunity was presented to him. It transpired that one of the Jacobite enlisted men knew of a narrow path through the morass. Travelling at times in Indian file, the Jacobite army picked its way through the marsh in the darkness and fell on Cope's flank at first light. Cope's big guns were captured first, after the inexperienced gunners had fled. Then wave after wave of clansmen, chanting their bloodcurdling slogans as they charged, smashed into the Hanoverian army. The cavalry broke and fled, and panic spread to the infantry. The short-lived battle turned into a rout. The Highland officers lost control of their men for a time and many of the fleeing infantry were scythed down by the claymore. Cope's army lost about 300 dead and 400 wounded, while Jacobite casualties barely got into double figures. Cope fled to Berwick, where legend and song has it (incorrectly) that he was the first general in history to come with news of his own defeat.

The consequences of Prestonpans were several. All Scotland, except for isolated strongholds like Edinburgh and Stirling castles, was in Jacobite hands. The prince had conceived the fatal notion that his Highlanders were invincible. In London a financial crisis ensued, and the duke of Newcastle and George II at last began to form an idea of the crisis that was upon them. Most important of all in its potential results, the French now decided to support Charles Edward in earnest and began to lay plans for a descent on the south coast of England. Unfortunately, they moved too slowly to be able to coordinate their actions with the Stuart prince, even though he remained in Edinburgh for a month after his triumph at Prestonpans. The problem, as always, was that of numbers. The prince spent October trying to get ambivalent clan leaders and other Scottish grandees like Lord Lovat to commit themselves. In the meantime Newcastle and the Whigs made preparations for the invasion of England that was now considered inevitable.

The wisdom of Charles Edward's decision to invade England was queried then and has often been queried since. In fact the decision to proceed south of the border was taken narrowly, by one vote, at the prince's Council in Edinburgh. It seemed a sounder policy to dig in, defend Scotland against counter-attack from England, and await reinforcements from France. There was a very good chance of an independent Scotland under the Stuarts being recognised by Louis XV, and also that the new kingdom might be recognised *de facto* by the Whigs as part of a general peace package. More immediately, the prince seemed to lack sufficient numbers for an invasion. Here the defections of MacLeod and MacDonald of Sleat, plus the English naval blockade, played a decisive role. Furthermore, a move in strength across the border by the Highland army would almost certainly lead to the reoccupation of much of Scotland by the English army. In addition, the Highlanders had lost the element of surprise. A strike south in September, or immediately after Prestonpans, might have achieved much, since England was practically bare of regular troops. By November large numbers had been withdrawn from Flanders and these were stiffened by phalanxes of mercenaries: Dutch, Swiss and Hessians.

But against these cogent arguments, urged by Lord George Murray, Lord Elcho and others, the prince could muster others, even more telling. First, there was the question of money. The Highland army lived off the land and by regular collection of the public money, the cess and the excise, for which they gave regular receipts through their paymasters. It was already clear by October that, even with the sympathetic attitude of the Edinburgh banks, the revenue base of the Highland army was too slender and was shrinking. Only guaranteed subventions from France could help, and these seemed either uncertain to be sent or, if sent, uncertain to reach Scotland. An advance to collect the much richer pickings in England promised the provision of regular and substantial sums of money. There also seemed a question mark over the stability of the Highland army. Clansmen rarely stayed together in an army for any length of time: after a victory they were accustomed to disperse to their homes and glens. Charles Edward reckoned that the longer the period of inaction in Edinburgh, the greater the probability of large-scale desertion. Somehow he had to sustain the momentum created at Prestonpans.

Finally, and of crucial importance, it was far from certain that the French would land in strength if the Jacobite successes were limited to Scotland. As the events of 1744 demonstrated, the French aim in supporting the Jacobites was the defeat of England. There was not a really powerful incentive for them to restore the Stuart dynasty simply to Scotland, quite apart from the much greater logistical problems of mounting a full invasion of Scotland. England was therefore the only credible French target.

Curiously enough, both Charles Edward and Louis XV concurred here. The prince wanted to be king of the three kingdoms or of none; the French wanted the destruction of England, not the creation of Jacobite enclaves in Scotland and Ireland. But the French had always sworn that they would only face the terrors of the Channel – both the elements and the Royal Navy – if they could be assured of a substantial Jacobite fifth column and the appearance in the field of an English Jacobite army. Charles Edward knew in his heart that the English Jacobites, left to themselves, would always find an excuse not to appear in the field when there was any risk to life, limb or property. If, on the other hand, he pushed into England with his highly disciplined force, he could sweep up with him those Jacobite elements who were fearful to show their true colours without a protecting army. In this way, the French could have no excuse for inaction and would be given every encouragement to make their move. The French commander would have a clear advantage over Saxe in 1744, in that he could catch the English forces in a pincer, between his own veterans of Fontenoy and the victors of Prestonpans. Charles Edward's strategy, then, was to move into England, score a quick victory over Marshal Wade in the north, incorporate the levies he expected from Lord Barrymore and Sir Watkin Williams Wynn, keep the English guessing about his destination until the last moment by taking the north-western route into England, and then race for London to link up with the French invaders.

The plan was a good one, but it had three flaws that were to prove fatal. The intelligence, communication and espionage service of the Highland army was lamentable. The prince had lost touch with the French, so that he did not know the stage their preparations had reached and did not coordinate with them. He had not lost touch with the English Jacobites for the simple reason that he had never bothered to establish contact in the first place. He apparently expected a spontaneous rising from them as soon as he appeared across the border. Finally, he had no accurate intelligence on enemy strength and movements, and this was to prove calamitous at Derby.

Until Derby the prince achieved spectacular success. The town and castle of Carlisle collapsed before him like a house of cards. Wade's relieving force, marching from Newcastle, got bogged down in Pennine snowdrifts and had to retreat ignominiously. Pressing southwards via Lancaster, Preston and Manchester, the prince's rate of advance confounded and confused the Whig commanders Ligonier and Cumberland, who had hoped to intercept at the Mersey. When Cumberland barred the way to London in Staffordshire, Lord George Murray sent him the wrong way in a brilliant feint towards Wales while the Highlanders moved down to Derby. The arrival of the Jacobites caused consternation in London – 'a panic scarce to be credited' was Fielding's description – a run on the banks, and a realisation that only some inferior guards and other picayune forces stood between the Stuart prince and the capital. Cumberland, meanwhile, realising his mistake, desperately tried to get between the Highlanders and London, though by now his forces were exhausted, disoriented and demoralised.

But at Derby on Thursday 5 December 1745 the fortunes of the Stuart dynasty were decided forever. Charles Edward found himself paradoxically the victim of his own incredible success. Precisely because of the speed of his advance, he was now just over 120 miles from London without having heard from either the French or the English Jacobites. Actually, as he himself sensed, he was on the verge of a world-shattering victory even without them, for even if Cumberland could have interposed his army in time, in its weakened condition it would surely not have withstood the onslaught of the charge of the clansmen.

Yet it was at this precise point that Murray and the clan leaders lost their nerve. All the doubts expressed earlier in Edinburgh about the wisdom of the English venture now rose to the surface. The Scots did not share Charles Edward's automatic enthusiasm for a Stuart dynasty in England. They felt dangerously exposed, were misled by one of Newcastle's most brilliant secret agents, Dudley Bradstreet, about the strength of the armies that lay before them (Wade, who was said to be on their flank, was in fact no farther south than Wetherby on this day). They even doubted Charles Edward's sincerity in his assurances about the French and the English Jacobites and asked to see documentary evidence of support from these parties, guaranteeing their participation. Naturally, the prince was unable to provide it. Clearly the clan leaders' circumspection was absurd at this stage of the game. A man playing poker for high stakes cannot expect a watertight guarantee of success. Nevertheless, this was in effect what they demanded at Derby, and against the prince's strenuous protests they insisted on retreat.

The success of Lord George Murray in getting the army back to Scotland exposed the shallowness of his own fears, for if the forces arrayed against him were as formidable as he had alleged in the Council at Derby, he would never have been able to manage the task. Cumberland's forces were too exhausted to commence the pursuit until a full three days after the Highlanders had quit Derby, and even then he took with him only his cavalry and some mounted dragoons. Wade, having bungled things on the Scots' southward drive, now compounded his spectacular feat of incompetence by failing to cut them off from the border. Thanks to Charles Edward's rash insistence on slowing down the retreat to Scotland to make it appear a 'tactical withdrawal', Cumberland's vanguard caught up with Murray and the Highland rear at Clifton, two miles south of Penrith. In a moonlit encounter at five o'clock on the evening of 18 December, the last clash of arms between rival armies took place on English soil. Murray's clansmen had the best of the ensuing half-hour skirmish, Cumberland broke off the pursuit and the Jacobites disappeared safely across the border.

On any analysis the campaign of the Jacobites in England during November–December remains an outstanding military exploit. History records only a handful of occasions when a small army, substantially outnumbered by an enemy, has penetrated deep into hostile territory and emerged again virtually unscathed. There have been greater triumphs of sustained marching (the 'Long March' of the Chinese Red Army in 1934 is an obvious example) and of mobility within enemy terrain (the great campaign of the Mongol general Subedei in 1221–22 comes to mind), and even of the withdrawal of large numbers from danger (Manstein's fighting retreat in the Crimea in 1943, for instance), but geographical, logistical and infrastructural factors were usually more favourable on those occasions. The most illuminating comparison for the feats of Charles Edward's men is with the withdrawal of the 10,000 in Xenophon's *Anabasis*.

One can identify both negative and positive reasons for the success of the Highland army in this extraordinary campaign. Negatively, the vital element was the extraordinarily inept performance of Marshal Wade. In retrospect it seems almost incredible that Wade should have failed to bar the Highlanders' return to Scotland, and even more so that he escaped official censure for his actions. When one considers that the Hanoverian officers General Oglethorpe, Sir John Cope and Colonel Durand all faced courts-martial for their actions in the '45 – and, with the exception of Cope, none was as culpable as Wade – it seems odd, to say the least, that no one pointed the finger of accusation at the elderly marshal. On the positive side, the single greatest cause of the successful Jacobite retreat was the generalship of Lord George Murray. Throughout the English campaign he consistently outthought Cumberland and revealed a tactical genius of a high order. Had Murray ever held command in the British army as a general, he might have been the one man to stretch Marshal Saxe to the fullest.

The second Scottish campaign, from January to April 1746, was marked by a steady decline in Jacobite fortunes, caused mainly by the ever-tightening naval blockade of Scotland, which cut off the possibility of French aid at the time it was most needed. Seapower really came into its own in these closing months of the '45. The French, in any case, having planned for an invasion of England, found it extremely difficult to switch their planning for a descent on Scotland. The revenue base of the Highland army continued to shrink: by the time of Culloden both officers and men were paid in provisions only and there was little enough of those. Most of the clansmen in the ranks on Drummossie Moor on the fateful 16 April 1746 were suffering from acute hunger as well as fatigue. The Jacobites had condemned themselves to this fate by their decision to retreat into the Highlands after the battle of Falkirk, thus depriving themselves of the possibility of collecting the public monies. Finally, the prince, by now severely demoralised by the refusal of the members of his Council to abide by his decisions, assumed command of the army in the field and proved himself a disastrous tactician.

Having crossed into Scotland, the Highland army raised a levy on the Whig town of Glasgow before commencing, in singularly inexpert fashion, the siege of Stirling Castle. General Hawley, having taken over command of Wade's forces, moved north to meet them. The two armies, both about 8,000 strong – for the prince had now been joined by the forces he had left behind in Scotland in November under Lord Strathallan and also by over 1,000 men of the Irish Brigade in the service of Louis XV who had evaded the blockade and landed on the east coast in December – clashed at Falkirk on 17 January. Hawley was caught off balance, as he had assumed the Jacobites would not dare to attack him but would await his onslaught on them. The battle of Falkirk was a dramatic engagement, being fought during a violent storm and driving rain which, thanks to Murray's dispositions, bore most heavily on Hawley's army. In the fading light of a winter afternoon another short-lived battle took place, but this time the result was not quite so decisive as at Prestonpans. Having broken up a cavalry charge with disciplined and devastating fire, the Highland right charged Hawley's infantry, routed it and continued in pursuit. The Hanoverian right, however, under General Huske, held up well, and night came on before Murray could rally his troops, scattered in undisciplined pursuit and plunder, to deal with it. Hawley retreated back to Edinburgh, while the Highlanders entered Falkirk, so on paper the victory was the prince's, but his captains were displeased with the result. Even though the Jacobites lost only about 50 killed and 60 or 70 wounded, as against over 300 dead in the Hanoverian army, they seemed to lack the resolution to pursue Hawley.

This was a psychological turning point for the Jacobites, as decisive in its effects on the Scottish campaign as Derby had been on the English venture. The Jacobites should at this point have turned south instead of proceeding with the futile siege of Stirling. Instead, a few days later the regimental commanders petitioned the prince to retreat to the Highlands, since desertions had thinned the army and left it unable to face the Hanoverians under their new commander, the duke of Cumberland. Once again, as at Derby, the prince resisted fiercely, pointing out the inevitable consequence of such an action, and once again he was overborne and outvoted. Once again, too, the prince's strategic grasp was demonstrated to be superior. He pointed out that to retreat now would be to throw away all gains made, to give the enemy an immense psychological boost, to lose the Jacobites' cannon and heavy artillery, and above all to dissuade the French from coming to the rescue. When he could not carry the clan chiefs with him, Charles Edward sullenly acquiesced in the retreat, having disclaimed all responsibility for the consequences in writing.

The first stage of the withdrawal took the Highlanders to Perth, where an acrimonious council of war was held. It was resolved to retreat to Inverness, one column proceeding there by the coast road, the other across country. Once arrived there, the clansmen undertook several military tasks without any coherent policy for combating the advance of Cumberland. Fort Augustus was besieged and taken, Fort William was invested but it held out, while there were Jacobite probes into Dornoch, Badenoch and Atholl.

Cumberland, who had moved up to Aberdeen, where he remained for six weeks, commenced serious operations at the beginning of April. The Jacobites failed to take their opportunity by opposing his passage of the river Spey. Cumberland arrived in Nairn on 14 April. Meanwhile the prince, using his crony John William O'Sullivan as military adviser, had decided to offer battle on Culloden Moor. As Lord George Murray pointed out, no more disastrous choice for Highlanders could be imagined, as it was open moorland, affording full scope for the enemy's superiority in cannon and none at all for the clansmen's devastating charge. But Murray was no longer commander in the field. The decision to offer battle in the first place was a consequence of the failure of the French treasure ships, especially *Le Prince Charles*, to get through to Scotland with financial aid. This explains the desperation and obstinacy behind the prince's decision to fight Cumberland at all costs and at the earliest opportunity, a decision all the more astonishing at first sight, since nearly half his army, including some of the best regiments, were not present at Culloden.

At Culloden on 16 April the Highlanders were beaten before the battle even began. Not only did the chosen terrain entirely favour Cumberland, who had 8,000 men to the prince's 5,000, but the wretched Highlanders were half-starved and physically exhausted, after marching all night on a hare-brained scheme to fall on the duke's army at Nairn in a night attack. The night march had turned into a total fiasco. Bitterness between the prince and Lord George Murray, which had bedevilled the Jacobite campaign from the very beginning, now reached a peak, on the morning of a decisive battle. With his officers in disarray, his commissariat broken down, his men half-starved and sleepless, facing a numerically superior army with powerful artillery on a field that overwhelmingly favoured them, how could Charles Edward's battle at Culloden have had anything other than a disastrous end?

And so it came to pass. The Jacobite army was destroyed in half an hour in the early afternoon of this April day, but not before it had demonstrated its calibre against all the odds. For the last time on earth the cry of 'Claymore' was heard as Highland clans bore down on an English army. There was no lack of valour on the Jacobite side, and all that could be achieved by courage alone was done. The charge of Clan Chattan on the right blunted the enemy line but failed to penetrate it. The Jacobite left, however, failed to take any real part. Outgunned and out-numbered, the clansmen fell in droves. Retreat was ordered and honour saved only by two gallant rearguard actions, that by Brigadier Stapleton and the Irish picquets on the Jacobite left, and by Lord Elcho and his mounted Lifeguards on the right. But whereas the Highland right retreated in good order, the left degenerated into a confused shambles and many of the Mac-Donalds on this wing were slaughtered by Cumberland's pursuing cavalry.

The battle of Culloden, though a decisive battle in hindsight, was not immediately regarded as such by contemporaries. The clans had been seriously checked but by no means annihilated, and many of the crack regiments, like the MacPhersons, had taken no part in the battle. Lord George Murray looked forward to a return contest with Cumberland, when he hoped 'to do to them what they have done to us'. What transformed matters completely was Charles Edward's decision to throw in the sponge. Issuing a *sauve qui peut* order, he declared his intention of returning to France to bring back a French army of invasion. Ironically, it was to take him five months to escape from Scotland, whereas some of his captains got away to France almost at once. So ended for all time (though of course no one at the time realised it) all armed attempts to restore the Stuart dynasty to the three kingdoms.

With hindsight the defeat of the Jacobite rising seems inevitable. The dissolution of the clan system as a result of both the purging of its human element in the pogroms of 1746–47, and the legal attacks on it in the form of the abolition of wardholding and hereditary jurisdictions and the interdiction on the wearing of the plaid, all seem part of the ineluctable process whereby Scotland was integrated into a mercantile-capitalist society, ready for 'take-off' into industrial capitalism. In some ways this seems a microcosm of the nineteenth-century process whereby whole societies of a traditional or 'backward' kind were integrated into a world system of capitalism by war and conquest. Yet this view of

1   The birth of Jacobitism: a Protestant view of the flight of James II, and
the Protestant triumph at the Battle of the Boyne, 1690

2   The Old Pretender, James Francis
Edward Stuart, about 1712

3 The '15: a later impression of the earl of Mar's Council of War. 'Bobbing John' Erskine, earl of Mar, was as much a Jacobite for King George I's slights and insults as for any loyalty to the House of Stuart

4 The Highland army leaves Perth in despair, 1716

5   Lord Lovat, after William Hogarth

6   Charles Edward Stuart, the Young Pretender, 1738

7   Henry Stuart, cardinal and duke of York, the
last of the Stuart claimants to the throne of
Great Britain

8   Clementina Sobieska, the ill-fated wife of
James Francis Stuart

9   The battle of Prestonpans, 1745. The Lochaber axe and the broadsword
proved superior to the English musket and bayonet at close quarters

10   The heroic entry of Charles Edward Stuart into Edinburgh, a romantic
nineteenth-century version

11 The '45: the advance into England. The Highland army arrives at
Manchester

12 The '45: the retreat. Charles Edward Stuart disposes of his prisoners after
the battle of Falkirk, 1746

13 The penalty of failure: the execution of Fergus MacIvor and Evan Dhu outside Carlisle Castle, 1746

14 The final act: the Lords Kilmarnock and Balmerino are executed on Tower Hill, surrounded by a vast and enthusiastic crowd

the 1745 rising as following some 'inevitable', predetermined course to destruction depends heavily on *ex post facto* rationalisation. A century like ours which has seen humanity return to the Dark Ages cannot afford to be too glib in its pronouncements on the impossibility of 'putting the clock back', even if we allow that this was the aim of the Jacobite rising.

Denial of the inevitability of the defeat of the Jacobites in 1745 raises two issues: could the rebellion have been successful, and what would the consequences of a Stuart restoration have been? Historians notoriously dislike the 'counterfactual conditional' involved in speculation on what-might-have-been, but as Max Weber long ago pointed out, such a method is at the basis of any possible theory of historical causality. To deny this is to assert that historical events could only have turned out the way they in fact did. This kind of determinism would automatically make the quest for causality otiose, and history would then simply be what the young Jane Austen imagined it was – a crude recital of events and dates.

The Whig position in Scotland, which had been seriously undermined in the 1730s, could, without the work of men like Duncan Forbes, have become untenable by 1745. It was the particular attention paid to the clans by Forbes and his 'divide and rule' policy which meant that not all clans were Jacobite and that not all of the Jacobite clans rose in rebellion. There was nothing inevitable about the disarray of the clans. This point is not always fully understood by commentators on the Jacobites. One recent reviewer stated: 'Ultimately England possessed the military and economic power to crush any rising based in Scotland.' This was true only if ceaseless work was done in Scotland to keep the clans divided. The total fighting strength of the clans and families of northern Scotland was about 30,000. When one considers what Charles Edward achieved at Prestonpans with 2,500, in England with 5,000 and at Falkirk with 8,000 men, who can doubt that a Jacobite army of 30,000 would have swept all before it, especially since the probability of a rising in England or an invasion from France would then increase as a multiplier effect.

It is often said that the clan system had two fatal defects. Like the ancient Greek city-states the clans found it impossible to cooperate for any length of time, and moreover they represented a closed society impervious to change. The evidence of the '45 campaign and particularly the three battles of Prestonpans, Falkirk and Culloden does seem to suggest that collaboration between the clans was no easy matter; nonetheless after eight months in the field this was not the reef on which the Jacobite army foundered. The issue of the non-cooperation of the clans is largely irrelevant. Solidarity among them in peacetime would never have averted Whig policies unless other factors came into play. And in a rising it was inconceivable that the clansmen would need to act together for more than the eight months during which they did collaborate in 1745–46, before the military issue was decided one way or the other. The argument that the clan system was impervious to change ignores the extent to which clan leaders had been able to develop their interests as minor capitalists. Donald Cameron of Lochiel is a good example of this tendency. And it is often precisely the critics who play down the reality of the clan as an institution, on grounds of fictitious kinship or the assimilation of the feudal and clan principles, who stress that it was an outmoded social form. But in that case it cannot, by definition, have been outmoded through being resistant to change.

The argument from inevitability can be posed in another way. If the Stuarts had been restored in 1746, would not their regime have been a 'fetter' on the development of the Industrial Revolution in England? After all, it can be argued, it was only the acceptance of the principle of non-intervention by the government in the realm of private property after 1688 that made possible the growth of financial capitalism based on joint-stock companies. Would not Stuart absolutism have led inevitably to a bloody revolution like that in France? Here a distinction has to be drawn between inevitable developments in technology and the political forms in which technological change manifests itself. In the first place the French Revolution of 1789 was itself not 'inevitable' – both its causation and its development depended on a series of aleatory factors. And not until 1871 did a truly bourgeois republic emerge in France, even though the economic system which seemed to require such a political superstructure had been in existence for decades. Secondly, it was doubtful (as many of the shrewdest observers of the '45 pointed out) whether the Stuarts could truly be seen as an anti-capitalist force. As O'Heguerty pointed out in his analysis of the consequences for Ireland of a Stuart restoration, it was unlikely that a mere change in dynasty in England would greatly alter underlying trends and policies. For very many Jacobites the Stuarts were a marginal first choice over the unappealing Hanoverians with their prodigal expenditure and corruption. The restoration of the Stuarts was not connected in most Jacobite minds with profound changes in the socio-economic system. In a word, there was no widely held belief that a Stuart monarchy was incompatible with the development of capitalism. Indeed, it can be maintained that the Hanoverians were more of a fetter on the burgeoning of the Industrial Revolution. By encouraging reckless speculation of the South Sea Bubble kind, the regime of the early Hanoverians produced a backlash where economic caution was uppermost and innovation and experimentation discouraged.

On the other hand, it is clear that some of the possible consequences projected for the restored Stuarts are merely chimerical and fly in the face of technological determinants. For example, it was once argued by John Buchan that if Charles Edward Stuart had become king, there would have been no American Revolution. This choice of counterfactual hypothesis is particularly unfortunate, since if there is one process that was clearly overdetermined in the eighteenth century, it was the revolt of the North American capitalist class. The difference in kind between the Jacobite rising and the revolt of the American colonies emerges in the futile attempts by the British to suppress the latter, predicated on the idea that the American colonists were engaged in a purely political struggle. A political struggle waged within certain parameters where economic power is not the primary goal is clearly a different matter from an unalloyed clash of economic interests. Just as the entire weight of the socio-economic substructure favoured the colonists in their rebellion against the mother country in 1775, so too the infrastructure would have tipped the scales heavily in favour of the Whigs if the Jacobite rising had been a full-blooded anti-capitalist reaction. Whereas its rhetoric suggested this, the reality of Jacobitism was much more taken up with its role as a marginally preferable way of managing an agreed and irreversible social and economic system.

There is another way in which the inevitability of the defeat of the '45 looks an implausible thesis. In contrast to the 1715 rising, the '45 was launched in the most unpropitious circumstances. Political preconditions for Jacobite success were far more favourable in 1715 than thirty years later and yet the '45 came much closer to military success. Had the leadership available to the Jacobites in 1745 been present in 1715 when the structural factors favouring a Stuart restoration were stronger, the likelihood of Jacobite triumph would have been much increased. The contrast in leadership between James Stuart in 1715 and Charles Edward in 1745, or between 'Bobbin John' Mar and Lord George Murray, makes this clear.

This brings us to the final, 'dialectical' aspect of the rising. A very different interpretation can be put on the likelihood of the rebellion's success, depending on whether emphasis is laid on structure or conjuncture. On the face of it, few attempts at revolution or counter-revolution have taken place in a less promising climate than the '45. Nearly all the factors generally considered to constitute the 'objective conditions' for successful revolt were absent in 1745. The long existence of an Augustan calm fostered a general atmosphere of satisfaction within England, augmented by two generations of envious praise from the Continent. Public opinion was apathetic and unreceptive to change (one more reason why radicalism found its most congenial home among the Jacobites). Perhaps the most characteristic figure of Great Britain in the 1740s was Hume, whose political writings reflect an era of stability midway between the convulsions of the seventeenth century and the turmoil to come at the end of the eighteenth – an epoch when the threat to the established order from the Jacobite was fading and that from the Jacobin was still to come. Throughout the early Hanoverian period there was a remarkable stability in population and the general level of prices and wages. The agricultural depressions of the 1730s and 1740s had bankrupted many of the lesser gentry but produced lower prices, so increasing the purchasing power of the lower classes. The population of England, around six million in 1715, remained static until 1745, when it began to rise. In the same thirty years imports and exports were virtually stagnant. Only after 1745 did the principal sectors of the economy – agriculture, commerce and industry – begin to expand in a dramatic way (the decade 1745–55 was a boom period comparable to the 1780s). Above all, whatever changes had taken place in the balance of power between gentry and aristocracy, the common people were not yet sufficiently confident or politically conscious to be a serious factor in politics.

In any case, the '45 was probably the last chance for the

Jacobites to enlist on their side any significant element of 'working-class' support. The occupational groups that appeared so significantly in Charles Edward's army – artisans, shopkeepers, farmers and labourers – were being rapidly weaned away from Jacobitism to the new creed of Methodism; John Wesley, the sect's founder, was rapidly opposed to the Jacobites. The non-clan regiments in the Jacobite army of 1745–46 contained a strong component of weavers, shoemakers and drapers, exactly the same kind of skilled men who by the 1760s were following the banner of 'Wilkes and Liberty'. The irony here is that the anti-Scottish and anti-Catholic sentiments of the Wilkesites were sometimes cited as evidence that the English mob could never have held Jacobite sympathies. The truth is rather that in an era of aristocratic politics the urban masses would follow whichever deviant political dispensation seemed to pose most of a challenge to their 'betters'.

The Jacobite rising of 1745 posed a more profound threat to the Whig supremacy than most historians now feel disposed to admit, and came amazingly near to military victory. Against all the odds and the apparent indices, the Jacobites were close to a world-shattering victory. The reasons why the '45 was such a threat have already been stated. Further evidence for the gravity of the rebellion can be discovered in the seriousness with which, right up to 1759 and despite the ferocious Whig backlash of 1746–47, it was feared that the Jacobites would rise again. Until Hawke's victory at Quiberon Bay, no one could be certain that Charles Edward would not come again to Scotland for another trial of strength.

Britain in 1745 was faced with what in modern parlance would be termed a 'legitimation crisis', that is to say one of those crucial periods in history when the rightfulness, competence and efficiency of a regime are simultaneously challenged. Contemporaries feared that twenty years of Walpole had reduced a once-proud nation to the level of a satrapy for an over-powerful monarch. They feared too that the French were winning the global struggle for hegemony and that the Whigs were impotent to do anything about it, as the interests of the Hanoverian kings dictated a 'Europe first' foreign policy. They were apprehensive about the possible future cataclysmic consequences of the National Debt. Whole sections of society were excluded from the privileges of the Whig ascendancy: the country squirearchy, the

Tory party *en masse*, Catholics and non-jurors. Heavy taxation descended on one group of 'outs'; penal laws were visited on another; on yet another, the working class, the most draconian system of laws yet devised to protect private property fell with ferocious impact. Many men feared the consequences of a nation permanently divided on the succession issue. Ideologically, no watertight case for 1688 had ever been produced. The Jacobite philosophy not only survived intact in 1745 but looked increasingly attractive to those who had doubts about the kind of society that had appeared since the late seventeenth century. Until the appearance, at the end of the century, of a fully fledged theory of liberalism, capitalism, albeit at this juncture mainly of the financial and mercantile kind and not the industrial variety, lacked an intellectual justification in terms of ideology. The classical humanist tradition seemed ineradicably hostile to capitalism, and in the early eighteenth century this ideological struggle took the form of Court versus Country. So it was that the rebellion of 1745 drew its inspiration from many different chronological strata. Some of the issues, over abbey lands for example, dated back to the Reformation. Others, such as the question of kingly power, were as old as the Civil War. The Court/Country dichotomy was presaged in the Restoration period. The National Debt dated from 1689, but specific forms of Walpolian corruption from the 1720s and the Hanoverian dynasty itself from 1714.

As if all this were not enough, Scotland contributed a specific Jacobitism of its own, thus helping to overdetermine the general legitimation crisis of 1745. The rising that year in Scotland produced a genuine civil war, almost along the lines of the North/South divide in the American Civil War basically between those who had done well out of post-1688 mercantile and financial capitalism and those who had not. In political terms, this manifested itself in respective support for and opposition to the Act of Union of 1707. Cutting across this distinction was the more archaic struggle within the clans, and in particular the last attempt to curb the power of the Campbells, who had hitched their fortunes to the star of 1688. The civil war in Scotland made the crisis look more acute there than in England, and what seemed like a Scottish invasion of England in November–December 1745 masked the profound divisions in English society.

Historians, writing with hindsight, have underrated the '45

because they have set the full acceptance of the Hanoverian regime in Britain earlier in time than its actual occurrence. This acceptance in reality only came to pass after the glittering British triumphs in the Seven Years' War. It was not there during the War of Austrian Succession, and historians who say that Charles Edward Stuart mistook opposition for disaffection have, it seems to me, mistaken the legitimacy of the regime (in the Weberian sense) *after* 1760 under George III for the quite different set of circumstances under George II. Here too we can see the dimensions of the French error in 1745. France had it within its power to knock out its chief competitor for global supremacy by supporting the Jacobite rising to the hilt. By failing to take its chance at the time when the British political sytem was at its most brittle, France condemned itself to the later indignities of the Treaty of Paris in 1763.

Chapter 8

The bitter fruit:
exile and diaspora

But good the hour, the friendly hour, that brings the battle near.
That brings us on the battle, that summons to their share
The homeless troops, the banished men, the exiled sons of
 Clare.

Emily Lawless, With the Wild Geese

Madam, there are 50,000 slain this year in Europe, and not
one Englishman.

Robert Walpole (to Queen Caroline in 1734)

We'll o'er the water, we'll o'er the sea,
We'll o'er the water to Charlie,
Come weel, come woe, we'll gather and go,
And live or die wi' Charlie.

Hogg, Jacobite Relics

The consequences of failure in the Jacobite risings were serious.
Leading lights in the rebellions could expect execution: for nobles
this meant the headsman's axe, but for the mere gentry and other
commoners there was the more horrible punishment of being
hanged, drawn and quartered. The victim was dragged to the
place of execution (in London this was Tyburn) on a horse-drawn
sledge or hurdle. He was then hanged on a gallows but taken
down before actually dead. Revived and brought to consciousness
with cold water, he was then laid on a table and had his stomach
cut open – the executioner often doubled in ordinary life as a
butcher of livestock. The victim's intestines were then pulled out

and burned and his body hacked into four quarters, which were 'at the king's disposal'. This usually meant that they were displayed in some public place as an example to others. This grisly butchery was watched by huge, eager crowds. The eighteenth century provided a lot of support for Nietzsche's dictum that only at bullfights and crucifixions is mankind truly itself. The moment of death for the victim largely depended on how much the executioner had been tipped. A generous bribe meant that you would be dead before being taken down to be disembowelled.

In both the Jacobite risings of 1715 and 1745 most of the leading 'rebels' made good their escape to France and elsewhere. The story of the Stuarts and their followers is full of escapes of all kinds: King Charles II after the battle of Worcester, Princess Clementina Sobieska from the Schloss Ambras in Innsbruck in 1718, Lord Nithsdale (described below), and, most famously, Charles Edward Stuart himself from Scotland in 1746. In 1715 the Hanoverian backlash was comparatively mild. Only two Jacobite peers went to the block: the young earl of Derwentwater and Viscount Kenmuir. And only four men suffered the torments of being hanged, drawn and quartered. In Scotland a conciliatory line of 'boys will be boys' was pursued. Jacobite families were gradually permitted, through informal deals, to bring back the attainted estates to their kinship fold. The number of deportations was small, and there were few deaths in prison.

In 1746 it was otherwise. Though most of the Jacobite leaders were not captured, Lords Balmerino, Lovat and Kilmarnock were beheaded, and large numbers of the ill-fated Manchester regiment were hanged, drawn and quartered. The Whig reaction to the '45 was as severe as their shock and fear had been when the rising came so close to success. As Cumberland remarked about Scotland: 'I tremble for fear that this vile spot may still be the ruin of this island and our family.' Jacobites were transported to the New World or died on the prison hulks in the Thames in their hundreds. Altogether there were 120 executions, nearly 100 deaths in prison, and over 1,000 banishments and transportations.

In Scotland Cumberland instituted the reign of terror that has made his name a byword for savagery. His 'martial law' consisted in letting his troops rampage through the Highlands without let or hindrance, provided all truly valuable booty was reserved for the officers. When his army had done its worst, London moved in with its laws, designed to extirpate Highland society once and for all. In express violation of the 1707 Act of Union, the heritable jurisdictions were abolished. So too was wardholding. The plaid and other forms of Highland dress were forbidden. Shorn of their traditional powers, the Highland chiefs became mere landlords, concerned with rents not claymores. In addition, this time forfeiture of the 'rebel' estates was taken seriously. Two separate Acts of Parliament, the Vesting and Annexing Acts, made sure that forfeited property remained firmly in government hands. These measures taken together sounded the death-knell of Jacobitism in the Highlands, even though it is important to appreciate that they merely accelerated a process of decay that was under way even before the '45.

Almost the only consolation Jacobites could derive in the aftermath of both rebellions was from the spectacular escapes from prison by their men. In August 1716 eighteen prisoners escaped from Edinburgh Castle by climbing down the 'escape proof' rock. Earlier that year the earl of Nithsdale had made a daring escape from the Tower the evening before he was due to be executed. The planners used the oldest device in the book: the woman who changes both clothes and places with the captive. Dressed in cape and hood, Lord Nithsdale simply walked out of the Tower and holed up in London for a week before travelling to Dover and escaping to France.

Another escape route, via a lavatory, was successfully essayed by the Jacobite commander Tom Forster. Those favourite items of high adventure, the nightgown worn over day clothes and the duplicate key, featured in this escape. Continuing the sequence of one major escape a month, in May 1716 came the mass break-out of Old Borlum Mackintosh and eight of his men. They simply rushed the guards in the exercise yard and poured out into the streets. Within three months, then, three of the major Jacobite rebels, Nithsdale, Forster and Borlum, had escaped from custody. This revealed such massive incompetence on the part of the authorities that bribery of prison governors or collusion in high places was suspected.

By 1746 the London authorities had learned their lesson. Security was far tighter. Of the fifty-eight successful escapes in the aftermath of the '45 rebellion, forty-five were from jails in Scotland, where the prisons were antiquated and the jailers either more sympathetic to Jacobitism or more venal. To escape from a

London jail in 1746–47 required real skill and courage. Only one man is recorded as having managed to do so from a major London prison: Alexander MacLachlan of the Atholl Brigade, who successfully used the time-honoured lavatory escape route. In the iron grip exerted on Jacobite prisoners, as in so many other ways, the '45 was a much grimmer experience for the captured than the '15 had been.

Yet in all the Jacobite risings most of the leading lights, those specifically named in Acts of Attainder, made their way safely to France. There very different fates awaited them. For the junior officer it was a choice between penury or starvation in a Paris slum or service with the Irish Brigade on behalf of France. For the clan leaders and regimental commanders things were much better. Charles Stewart of Ardshiel, who had commanded the Appin Stewarts in the '45, was only one of many clan grandees who received his normal rents from his Highland tenants; they were thus paying a double rent, one to the landlord implanted by the Commissioners of Forfeited Estates and one to the laird in France. Some of the chiefs, such as Donald Cameron of Lochiel, had taken security for their estates before 'coming out' for the prince in the '45. In Lochiel's case the security consisted of a lieutenant-colonelcy in the French service which gave him a larger income than he had enjoyed before the rebellion. Yet he was plagued with guilt about the way he had thus emerged as a beneficiary of the rising. He wrote to James in Rome:

> Lord Ogilvy and others might incline to make a figure in France; but my ambition was to serve the crown and serve my country or perish with it. H.R.H. said he was doing all he could, but persisted in his resolution to procure me a regiment. If it is obtained I shall accept it out of respect to the Prince; but I hope Yr. M. will approve of the resolution I have taken to share in the fate of the people I have undone, and if they must be sacrificed, to fall along with them. It is the only way I can free myself of the reproach of their blood and show the disinterested zeal with which I have lived and shall die.

One is tempted to attribute Lochiel's death the following year (1748) from meningitis to some sort of death-wish deriving from guilt. The Lord Ogilvy Lochiel refers to *did* have a spectacular military career in France. A regimental commander under Charles

Edward in the '45, he went on to become a lieutenant-general in Louis XV's army.

Other Jacobite grandees positively throve on service for the king of France. It is hardly surprising to find that men exiled for the prominent part they had played in the Jacobite risings often went on to distinguished military careers. James Francis's half-brother, the duke of Berwick, accepted French nationality and became a marshal of France and one of the great captains of his day. Lord Clare (Charles O'Brien, 6th Viscount) was another Jacobite to receive a marshal's baton (from Louis XV in 1757). General Francis Bulkeley was another Franco-Irish commander of the Irish Brigade high in French military circles. Perhaps the most impressive of all was Earl Marischal's younger brother, James Francis Edward Keith, who became a field-marshal in the service of Frederick the Great and died a hero's death at Hochkirchen in 1758.

Yet these were only the best-known exiled Jacobite commanders. It is an amazingly little-known fact that the 'Wild Geese' provided field-marshals for all the major European powers in the first half of the eighteenth century. The diaspora of the Irish Jacobites to Eastern Europe was different from that to France and Spain. It was an affair of officers rather than NCOs and rankers. But what officers! Peter Lacy of Limerick began his career in 1699 on taking service with Czar Peter the Great. After two decades spent as the hammer of the Swedes, Lacy was appointed a marshal of the Russian army. During the War of Polish Succession which began in 1733, he was second-in-command to Prince Eugene of Savoy, following the Austro-Russian alliance. From 1736 to 1739 he fought against both Tartars and Turks before retiring as governor of Livonia, where he died in 1751 at the age of seventy-three.

His career resembled at many points that of Maximilian Ulysses Browne, field-marshal of the Imperial army, though Browne's career started later. He rose to prominence in the War of Austrian Succession, was created field-marshal by Empress Maria Theresa in 1754 and died at the siege of Prague in 1757. Some contemporaries rated him above Saxe as a great captain. Another Irish field-marshal in the service of Austria, of slightly different vintage, was James Robert Nugent, who came to prominence in the Turkish war of 1737.

But the greatest rallying point for Jacobite exiles was

undoubtedly the French army. Of all its units perhaps the most famous in the Jacobite period was the Irish Brigade. There had been earlier flights of the 'Wild Geese' – the name given to those Irishmen who preferred to emigrate from Ireland rather than live there under English domination. 'The flight of the earls' in 1607 opened an era of military emigration. By 1688 there were already 6,000 Irish troops in France. But after the Glorious Revolution the exodus of Irish fighting men reached epidemic proportions. Scholars have disagreed on the numbers involved in the exodus. A high of 250,000 between 1690 and 1766 and a low of 50,000 have been mentioned, but certainly in the last ten years of the seventeenth century at the most conservative estimate 40,000 'Wild Geese' quitted Irish shores.

A brigade under Lord Mountcashel left Cork in the spring of 1690 as a swap for the 6,000 French veterans Louis XIV had just landed. And in 1691, after the ill-fated Treaty of Limerick. Patrick Sarsfield, the hero of the Irish Jacobite wars, led between 11,000 and 12,000 Irish soldiers into exile with him in France. It was a condition of the treaty that soldiers serving in the Irish army could volunteer to leave the country with all the honours of war to join Louis XIV's forces in France. Four thousand dependants accompanied them, but many more were left behind, as Gerald O'Connor, Sarsfield's ADC, described: 'Loud cries and lamentations broke from the wives and children who had been left behind; some dashed into the stream and perished in its depths; some clung to the boats that were making off from the shore; many of the men, husbands and fathers, plunged into the waters.'

The Brigade landed at Brest, where it established its headquarters. In 1692 its total strength was estimated at 30,000 men. This included the 1690 Mountcashel detachment and those already serving as a consequence of earlier flights. There was now a standing Jacobite army in France paid for by Louis XIV until 1697, when its regiments were either disbanded or absorbed into the French army. But the Wild Geese still retained their distinctive identity as an Irish Brigade until the Seven Years' War, when the Brigade was split up and Irish regiments fought as attachments to French units. These regiments in turn continued their existence until the French Revolution. The Brigade was formally dissolved in 1791.

From the court at St-Germain James II welcomed the Brigade

with fulsome oratory in a letter dated 27 November 1691: 'We shall never forget this act of loyalty, nor fail, when in a capacity to give . . . particular marks of our favour.' James soon showed what he meant by these 'particular favours'. He struck a deal with Louis XIV whereby he would receive a sum from the Sun King corresponding to pay and allowances at Irish army rates but would then pay the Brigade at *French* army rates, considerably lower. James salved his conscience by promising that when he was restored he would make up the difference in arrears.

This was only the first of many blows to rain down on the Wild Geese during the 1690s. At first there were propitious signs. Sarsfield's Brigaders were concentrated in Normandy ports in 1692 preparatory to the invasion of England. But the French defeat at La Hogue in May changed everything. Once it was realised that plans for a descent on the British Isles would have to be laid aside for the time being, the Irish troops were dispersed throughout Europe. They were sent to join the French armies in Flanders, Germany, Spain and Italy. About 14,000 men remained in France as the Irish Brigade proper. A similar number were dispersed, a diaspora within a diaspora. The dispersed regiments gave a good account of themselves throughout 1692–93, at Steenkirk in Flanders (a victory over Williamite armies), Lauden (where Sarsfield was killed), and at Maraglia in Italy (facing Eugene of Savoy). The fame of the Wild Geese was particularly high in Spain, where they played a notable part in the successful 1697 siege of Barcelona.

Then disaster struck the dispersed Irish. Peace proved a greater danger than enemy guns. Following the Treaty of Ryswick in 1697, Louis XIV was compelled to cut back on military expenditure. As a target for his economies he fastened on the Irish units in Flanders, Italy, Germany and Spain. While the Irish Brigade proper was now firmly entrenched within the French military establishment, their luckless compatriots were disbanded, leaving the common soldiers penniless and starving. The irony of this situation was that the demobilised units had borne the brunt of the fighting in Ireland during 1690–91. It was those who had shipped out early, in 1690, who, in the main, formed the Irish Brigade proper.

An Irish ranker, destitute in a foreign land whose language he could not speak, was in the circumstances almost bound to turn to crime. Contemporary chroniclers spoke of gangs of Irish highwaymen infesting the road between Paris and St-Germain. Their methods of robbery were brutal, but less so than the penalty usually visited on them if they were caught by the authorities. Being broken on the wheel was the favoured punishment in France for all brigands and highwaymen.

The officer class was not in such desperate case. They survived, just. In 1698 they appealed to Louis XIV, pointing out the flagrant injustice of their treatment. Louis, foreseeing that the struggle with England and the Empire would soon have to be rejoined, formed the officers into a special corps, earmarked for personal duties to the monarch.

The opportunity to use them came in 1701 when the War of Spanish Succession broke out. Once again the unofficial Wild Geese (as distinct from the official Irish Brigade) found themselves in action in Italy. Their campaign started badly with the rout of the French by Prince Eugene of Savoy at Chiari. But the Irish soon retrieved their laurels. In 1702 Eugene's surprise attack on Cremona came within an ace of success. The carousing French were taken completely by surprise. Only the stubborn resistance of two battalions of the Irish prevented an Imperial walkover. The stalemate around the Po gate encouraged the French. They rallied from their debauchery and fought in their nightshirts in the winter cold, officerless and without food, for ten hours until Eugene was beaten back.

Both sides raised their stakes. At Luzara in 1703 Marshal Vendôme collided with Eugene of Savoy. Slaughter on the Malplaquet level was the outcome. More than 10,000 Irishmen, nearly a third of those taking part in the battle, were killed. But the later years of the Spanish Succession war brought better fortune for the Irish, especially when the duke of Berwick joined them as commander in Spain. The Irish Brigade proper was meanwhile engaged in the series of battles against Marlborough, but did little to enhance its reputation in a failure opposite Schulenburg at Malplaquet in 1711.

The irony of the situation of the Wild Geese was that throughout the wars under Louis XIV they were never once able to come to grips with their ancient enemy the English. It was 1745 before they could challenge in battle the nation that had forced them into exile. The battle of Fontenoy marks the apogee of achievement by the Irish Brigade. It now occupies a legendary position in the annals of the Wild Geese, helped by Emily

Lawless's poem (quoted on p. 126) and Hamilton Harty's symphonic study. It presented a welcome compensation both to Marshal Saxe and to the Irish Brigade for the cross-Channel débâcle of 1743–44. It was also instrumental in deciding Charles Edward to go it alone on his voyage to Scotland.

The War of Austrian Succession was five years old by the time Fontenoy was fought. In May 1745 the British braced themselves for a bloody clash. Two armies of about 60,000 each faced each other in Flanders. The legendary Marshal Saxe commanded the French, Cumberland, not yet the 'butcher of Culloden', the British and their allies. In the French ranks were all the glittering names of the Irish Brigade: the six regiments of Clare's, Dillon's, Bulkeley's, Roth's, Berwick's and Lally's, plus Fitzjames's horse.

On the morning of 11 May 1745 Cumberland ordered his centre to advance, and 16,000 of them moved up the slope to Fontenoy. Murderous fire from the French redoubts mowed them down in heaps, yet they moved steadily on, taking terrible losses all the way. By this stupendous feat of valour the British took the French centre. After conference with Louis XV, the duc de Richelieu and Lally, Saxe decided to throw the six Irish regiments into the fray in a do-or-die attempt to dislodge Cumberland's men. To the strains of 'The White Cockade' the Irish fixed bayonets and advanced. The four massive Irish cannon raked chasms in the British wall. Through this wall, on the right flank, the Brigade charged. Bitter hand-to-hand fighting with the British Brigade of Guards ensued. The Irish had centuries of oppression to avenge, and avenge it they did, though at a terrible cost. More than 700 out of the 4,000 engaged were casualties. Yet they won the battle for Saxe and broke the back of the Allies' 1745 campaign. The French lost about 5,000 at Fontenoy, the British and their allies three times that number.

The morale of the Irish Brigade was never higher than during that winter, when it stood ready in the Picardy ports under the duc de Richelieu, poised for an invasion of England to link up with Charles Edward's southward thrust from Scotland. Among the most zealous of Richelieu's supporters that winter was the Irishman Thomas Arthur Lally-Tollendal, commander of Lally's regiment. Lally was singled out for praise by Voltaire in his *Précis du Siècle de Louis XV* for his Jacobite commitment. Certainly it contrasted with the defeatism of Clare, who was content with his position in the French military hierarchy and wanted nothing to do with the '45 rising. Yet, as so often, it was the cynic who prospered and the man of commitment who suffered. While Clare went on to be marshal of France in the Seven Years' War, Lally was executed for his role in that conflict, in one of the most hideous miscarriages of justice in French history.

Sent to India in 1757 to retrieve French fortunes there, Lally ran up against the massive corruption of Admiral d'Aché and the French East India Company on the one hand, and the generalship of his countryman Eyre Coote, fighting on the English side, on the other. Arriving in India in 1758, Lally set about the conquest of Madras. Disaster followed disaster in a series of losing battles. The French were forced back to their final stronghold at Pondicherry, which surrendered in 1761, thus ending French inroads into India. Lally was taken to England as a prisoner-of-war. Meanwhile his enemies in India, like the Admiral Comte d'Aché, accused him of gross incompetence in the loss of Louis XV's Indian possessions. The duc de Choiseul, French Foreign Minister and a kinsman of d'Aché, listened to the allegations. Naively, Lally asked Pitt for parole to return to France to face his accusers. This was granted, but on landing in France he was thrown into the Bastille. After languishing there for four years, he was found guilty of having 'betrayed the interests of the King, the State and the Company of the Indies' and was sentenced to death by beheading.

To the horror of Voltaire, who later likened the case to that of Byng, Lally was decapitated clumsily by the Paris executioner. Louis XVI, who disliked this aspect, as so many others, of his predecessor's policies, publicly rehabilitated Lally's reputation in 1778, though it was not until 1929 that the French army ceremonially exonerated the luckless Irishman. But as far as the Irish Brigade itself was concerned, the damage was done. Morale plummeted, the brigade was near to mutiny, and recruitment tailed off to a trickle. The Irish were stupefied at Louis XV's perfidy and ingratitude. In Ireland disillusionment set in and a sense of futility, underlined by the final doom of the Stuart cause at Quiberon in 1759.

In naval affairs the Jacobite role was not so significant, though far from negligible. Men like Robert Dunbar served in the Picardy ports as privateers. And it was the Jacobites who built up the Russian navy under Peter the Great. Thomas Gordon, a

Royal Navy captain dismissed as a suspected Jacobite in 1715, entered the Czar's service, recruited officers for him from the Royal Navy and was made an admiral. Another Jacobite admiral in the Russian navy was Christopher O'Brien.

The military role of the Jacobites in the diaspora was almost entirely an Irish affair. It is true that after 1715 Scotsmen enlisted in the French army and that there were 5,000 of them in the Royal Scots regiment which was earmarked for service in the '45. But mostly the Scottish diaspora was to North America, to which they were either transported as rebels or emigrated of their own will like the Ulster Scots. Sons and grandsons of the men of the '45 fought on opposite sides in the American War of Independence. While those still in French service fought under Lafayette, the Scottish descendants of the 1745 Jacobites largely stayed loyal to George III. As a result, by a supreme historical irony, they had to suffer a second exile, this time to Canada, when the American colonists were victorious.

Apart from soldiering, what other opportunities were there for the refugees? The Jacobite diaspora, unlike that of the Huguenots which it closely followed, was aristocratic in character rather than bourgeois and was a political, not a religious, phenomenon. It presented the peculiar spectacle of an entire section of a given aristocracy following its sovereign into exile. But this very fact brought its own advantages. Cultural and social solidarity between elites on a transnational basis made it easier for the Jacobites to find niches in diplomacy and administration. The most famous such Jacobite diplomat was George Keith, hereditary Earl Marischal of Scotland, who was 'out' in the '15 and the '19 and later entered the service of Frederick the Great. He achieved great things in the Prussian foreign service. He was Ambassador Extraordinary to the French and Spanish courts, was decorated with the order of the Black Eagle, and was governor of the Prussian canton of Neuchâtel when Rousseau was in temporary residence there.

But though less famous than Marischal, some of the Jacobites scaled even greater heights. A Scotsman like Douglas could be found right at the heart of Louis XV's secret parallel foreign policy, *le secret du roi*. Ricardo Wall, a protégé of the duke of Liria, became a Spanish diplomat, served at the English court and was later Spanish chief minister and Secretary of State for Foreign Affairs, where he was in office in 1759 during Choiseul's English invasion project. Patrick MacNeny became Secretary of State for War in the Low Countries, and his sons were advisers at Vienna to Empress Maria Theresa and an important influence on Belgian affairs.

At a slightly lower level, the Jacobites made impressive careers as administrators, particularly in the French Empire. La Compagnie des Indes had the same sort of predilection for Irishmen as administrators as the British Empire did later for Scots. *Commis de bureaux* positions were held in the French Foreign Ministry by men like Charles Clarke (Martinique), O'Heguerty (Ile de Bourbon) and MacMahon (Louisiana). Gubernatorial assignments were given to Baron Copley in Guadaloupe, and to Conway and Lally in India. In the Low Countries the administration of the Ostend Company was almost entirely a Jacobite affair. And in Spain the economist and philanthropist Bernard Ward was commissioned by Ferdinand VI to make a grand tour of Europe between 1750 and 1754 to investigate how the Spanish economy could be regenerated on the Northern European model. Ward's economic thought deeply influenced the *philosophes*.

In sum, then, the Jacobite emigration from the British Isles produced a nucleus of politicians and administrators for the European powers. The aristocratic nature of the Jacobite movement evoked oligarchic solidarity and therefore the exiles were treated as honoured guests. There were no Jacobite ghettos; their principal problems were not economic but those of divided loyalties and dual nationalities. Even the problems of strange languages and cultures were mitigated to some extent by the aristocratic tradition of the Grand Tour, which made life abroad seem more feasible and more palatable.

The prominence of the Jacobites in the armed services, diplomacy and administration is therefore not really surprising. More intriguing is their dominant role in commerce and their excursions into financial, and later, industrial capitalism. The natural tendency of the Jacobites at home was to find a niche in the squirearchy. But under the pressure of events when abroad they turned to other occupations and outdid the Whigs at them. In Britain mercantile activity was respected. It was accepted that aristocrats could engage in it without loss of dignity. The Jacobites overseas abandoned 'Country' ideology, stole the Whigs' clothes and in time changed the image of the French nobility. Their penetration of French commerce was made easier by the persistent disdain for trade of the *noblesse*. Indeed, it could be argued that it was easier for Jacobites to find openings in commerce than in politics or administration, for there were no linguistic barriers, restrictive laws or xenophobia to surmount.

Jacobite merchants settled in ports like Dunkirk, Rouen, St-Omer, Boulogne, Dieppe, Le Havre, St-Malo, Brest, Nantes, L'Orient, Bordeaux and La Rochelle, being particularly attracted to the Breton ports because of Gaelic cultural solidarity. This new breed of Jacobites did not mind getting their hands dirty. Antoine Walsh, the Franco-Irish Jacobite privateer owner from Nantes, who sailed Charles Edward to Scotland in 1745, was heavily involved in the slave trade. In the explosion of trading companies launched onto the ocean in the early eighteenth century there were always Jacobites to be found. There was the Jacobite-dominated Ostend Company, particularly associated with names like MacNemy and Ray. There was Colin Campbell, director in Gothenburg of the Swedish East India Company. There were the Jacobite business communities at Bilbao, Cadiz, Seville and Malaga. Even the Danish East India Company, which was not Jacobite at first, became so after the '45, when many of the veterans of Culloden fled to Denmark and set up business houses in Copenhagen and Elsinore. In general, it can be said that, by their mercantile activities outside France, the Jacobites struck back at their tormentors by revealing to the Austrian and Nordic princes the extent to which world markets were monopolised by the English, Dutch and French and encouraging them to destroy this monopoly.

Although the main thrust of Jacobite activity lay in the mercantile sphere, they had their representative in the field of banking too. John Law, a Jacobite confidant of the Oglethorpe family, was comptroller-general of French finances in 1720. Other prominent Jacobites in high finance were George Waters & Sons, bankers to the Stuart court, and Robert Gordon, another familiar figure in banking circles. Jacobite exiles made their mark in agriculture too, introducing the methods of 'Turnip Towns-hend' to the Continent.

Only after the '45, with the second great wave of exiles, did the supporters of the House of Stuart begin to make their mark also as manufacturers and industrialists. The Alcock brothers had a thirty-year stranglehold on the manufacture of iron and associated metals in France. But undoubtedly the most important member of this post-1745 group and one of the great figures in industrial history was John Holker. Born in 1719 at Stretford in Lancashire, he served his apprenticeship in Manchester and joined the Manchester regiment, which was formed when Charles Edward arrived there in November 1745. Imprisoned after Culloden, he escaped to France, and after a short period in Lord Ogilvy's regiment, set up business in Rouen in 1749. Holker brought over the necessary machines and men from England to begin a textile industry in France.

The comptroller-general of finances, M. Machault, promised to make him manufacturer-royal if he could beat the English at their own game. The Holker factory soon became the base for a thriving French textile industry. In 1755 Holker was made inspector-general in charge of supervising foreign manufacturers, and in 1766 he became a naturalised French citizen. In 1771 he brought back from England the first 'spinning jenny' and followed this with Arkwright's shuttle in 1779. These quickly spread through France. For this service Holker was raised to the French nobility, while his son succeeded him as inspector-general. Even though he died in semi-disgrace at Rouen in 1786, compromised by his son's American industrial deals, his contribution to French industrial 'take-off' was everywhere recognised.

But in the opinion of some scholars the most important contribution of all made by the Jacobite diaspora was in the dissemination of Enlightenment ideas. Bolingbroke in his brief Jacobite period had singled out Voltaire as the vehicle by which English ideas could be spread in France. Although his was the single most important contribution to the percolation of these new concepts, Bolingbroke soon renounced the Stuarts. But other Jacobites continued his work. Atterbury was an important 'transmission belt' for spreading the ideas of Locke and Newton, while the Chevalier Ramsay had close contacts with Hume.

Sometimes the new ideas originated with the Jacobites themselves. Among Jacobite figures who made an important contribution to scientific thought on the Continent were the physicist Joseph Black and the naturalists Michael Adamson and John Turberville Needham. The mania for all things English in eighteenth-century France helped this process.

The most controversial intellectual role played by the Jacobites on the Continent was in the area of Jansenism and freemasonry. These were particularly tricky waters to swim in because of the attitude towards them of the Catholic church, the official protector and champion of the Stuart dynasty. There is no question but that the Jacobites had a crucial influence on the development of freemasonry – to such an extent, indeed, that later witnesses went so far as to describe freemasonry as a gigantic Jacobite conspiracy. Men like the duke of Wharton in Spain, Patrick Gordon and James Keith in Russia, George Hamilton in Switzerland and Lord Winton in Rome all set up Jacobite lodges. The intellectual of the Franco-Irish ship-owning fraternity, Pierre André O'Heguerty, was a good example of the typical Jacobite freemason. And the Radcliffe family (which included Derwentwater of the '15) were also prominent in freemasonry. Perhaps the most important of all of them was the Chevalier Ramsay, the political theorist and one-time tutor to Charles Edward, whose eccentricity so irritated James Stuart, although his exact role in the movement is still shrouded in mystery.

The real problem with the Jacobite freemasonry connection came in 1738 when the masonic movement was condemned by Pope Clement XII. The role of the Catholic church in the Jacobite diaspora was crucial, since in order to make any progress in a chosen career in a Catholic country, a Protestant Jacobite exile had to undergo conversion. So, for example, the duke of Perth was introduced into the church by Bossuet and John Law by Abbé (later Cardinal) Tencin. This represented a sort of penal law in reverse.

Moreover, the pope's condemnation of freemasonry, in which the Jacobite exiles were so deeply implicated, had other complications. The predominant strain in intellectual Jacobite Catholicism was Jansenism, itself increasingly under suspicion from the Holy See. Jacobite Catholics who subscribed to the mystical tenets of Fénelon were often instrumental in furthering the growth of the masonic movement. Chevalier Ramsay, prime representative of Scottish mystical Jacobitism, is an obvious example.

This complex of mysticism/Jansenism/freemasonry made the intellectual relationship of the Jacobites with the papacy an uneasy one. But it did enable the Jansenists to build bridges to the English Protestants after 1716. This ecumenical tendency encouraged hopes that James's religion might not after all be an insuperable barrier to his being restored. The Catholic mystics within the Jacobite movement stressed the fact that James's version of the faith of his fathers was not necessarily the one espoused in the Vatican. Even though his supporters held out no hopes that he would actually abandon his religion for Protestantism, they encouraged his animus against the Jesuits. One of them counselled him as follows: 'Take six Jesuits, land in England, set up a number of gibbets and hang them.'

The mystical strain in Jansenism had other dangers for the Jacobites, since it threatened to alienate the temporal as well as spiritual powers. Bishop Fitzjames of Soissons condemned Louis XV for sexual immorality and attacked successively the king's mistresses Madame de Châteauroux and Madame de Pompadour, and as a result he fell from royal favour.

The story of the Jacobite diaspora in general is a story of triumphant recovery from adversity. The uncertainty and anguish of exile gave way to a fighting spirit which carried the Jacobites to remarkable heights of achievement. Their exploits should be enough to convince lingering doubters that the Jacobite movement was not simply a clique of fossilised ultramontane reactionaries but, by contrast, contained within its ranks some of the finest talents of the age, either persecuted for their religion or driven into exile because of a genuine detestation of the corruption of the Whig oligarchy. 'Every man has his price,' Walpole sneered. The Jacobites showed convincingly that most men had their value too.

Chapter 9

The cultural milieu of Jacobitism

Men some to bus'ness, some to pleasure take
But every woman is at heart a rake.
Men, some to quiet, some to public strife,
But ev'ry lady would be Queen for life.

Pope

Women are much more like each other than men: they have,
in truth, but two passions, vanity and love; these are their
universal characteristics.

Chesterfield

Women are like tricks by slight of hand
Which, to admire, we should not understand.

Congreve, *Love for Love*

It is difficult to measure the huge distance between the eighteenth
century and our own except impressionistically, by a series of
snapshots. Families in the eighteenth century lived in the presence
and expectation of sudden death as much as the ancients had.
Infant mortality was high and life expectancy low. We are
accustomed to theatrical knights, but in eighteenth-century
England even the most distinguished thespians could not be hosts
in the best society, and in France actors could not receive
Christian burial. And so on. But one proposition can be asserted
with certainty: the Jacobites lived in a world that was at once
savage and extremely sophisticated. The same people who
pondered Berkeley's and Hume's treatises on sense-data thought

nothing of hanging, drawing and quartering 'rebels' or hanging highwaymen at Tyburn. Louis XV's court at Versailles, which offered patronage to Voltaire, Rousseau and other doyens of the Enlightenment, scarcely batted a collective eyelid when Damiens was put to the most horrible torture for an assassination attempt on the king. In the very month of the outbreak of the '45 the *Dublin Journal* recorded in the most matter-of-fact way the execution of a number of youths for sheeplifting and cattle stealing. The truth was that the 'lower orders' were treated with casual cruelty and abominable callousness by aristocrats who quoted Homer and Virgil to each other.

One result of this was endemic crime on a level that would appal the average twentieth-century citizen. Outside the city limits, even as close to the metropolis as Hampstead or Hounslow heaths, lurked the highwaymen with their dreaded cry of 'Stand and deliver', some of them colourful personalities like Robert King or Dick Turpin (hanged at York in 1739), more often journeyman cut-throats or the truly desperate.

This tendency to crime was not ameliorated by the physical environment of the great cities like London (with close to a million inhabitants in the Jacobite period). The 'great wen' was a cockpit of disease. Syphilis was rife. Infant mortality was about one in four. Houses were infested with fleas and lice. The narrow city streets did not gain in attractiveness from having early 'skyscrapers' – houses eight or nine storeys tall – built on to them in Edinburgh. Life for the ordinary man and woman was Hobbesian: 'nasty, brutish, and short.' The most flagrant social inequalities and injustices were regarded by society's beneficiaries as being part of the natural order, and any assault on privilege was punished murderously. Given the foulness of their physical surroundings and the oppressive poverty and injustice which daily ground them down, the masses for their part regarded brutality as in the natural scheme of things. An early 'Jack the Ripper' figure in Germany, who specialised in eviscerating pregnant women and ripping out the embryos, was himself executed by having his body 'torn' with red-hot tongs and then broken on the wheel. This meant being stretched so that your arms and legs were disjointed prior to having your bones broken with a crowbar.

The London mob was a particularly vicious creature from whom no foreigner, Jew or Catholic was safe. Life was held to be cheap; unwanted babies were left out in the street to die or were thrown into dungheaps or open drains. As if the brutality of the mob were not enough, their 'betters' joined in the mayhem. Their speciality was tormenting their social inferiors: servants, maids, prostitutes, and all women who were not protected by the iron law of oligarchy. Rape was a commonplace. The age of consent was twelve, but unless the rape victim was murdered or was an aristocrat, there was next to no chance of a conviction, especially as the rapist was likely to be a vicious and idle 'young buck' – a scion of the aristocracy or gentry.

Man's inhumanity did not stop with his fellow man. Animals were subjected to dreadful torments. Dropping cats from a great height, goose-riding, bear-baiting, bull-baiting, cockfighting – all were on a long list of atrocities visited on the dumb creatures.

Overlaying the poverty, brutality and injustice in London was the demon drink. Those who wonder at the Methodists' apparent obsession with alcohol should remember that John Wesley and his followers came to the fore in an era when the gin-shop was the most common sight in the English capital. Gin was a penny a quart and cheaper than milk, which was why mothers fed it to their babies to keep them quiet. Drunkenness was also endemic. One investigator counted 1,411 people going in and out of a gin-shop during a three-hour period one evening. In the late evenings the streets of inner London were strewn with the recumbent bodies of inebriated men, women and children.

As if all this were not enough, the common man and woman took the brunt of natural disasters. The famine in Ireland during 1739–41 gave a foretaste of the great hunger of 1845. The calamitous frosts of 1739 killed off the potato crop throughout Ireland. Consequent market forces took the price of corn and bread way beyond the reach of the poor. The result was starvation on a grand scale. One of the Wild Geese, in Ireland at the time, left this description of the famished:

> Out of every corner of the woods and glens they came,
> creeping forth upon their hands, for their legs would not bear
> them; they looked like anatomies of death; they spoke like
> ghosts crying out of their graves; they did eat the dead
> carrions, happy when they could find them.

All this was the background to the Jacobites' world rather than their milieu itself. The true Jacobite environment was the country. In more senses than one a 'Country' ideology was attractive to them. Yet this was not an era when the beauties of the countryside were appreciated for their own sake. In *Kidnapped* Stevenson accurately has his characters refrain from drawing attention to Highland scenery. No mid-eighteenth-century sensibility would have found the Highlands beautiful. Surrounded by all the grandeur of Inverness-shire, Captain Burt claimed to prefer the view from Richmond Hill. In an age before easy communications, when the roads were in many respects in a worse condition than two centuries before, the eighteenth-century traveller was too concerned with the difficulties of terrain like the Highlands to have room for contemplation of its beauties. As Macaulay remarked in the same context:

> A traveller must be freed from all apprehension of being murdered or starved before he can be charmed by the bold outlines and rich tints of the hills. He is not likely to be thrown into ecstasies by the abruptness of a precipice from which he is in imminent danger of falling two thousand feet perpendicular; by the boiling waves of a torrent which suddenly whirls away his baggage and forces him to run for his life; by the gloomy grandeur of a pass where he finds a corpse which marauders have just stripped and mangled; or by the screams of those eagles whose next meal may probably be on his own eyes.

True enough, as far as the Jacobite grandee was concerned. For him the countryside was, rather, the repository of virtue, and land the true index of patriotism. A man with stocks and shares could quit his country in times of peril with his wealth intact. One whose wealth lay in real estate would have to stay and fight when his country was in danger. The typical Jacobite would have agreed with the entry by François Quesnay (1694–1774) in the *Encyclopédie*, against 'grain': 'Commerce, like industry, is merely a branch of agriculture. It is agriculture which furnishes the material of industry and commerce and pays them.'

The key to the normal Jacobite sensibility lies in the fact that the Jacobite era at its zenith was located in a period of Augustan calm, before the Industrial Revolution and before the first self-conscious social revolution in France. David Hume, though no Jacobite, was in many ways an archetypal figure of this period, able to take for granted all kinds of social premises no one in the following century could dare to. The notorious inconsistencies in his social and political thought occur largely because he was not forced by general social crisis to define his position clearly, as he would have been compelled to do had he lived at the time of the French Revolution. Because not even the Jacobite risings were ever a challenge to the *social* regime, though a very serious one to the *political* regime, both Jacobites and their opponents could take a relatively cavalier attitude even to the kind of middle-range political problems that beset the Founding Fathers at the Philadelphia convention in 1787. The common view was that of Pope in the *Essay on Man*:

> For forms of government let fools contest,
> What e'er is best administered is best.

Another crucial aspect of the Augustan culture in which the Jacobites throve is that it pre-dated the Romantic movement. It is true that the world of the Jacobites was a pre-industrial one – and the Romantic movement was in part a reaction to the Industrial Revolution, but that is not the whole story. The forerunner or 'prodromos' of the Romantic movement was Jean-Jacques Rousseau, a contemporary of the later Jacobites, friend and confidant of Earl Marischal Keith, and a man who knew a good deal about the Jacobites. Once, early in his career, he masqueraded as a Scottish Jacobite called Dudding in order to win the favour of a rich lady.

Yet our generalisation may be allowed to stand, for Rousseau's real influence came later in the eighteenth century. In the Jacobite period proper he was a lone wolf, a prophet crying in the wilderness, persecuted by potentates and pursued from principality to kingdom by powerful enemies. The Jacobite era was predominantly a classical one in all senses of the word. Reason was still considered superior to instinct or '*sensibilité*', order and tradition to the radical and the innovative. As an illustration of the other sense of 'classical', it is worth recalling that Lord Hardwicke and Archbishop Herring found themselves unable to correspond during the '45 without quoting huge chunks of Virgil at each other. A knowledge of the classics was considered a prerequisite of the true gentleman. Jacobite and Whig shared this viewpoint.

Classical allusions permeated the sensibility of the educated classes in the eighteenth century. 'Country' theorists took their cue from Polybius, with his idea of the separation of powers, or from Machiavelli, who in turn relied heavily on the classical authorities. The typical English Jacobite would have endorsed Xenophon's perception of trade (in the *Oeconomus*) as 'banausic', though this attitude had to change when the Jacobites were driven into exile. But the key figure for the squirearchy was the archetypal classical, the poet Horace (the quintessential Apollonian in Robert Graves's sense). Horace was the ancient authority to whom, above all else, the exponents of Country ideology looked when they sought a classical sanction for their views. '*Odi profanum vulgus et arceo*' ('I hate the vulgar mob and I keep them at arm's length') expressed the distaste of the Jacobite grandee for the common herd. '*Persicos odi, puer, apparatus*' ('I hate Persian luxury, boy') denoted their Country austerity.

Another eighteenth-century curiosity was the admiration of Sparta. Athens was regarded as typifying the spirit of commercialism and economic imperialism. The intense admiration for Athens and distaste for Sparta that we are familiar with nowadays came in only with the nineteenth century. Following Machiavelli, Country ideologues located the beginning of republican *virtù* in Lycurgus and the ancient Spartans. This was a motif very widely taken up, and it survived into the Romantic movement, as did the idea of virtue being found in the countryside and not the town. It is savages and peasants who are noble in Rousseau, not the 'proletariat'. Of course, this admiration for Sparta was more than a little inconsistent with other strands of Country ideology. No plank in their platform was stronger than dislike of a standing army, yet the whole point of Spartan society was that it was based on just such a standing army.

Another point to note about the intellectual society of the Enlightenment of which the Jacobites were a part is that it was a small, closely knit world, where most of the luminaries knew each other. The Chevalier Ramsay was at one time tutor to Charles Edward and confidant to James. He was also a close friend of David Hume. Hume, perhaps naturally as a Scotsman, was always fascinated by the Jacobites, and was responsible later in life for disseminating some of the grosser calumnies against Charles Edward. Hume, of course, had close connections with Earl Marischal and Rousseau, with whom he had a famous (or infamous) quarrel. Marischal was in the employment of Frederick the Great, who was a patron of Voltaire. Voltaire in turn was a great admirer of Charles Edward and sympathetic to Jacobitism. In 1745 he had been special assistant to his friend the marquis d'Argenson (then Louis XV's Foreign Secretary) and instrumental in promoting the French expedition of that year. Voltaire described d'Argenson as suitable for the post of foreign minister in Plato's *Republic*. The commander of the 1745 expedition, the duc de Richelieu, was also pro-Jacobite and at one time patron to Rousseau. Montesquieu was another Enlightenment figure with two-way links, corresponding with both Hume and Charles Edward. When there was a liberal pope in the Vatican like Benedict XIV (1740–58), who took a conciliatory attitude to the *philosophes*, the interlock of cultural elites was even closer. Voltaire dedicated his *Mahomet* to Benedict, even though he revealed his true attitude of amused contempt in a letter to the marquis d'Argenson in August 1745: 'I have just received a portrait of the chubbiest old Holy Father . . .'

The Jacobites, then, had contacts with all the important intellectual leaders in Europe. Jacobitism had an importance in European affairs during the first half of the eighteenth century that it is difficult for us to appreciate, but on contemporary evidence equally hard to overrate. As late as 1769 Blackstone in his *Commentaries on the Laws of England* thought it necessary to address himself seriously to the problem. Certainly there was not a figure of any consequence in the philosophical or literary world who did not have definite views on the Jacobites and their doctrines. There were those broadly sympathetic, like Pope, Samuel Johnson, Montesquieu, Voltaire and Smollett. There was a whole coterie of writers hostile to the Stuarts and all their works: Defoe, Fielding, Locke, Sterne. And there were many more who were ambivalent: Swift, Berkeley, Hume and Henry, Lord Kames. Even prominent figures from later in the century took up a view, whether to show the corruption of England at the time of the '45 (Gibbon), to inveigh against Scotsmen and Catholics (Wilkes) or to stress the virtues of republicanism (Rousseau). Even Benjamin Franklin sent his Whig friends a congratulatory letter when he heard the news of Culloden, though he was to change his tune on 'unnatural rebellion' thirty years later.

Yet another important element in the Jacobite sensibility was the propensity to secrecy. Since the Jacobites were a proscribed organisation in England, secrecy became a fetish. Many are the letters from English Tories to the Pretender which end with an earnest entreaty that the letter be destroyed, since correspondence with James was high treason. In time the Jacobites went beyond this prudential form of secrecy to a love of the recondite and the arcane for its own sake. The convoluted ciphers in the Stuart papers, often concealing messages of stupefying banality, and the plethora of 'cant names', tell their own story. So does the closet Jacobitism of the Welsh secret societies like the 'Cycle of the White Rose' in North Wales and 'The Sea Serjeants' in South Wales. The Jacobite connection with freemasonry is relevant here too.

In time the English Jacobites evolved elaborate systems of equivocation or 'doublespeak' to evade charges of treason. Dr King's speech at the Radcliffe Camera in Oxford in 1749, with its *leitmotif* of '*Redeat*' (referring clearly, though not explicitly, to Charles Edward), is an example of this. So was the well-known Jacobite habit of responding to a toast to the king by passing the charged glass over a bowl of water, indicating that it was 'the king over the water' whose health was being drunk. The issue of secrecy in English Jacobitism is important, for it alerts us to a neglected aspect of Jacobite historiography: that the papers of most of the best-known English Jacobites like Sir Watkin Williams Wynn were destroyed so as not to incriminate the writers. Consequently most of our archival evidence for English Jacobitism was destroyed also.

The Jacobite sensibility is well caught in an apothegm by Charles Maurice de Talleyrand (1754–1838): 'Both erudition and agriculture ought to be encouraged by government; wit and manufactures will come of themselves.' Whig propagandists often tried to build on this by claiming that the advantages of wit lay entirely on their side. Along with the fullest purses, swiftest swords, best heads and fairest women, they also possessed the sharpest tongues and the fastest repartee.

Wit, rather than humour, was a key to the eighteenth-century mind: in Pope's words:

> True wit is nature to advantage dress'd
> What oft was thought, but ne'er so well express'd.

However, just as there can be no distinguishing Jacobite from Whig in point of clan difference, occupation, commercial, financial or industrial acumen, or even cultural attainment, so we find the precious substance wit equally divided between the rivals. Indeed, at the height of the Jacobite threat the supporters of the House of Stuart probably had the edge in this department. The greatest of the Whig wits, John Wilkes, made his appearance on the political scene when the Jacobite threat to the Hanoverian dynasty was over. Who can forget Wilkes's classic ripostes? 'Wilkes,' said Lord Sandwich, 'you will die either on the gallows or of the pox.' Wilkes: 'That must depend on whether I embrace your lordship's principles or your mistress.' Or this: 'Wilkes, I will not tolerate being the butt of your remarks.' Wilkes: 'That can never be, for as my bibulous friends will tell you, I cannot abide an empty one.'

It has to be admitted straight away that no Jacobite ever attained those heights. But in the heyday of Jacobitism the Tory-Jacobite sensibility probably gave better than it got. A Fielding was no match for a Swift in this department, a Defoe for an Atterbury, or a Chesterfield for a Samuel Johnson. The flavour of eighteenth-century wit, depending as it does so heavily on a knowledge of the Bible and the classics, may not always be to our taste, but some of it loses little 'in translation' between the ages. The Earl Marischal remarked of Hume, famous both for his erudition and for his corpulence, *'Verbum caro factum'* ('The word is made flesh'). When Thurot made his daring raid on Ireland in 1760 in two small ships, achieving privateering wonders before the British caught up with him, Marischal remarked: 'I see the conquest of Ireland by M. Thurot has miscarried.' Displaying this sort of levity towards serious matters like French descents on the three kingdoms, it was no wonder that Marischal was far from being the Stuarts' favourite Jacobite.

But probably the finest of all Jacobite wits was Bishop Atterbury, who had an F.E. Smith-like ability to expose the fatuousness of an opponent's would-be crushing jibe. On one occasion Atterbury said in the House of Lords that he had prophesied last winter that a certain bill would be attempted in the present session and he was sorry to find he had proved a true prophet. Lord Coningsby replied that Atterbury had held himself out as a prophet, 'but for my part I do not know what prophet to liken him to, unless to that furious prophet Balaam, who was reproved by his own ass'. Atterbury replied: 'Since the noble lord has discovered in our manners such a similitude, I am well content to be compared to the prophet Balaam. But, my lords, I

am at a loss how to make out the other part of the parallel: I am
sure I have been reproved by nobody but his lordship.'

One of the most famous eighteenth-century wits was of
course Samuel Johnson, often taken to be the quintessence of the
Jacobite type. Hard-drinking, reactionary, taking his inspiration
from the classics, despising all egalitarian notions as 'cant',
Johnson conformed to the type so beloved of Whig propaganda,
and immortalised (and caricatured to the point of absurdity) by
Fielding in *Tom Jones* in the person of Squire Western with his
parrot cries of 'Hanover rats.' It is true that the Jacobite squires
were a bibulous lot. Sir John Hynde Cotton, one of the English
Jacobite leaders of the 1740s, was described by the Cambridge
antiquary Cole as 'one of the tallest, biggest, fattest men I have
ever seen' and he was reputed to be able to hold his liquor better
than any man in England. On being told that it would be better
for his gouty leg if he drank less, he replied that if it would not
bear his daily allowance of six bottles of wine 'it was no leg to
him'. Charles Edward himself, who in his latter days in Rome
disdained the light vintages of Frascati and the Castelli for his
daily intake of half a dozen bottles of Cyprus wine, can be
located in this tradition. But hard drinking was by no means
confined to the adherents of one particular political persuasion.
And in their portrait of the typical Jacobite Whig propagandists
forgot men like Johnson who could give as good as, and better
than, they received from old enemies like Chesterfield and
Horace Walpole.

Mention of Johnson brings us to a fascinating fact about
English Jacobitism that was never far from the surface in all the
Jacobite risings, and had fatal consequences at Derby in
December 1745: the mutual suspicion and dislike between
English and Scots. The fashion in England for hatred and
contempt of Scotsmen, which was played up by Wilkes and
which so distressed Hume, was as pronounced in the mid-
eighteenth century as was the Anglomania of the French. In
Johnson's writings we can discern the suspicion and dislike of
things Scottish that so often surfaced in the English Jacobite
leaders and prevented effective cooperation. It may be worth
citing a few of Johnson's dicta on Scotland. To Boswell he said:
'Norway too has noble wild propsects; and Lapland is remarkable for prodigious noble, wild prospects. But, sir, let me tell you,
the noblest prospect which a Scotsman ever sees is the High Road

that leads him to England.' His particular disdain was reserved for the Celtic revival in Scottish literature as exemplified by Ossian. When Boswell asked him if any man in a modern age could have written such poetry, Johnson replied: 'Yes sir, many men, many women and many children.' And again on the subject of Ossian: 'A man might write such stuff for ever if he would abandon his mind to it.'

Wit was permitted, even by absolutist rulers, over the entire range of human activities in the eighteenth century, with one exception: religion. It is significant that in his essay 'The Natural History of Religion' Hume delivers merely a sideswipe at Christianity and its practice of the Eucharist: 'Of all religions the most absurd and nonsensical is that whose votaries eat, after having created, their deity.' The really devastating fun poked at the 'infant or superannuated deity' is reserved for the posthumously published *Dialogues Concerning Natural Religion*. Despite the dithyrambs of the *philosophes*, Christianity was still an idol that could be questioned but not yet toppled. The curious limbo inhabited by the men of the Enlightenment between an age of genuine belief and the nineteenth century when science became the fetish no doubt accounts for the eighteenth century's curious predilection for quacks, fakers and nostrums. In some ways the master charlatan Count Cagliostro (Giuseppe Balsamo) is more representative of the era before the French Revolution than Voltaire himself.

But the increasing fashion for philosophical scepticism had its impact on the Jacobites. The Leslies, Atterburys and Ramsays of the early Jacobite period give way to men of a different breed: Lord Elcho, Earl Marischal, John Holker. The passage from pious belief to scepticism or indifference is nowhere better charted than in the distance between the Old and the Young Pretender. It is abundantly clear that Charles Edward had so little time for organised religion that he would have joined Wilkes, Franklin and the rest in the Hell-Fire Club if a profession of the principles of that organisation would have gained him the three kingdoms. Perhaps this sort of consideration provided the true interpretation of the otherwise puzzling Delphic utterance by Sir Charles Petrie when he says: 'as a whole the men who surrounded Charles Edward were not of the same calibre as those who fought for his forebears.' No, indeed. On any reasonable analysis they were of a far *higher* calibre.

Wit was also lavishly used to draw attention to the alleged shortcomings and deficiencies of women. Here is Pope:

> In men we various ruling passions find,
> In women two almost divide the kind,
> Those, only fix'd, they first or last obey,
> The love of pleasure and the love of sway.

Yet Pope's estimate is at least a higher one than the saying of the supremely unattractive Lord Chesterfield, doyen of Whig sensibility, which is quoted on page 142.

It would be truly anachronistic to expect from the eighteenth century late twentieth-century 'enlightened' views on the female sex, but a study of the era provides grounds for asserting two main and not unlinked assertions: that women were better placed in the eighteenth century than in the more constricting Victorian age; and that Jacobitism provided them with a more congenial home than Whiggery.

The eighteenth century was, at least when compared with its successor, a permissive age. It is to be expected, then, that the influence of the boudoir would loom large. No adequate history of the *ancien régime* can be written that neglects the influence of royal mistresses, whether the La Vallière, Montespan and Maintenon of Louis XIV or the Châteauroux and Pompadour of his successor. This, a conclusion unpalatable to modern feminists who affect to despise this sort of influence, may be partially mitigated by the consideration that many women who began their public career by becoming someone's wife or mistress went on to achieve great influence through their own merits. Whether those merits were for good or evil is another matter. Sarah, duchess of Marlborough, the woman whose hold over Queen Anne reduced Macaulay to spluttering indignation, is a good example. As a politician of the machiavellian variety she was far superior to her famous soldier husband. A similar type of woman in France was Claudine Alexandrine Guérin de Tencin. Beginning her rise to prominence as the mistress of Abbé (later Cardinal) Dubois, she had liaisons with most of the influential figures at Versailles in the first two decades of the eighteenth century. Her affair with Bolingbroke is sometimes credited with having torpedoed the 1715 rising. According to this view, it was Claudine who confided the plans of the '15 to Bolingbroke, and Bolingbroke who passed them on to the English.

For women of a certain rank, marriage to a 'gentleman', chosen by her parents for his rank or social status, was the inevitable fate. Spinsterhood was a precarious business even among the upper classes: only the cloister was considered suitable for spinsters of noble birth. These facts give us a clue as to why Jacobitism provided a congenial home for many women. It was obvious that matrimony under such circumstances was unlikely to bring fulfilment to an intelligent and ambitious female. But if she could enlist under the banner of a political cause, her talent could be put to some use. Jacobitism provided such an outlet. The Pretenders would accept all kinds of volunteers, regardless of sex. Women could use their ingenuity as secret agents, couriers and lovers to help the Jacobite cause. The most eminent of them would be rewarded by a personal correspondence with the *de jure* king of England. Moreover, since to subscribe to Jacobite principles in Britain created a sense of alienation from social norms and was as 'deviant' in its own way as being a thoroughgoing socialist in Britain today, women and Jacobitism could come together in a mutual embrace of the outsiders and the marginalised. Both were minorities, and each could find uses in the other.

To say this is not necessarily to say that the Jacobite ethos provided a special niche for women. The interests of Jacobitism and those of the female sex were ultimately no more (and probably a good deal less) compatible than those of socialism and modern feminism. But as an alliance of convenience it bore some interesting fruit. Not surprisingly, the Jacobites had experts in the art of love in high places. Olive Trant was one of the most formidable, a rival to Claudine Tencin for the affections of the Regent, the duc d'Orléans. There were the Oglethorpe sisters, Anne and Fanny, daughters of a Surrey Jacobite family who had followed James II into exile at St-Germain. Fanny Oglethorpe is converted by Thackeray in *Henry Esmond* into 'the Pretender's mistress' – a gloss that some historians have been prepared to follow uncritically.

Yet other women derived their influence from straight economic or political power, and in this connection it is the third Oglethorpe sister who is the really interesting one. Eleanor Oglethorpe, later the marquise de Mézières, was born into a staunch royalist family just before the Glorious Revolution and was brought up at the Jacobite court at St-Germain-en-Laye when her parents followed the Stuarts into exile. Saint-Simon described her as a shapely beauty when young, and she used these assets to contract an (at

first sight) unspectacular marriage with a minor marquis, de
Mézières, a career army officer. With the modest fortune thus
acquired she invested heavily in John Law's Louisiana scheme (the
so-called Mississippi bubble) and sold out her stock when share
prices were at their height, just before the bubble burst. With the
huge fortune she made from this speculation Eleanor lobbied the
French court incessantly on James's behalf and used the glamour of
the Stuarts to make spectacular marriages for her daughters.
Combining her money with James's patronage, she took her family
to the very pinnacle of the French aristocracy. She was one of those
women who loved the world of political intrigue, and was
formidable enough to be taken seriously by French ministers like
Maurepas. She was still engaging in intrigue at the age of seventy,
deeply embroiled in the Elibank plot.

As the eighteenth century wore on, the sentimental and
nostalgic glow surrounding the exiled Stuarts drew in more
female supporters. In this category belong many of the most
celebrated figures of Jacobite legend, like Flora MacDonald,
saviour of Charles Edward during his flight in the heather after
Culloden in 1746. Isabella Lumisden, another fervent Jacobite,
only consented to marry Robert Strange, the well-known
engraver, on condition that he fought for Prince Charles during
the '45. Some women went even farther in their zeal for the
Jacobite cause. The Mackintoshes of Clan Chattan were raised in
1745 by Lady Mackintosh, Lord George Murray's cousin, the
'Colonel Anne' of Jacobite lore. As soon as her husband, a
Hanoverian loyalist, departed to raise a company of militia for
King George, 'Colonel Anne' raised the Mackintoshes for the
prince. She then rode at their head in her tartan riding habit, with
a clansman's blue bonnet on her head. At the time she was just
twenty years of age. Such was her beauty that after Culloden she
had Cumberland's officers eating out of her hand, all except the
execrable and inhuman General ('Hangman') Hawley.

The female attachment to the Stuarts always rankled with the
Whigs, and whenever possible they tried to turn it to propaganda
advantage. Since Charles Edward had little interest in women,
artificial interest had to be whipped up around mythical females
like 'Jenny Cameron' of the '45 – 'the young Pretender's mistress'
– for whom Sophy Western was mistaken in *Tom Jones*. Hearing
that the coach with 'Jenny' in it had broken down near Kendal
and she herself had been taken, Fielding remarked in the *True*

Patriot: 'It is a great neglect in the Pretender either as lover or
general to leave his baggage with so slender a guard.' If you could
not discredit the Jacobite movement with women, it was not
beyond Whigs like Fielding to fabricate would-be incriminating
evidence or to pretend that the Jacobite sensibility was miso-
gynistic. 'Why, lookee, sister,' says Squire Western in *Tom Jones*,
'you know I don't love to hear you talk about politics; they
belong to us and petticoats should not meddle.'

The fact that women genuinely were attracted to the Stuart
cause was grudgingly admitted by the nineteenth-century anti-
Jacobite Thackeray, who naturally tries to explain it as the
'weakness' of the sex: 'With respect to the women, as is usual
with them, 'twas not a question of party but of faith; their belief
was a passion; either Esmond's mistress or her daughter would
have died for it cheerfully.'

What of the role of women in Jacobite thought in general?
Can we sustain the thesis that the Jacobites looked more
favourably on women than the Whigs? Some of the aphorisms of
Johnson and his ilk do not seem to support this view. 'Woman's
at best a contradiction still', was Pope's considered judgment. 'A
man is in general better pleased when he has a good dinner upon
his table than when his wife talks Greek' is a well-known
Johnson aphorism. In the same league is the good doctor's
prefiguring of Kipling's Kitty O'Grady and the colonel's lady:
'Were it not for imagination, sir, a man would be as happy in the
arms of a chambermaid as of a duchess.' Again, there is this from
the Jacobite Thomas Carte in a letter to Daniel O'Brien in 1738:
'Tho' men often sacrifice their honour to their interest, and either
of these to their resentment, I never knew any but a woman
capable of sacrificing both to their revenge.'

Lest all this be thought overly 'sexist', it must be remembered
that such sentiments were normal and unexceptionable in the
eighteenth century. The notorious womaniser the duc d'Orléans,
defended his promiscuity to his mother as follows: '*Bah, maman,
dans la nuit tous les chats sont gris!*' An almost word-for-word
transcription of this appears among Franklin's thoughts for the
year 1745. And it is worth recalling that Johnson's strictures on
women were mild compared with those of his Whig contemporary Lord Chesterfield, as stated in 1748: 'Women, then, are only
children of a larger growth: they have an entertaining tattle and
sometimes wit; but for solid reasoning good sense, I never knew

in my life one that had it, or who reasoned and acted consequentially for four and twenty hours together.'

The truth of the matter is that, whereas Jacobite attitudes to women might seem patronising to the late twentieth-century sensibility, they were chivalrous in the old sense of the word. The idea of the 'gentle sex' as naturally inferior came as second nature to men trained in a martial culture where the norm was for the male to honour women as a softening, civilising influence but, by the very definition of physical strength and fighting capability, not to regard them as the equal of the male – the very attitude that John Stuart Mill was later to excoriate. Two letters from James Stuart should make this clear. When his wife Clementina left him and retreated into a convent in November 1725 he chided her with these words: 'I feel no resentment against you, for I am convinced that the malice and cunning of our enemies have imposed upon your youth and *the weakness of your sex*' (italics mine). Eighteen years later, writing to Lord Sempill about the marquise de Mézières's role in the French plans for a descent on England, he remarked: 'This lady has a great vocation to meddle, but the French ministers are to be sure too prudent to trust or encourage her in such matters, though her sex and her good will require that we should carry with all civility towards her.'

The Jacobite attitude towards women, then, was as good as, if not better than, that of their Whig contemporaries, given the prejudices of the age. It was a rare mind indeed that could entertain the principle of sexual equality; such an imaginative leap called for the genius of a Rousseau. It is altogether heartening, therefore, to be able to record that one of the few who took this leap was the great and good Jacobite Lord Pitsligo, who recorded this opinion in his *Moral and Philosophical Essays*: 'It were neither kind nor civil in this argument to forget the women, for they speak too. But to say the truth, idleness and speaking for speaking's sake is not their general character. They are more active, more foreseeing and better managers than we. If a foolish education sometimes spoils them (and whom does it not spoil) the fault should be laid where it ought.' Those who deny that there was any essential moral difference between Charles Edward's men of the '45 and their Whig opponents would do well to collate and contrast Pitsligo's sentiments with those of Chesterfield quoted above.

Chapter 10

A moveable feast:
the Jacobite court in exile

There'll never be peace till Jamie comes home.

Hogg, *Jacobite Relics*

If someone inferred that demons by their natural power can work miracles he would be mistaken . . . As Estius correctly observes '. . .the demons do not teach any truth which they might want to confirm by miracle; nor do they work any miracles by themselves or through others, in order to testify to their sanctity which they do not have. Either one of these two intentions seems to be necessary to say that someone works a miracle.

Benedict XIV, *De Miraculis*

Thy sympathising complaisance
Made thee believe intriguing France
But woe is me for thy mischance
That saddens every true heart.

Hogg, *Jacobite Relics*

The Jacobite court in exile did not find a final resting place until it settled in Rome in 1718. During the high tide of French support for the Stuarts, until Louis XIV's death in 1715, the deposed King James II and his successors were domiciled at the château of St-Germain-en-Laye outside Paris. It was a cold winter day in January 1689 when James II and Mary of Modena took possession of their new abode, which had already housed previous Stuart exiles. Although Louis XIV himself never cared for the château of St-Germain – the memory of days spent there as a child during the Fronde was too painful – it had been his principal out-of-town retreat until the completion of the great palace at Versailles. It was therefore regarded as a particular mark of his favour that he should make over the Château Vieux to James and his wife. Louis had not stinted on his hospitality. Signs of his personal regard for his guests were everywhere apparent as the Stuarts inspected their new home. Mary of Modena's dressing room had been carefully prepared by Madame de Maintenon: it contained an exquisite set of silver, and in one of the silver caskets was 6,000 livres d'or for running expenses. The jewellery made over to the Stuarts by Louis more than replaced all they had lost in their flight from England.

The Château Vieux at St-Germain was a towering yellow brick and stone edifice, begun in the fourteenth century and completed in the sixteenth, which gave onto the Seine. Visible for miles around, this great fortress of the Ile-de-France provided a magnificent panorama of Paris from its terraces. Close by was a second château, the Château Neuf, birthplace of Louis XIV and deserted in 1689, but soon to be the quarters of the Jacobite courtiers and officers. Experts pronounced the St-Germain complex austere and forbidding, but there was no doubting the beauty of the gardens and surrounding parkland. The hanging gardens and grottoes of the Château Neuf housed statues of ancient gods and heroes. There were fountains, a bowling green and an ornamental lake. The terrace, completed in 1673 at a cost of nearly a million livres, ran as straight as a Roman road for a mile and a half along the park, overlooking the Seine.

The Great Park, in which nearly six million trees had been planted in 1664, was famous for its hunting. James had at his disposal an army of huntsmen and beaters and a veritable armoury of weapons, plus tents, nets, dogs, hunting hounds, hawks and falcons. According to the locals, deer, fox, heron, wild duck and even wolves and bears could be flushed out of the Great Park. Louis XIV's *grand veneur*, the duc de La Rochefoucauld, the Sun King's great Master of the Hunt, took to James immediately and spared no efforts to distract him from the loss of his kingdom with the pleasures of the chase. The woods around St-Germain echoed to the galloping of horses and the sound of the hunting horn. So great were the attractions of St-Germain as a game centre that the English ambassador asked La Rochefoucauld for the loan of the hounds, only to be told coldly that as Master of the Hunt he was exclusively at the orders of James Stuart, the true king of England.

At first James could not settle. His thoughts were on the Irish campaign. But when he returned beaten after the Boyne, he began to accept the easy rhythms of life at St-Germain. Points of etiquette and protocol in relation to the court at Versailles were ironed out, fêtes and open-air theatricals held in the vast grounds, and the ever-expanding Jacobite court supervised. As refugees from Dundee's and Sarsfield's campaign poured in, most of them destitute, the rooms in the Château Neuf were quickly filled and the Scots and Irish spilled out into the village. By the turn of the century there were an estimated 2,500 of them. The main problem of the Stuart court was money. Louis XIV's monthly pension of 50,000 livres began to cover less and less of the expenses. One by one Mary of Modena's jewels were sold to meet the running costs of the court.

The milieu into which the Jacobite court at St-Germain-en-Laye was increasingly absorbed was that of Versailles under the Sun King, a much-discussed subject. While Mary of Modena fitted well into this context and was on excellent terms with Madame de Maintenon, James soon began to attract derisive gossip, notably from his habit of standing with his sword, point uppermost, in his hands before him during the Credo, to emphasise his position as Defender of the Faith. In general, James was tolerated but despised at Versailles, but Mary Beatrice was universally popular. The same qualities that had bedevilled James's short reign in England adversely affected his standing in France: obstinacy, tactlessness, failure of imagination, lack of charisma and social grace, inability to read human personalities as his brother had. Even the reputation for bravery, which Condé and Turenne had attested to, had been badly tarnished by his flight from Ireland. As if in recognition of his social failure, James increasingly retreated from life, formed a close friendship with the Abbé de Rance, and spent up to four days a week in the monastery of La Trappe, the visits becoming more frequent the closer he felt the approach of death.

Meanwhile a shadow court had been formed at St-Germain. Lord Melfort was the first Secretary of State, followed by Lord Middleton. The feud between the two, originally over religious differences (the former being a Catholic, the latter a Protestant), gave rise to the first phase of factionalism at the exiled Stuart court, a feature that was never thereafter to be absent, wherever the court moved. Other courtly positions were established: Lord Chamberlain, Lord Chancellor, Ambassador to the Court of France, vice-chamberlains, ladies-in-waiting, and so on.

The presence of the Jacobite court transformed St-Germain. The quiet village, seemingly forsaken by Louis XIV, acquired a new lease of life. French spoken in Scottish and Irish accents echoed down the narrow streets. The atmosphere was over-whelmingly military. While the Château Vieux maintained a luxury and elegance surpassing that of the palace of Whitehall, the Château Neuf resembled nothing so much as a glorified barracks. In 1693 the French Ministère de Bâtiments complained that the denizens of the Château Neuf had filled their precious moat with rubbish.

Etiquette at the Château Vieux became more relaxed as James progressively withdrew to La Trappe and Mary of Modena became the dominant figure at St-Germain. After James's death in 1701 she became the symbolic representation of the Stuart court in French eyes and, since James Francis was only thirteen years old, the Queen Regent as well. Money problems continued to plague the exiled dynasty. By the Treaty of Ryswick William III promised to repay Mary of Modena's jointure of £150,000, but he soon reneged on the agreement, claiming that the money was to be paid only when Louis XIV ordered the Stuart family and their supporters out of France. This Louis refused to do. As a result the court at St-Germain was entirely dependent on the monthly payment from the French Treasury, carried from Versailles in a huge iron cart. Sometimes the Treasury forgot to send the money on the due date and panic ensued in the château until the mistake was rectified. Louis XIV tried to shore up the poverty of the Stuarts in tactful ways, like the delivery of fruit and flowers to the château every May and September, and by seeing to the upkeep of the Orangery and the gardens at his own expense.

In 1706 James Francis reached his majority. Suffering from poor health, exacerbated by the damp climate of St-Germain, he thereafter spent more and more time away from the château, either on expeditions like the '08 or with the duke of Berwick in Flanders. Mary of Modena meanwhile continued her stewardship for her son at St-Germain. She felt an affection for the place that James did not, and stayed on after the Jacobite court moved with

James in 1713, dying there in 1718 at the age of sixty-one.

When the Treaty of Utrecht in 1713 required Louis XIV to expel the Jacobites from France, the Stuart court began a period of peripatetic existence that was ended only with the acceptance of the pope's offer of a permanent home in Rome. The first port of call for the doubly exiled court was Bar in Lorraine, ruled by a duke who was a close friend of Berwick. Bar was a small, sleepy, provincial town, picturesquely set, with grey stone streets, many churches, convents and monasteries, and a castle overtopping all. Here James remained for two years until the planning for a new Stuart attempt that culminated in the '15 began.

After the failure of the rising and with the winds of change blowing through France after Louis XIV's death, the duke of Lorraine considered James a political liability and regretfully asked him to move on. Pope Clement XI urged him to make a permanent home in the Papal States but James demurred, feeling that the Jacobite cause would be compromised if it was too closely identified with the papacy and the Catholic church. As a middle-of-the road solution he chose Avignon, a papal dominion. This time it was the turn of a Provençal town to resound with Scots and Irish variants of the French tongue, as threadbare Jacobites thronged the streets. Avignon was a comedown after St-Germain and even Bar. The episcopal authorities there were unduly officious, fussing about the numbers of Protestants in the Jacobite ranks. James felt ill at ease. In July 1716 he wrote: 'These southern climates agree less with my inclination than with my health which, I thank God, is very good.'

Money problems were now more than ever acute: a new wave of refugees had joined the court in exile following the collapse of the '15. Factionalism at court had already entered a new phase. No longer just a matter of Protestant cliques against Catholics, the intrigues had broadened to set Scots against Irish and grandee against grandee, particularly Mar against Marischal and the duke of Ormonde. On top of this, George I was trying to force the pope to remove the Jacobites from Avignon by threatening to bombard Civitavecchia. Moreover, in 1716–17, in the aftermath of the Jacobite rising, a number of English assassins were apprehended by the French on their way to Avignon with murderous designs on the 'Pretender'. Yet James discounted stories of assassination attempts and took no extra precautions in his walks and rides around Avignon.

But by 1717 the pressure on him to remove from Avignon had become too great to resist. After meeting Clement in Rome in June, James consented to take up residence in the ducal palace at Urbino, with a pension of 12,000 scudi (about £3,000). For the next half-century James was to be domiciled in Italy.

The ducal palace at Urbino was a fairytale building, its picturesque round towers dominating the Appenine peaks in the background. Standing on the edge of a sheer, inaccessible rock and visible for miles, the palace was 1,500 feet above sea level, approached by a winding road from Pesaro through the Metaunus valley which ascended abruptly to Urbino on a series of zigzag hairpin bends. The twin pinnacles of the pink and brown palace dwarfed the town, with its cathedral and narrow, crooked streets. The gateway to the palace led from the piazza to an inner courtyard, lined with mathematical Corinthian columns. Inside the palace was a labyrinth of large, perfectly proportioned rooms. The detail of the doorways made Urbino one of the architectural sights of Italy. The doors were masterpieces of *intarsia* while their multicoloured woods were picked out in *trompe l'oeil* pictures of still life or martial and inspirational themes. One of the two chapels was built entirely in sculptured marble; the palace also boasted one of the finest libraries in Europe.

It was a superb location for a contemplative, but its very orderly perfection seemed to irk James. He complained of loneliness and isolation from the world. The Chevalier also found fault with the walks and drives, or rather the lack of them. All three roads suitable for driving petered out after a mile, all terminating at convents. During the day James reluctantly saw to social duties and in the evening would play a bored game of ombre or battledore and shuttlecock. Although he and his court were popular in Urbino because they brought trade and tourism and in general put the duchy on the map, James soon became seriously depressed at the sameness of life there. He asked the pope to allow him to reside elsewhere during the winter of 1718–19 and suggested Castelgandolfo, Clement's summer residence. This did not suit the pope. Pesaro, Albano, Perugia and Foligno were suggested in turn but James held out for Castelgandolfo. In the end, fearing that he might find the Pretender permanently ensconced in his summer palace, Clement used the occasion of James's marriage to Clementina Sobieska in

1719 to find a permanent place for him in Rome: the Palazzo Muti.

For the rest of the Jacobite period the seat of the Stuart court was in Rome. The Palazzo Muti was a small, unpretentious and undistinguished baroque palace, not to be remotely compared with the castle at Urbino in point of architectural beauty. Neither was the summer residence Clement provided for James (along with a papal pension): the Palazzo Savelli at Albano. But James loved the Albano retreat and spent many happy hours there, walking and hunting.

Now that he was married, with a pension from the pope, another promised from the French and a dowry of 25 million francs from the Sobieski family, the worst of the financial worries at the Jacobite court were over, at any rate for the time being. Gradually James and his band of exiles became a permanent fixture on the Roman scene. Despite major setbacks to his prestige caused by his turbulent relationship with his wife, James gradually eased himself into a way of life that would scarcely change over the next half-century. A papal guard was on duty daily outside the Palazzo Muti, the only residence besides the Vatican and the Quirinale to be so honoured.

Factionalism in James's court reached new heights during the years 1719–25 over the Inverness affair. The principal characters in this story, apart from James and Clementina, were Mar, Lord Pitsligo, James Murray of Stormont, John Hay (afterwards Lord Inverness) and his wife. Clementina accused Mrs Hay of having an affair with her husband. This was but the most melodramatic outburst of a neurotic, religiously maniacal woman, whose unbalanced tendencies were accentuated by life with the austere, melancholy and jealous James. There was no truth in the accusation of adultery, but in any case Clementina also objected to her sons being educated by Protestant tutors, so she decided to loose off a scatter-gun of complaints that would hit at least some of her targets. The end of the affair was Clementina's dramatic flight to the Ursuline convent in November 1725, whence she returned only when James consented to dismiss her *bête noire* Mrs Hay (titular countess of Inverness) and her husband. Even so she did not at first return to the Palazzo Muti but went to live in Bologna. Only in 1728 was James finally reconciled with his wife, but by this time she was hopelessly launched into religious mania, harbouring hopes of an immediate canonisation after her death.

Her demise in 1735, ostensibly through tuberculosis, was at least half self-induced.

Partly through feelings of guilt, James himself became a recluse after her death and turned to prayer and religious devotions. By the late 1730s the young Charles Edward was already the senior partner at the Stuart court. Although James accompanied his sons to parties and social gatherings, he invariably retired after an hour. Not a morning passed without his spending an hour in prayer in the chapel where his wife used to pray. At dinner he spoke little and retired immediately afterwards.

Perhaps Rome was never the right environment for the 'Old Pretender'. The Romans' attitude to religion jarred with his. Their attitude was emotional; it was stirred by splendour and lavish pageantry. The eighteenth-century Romans looked to their religion, their churches and their pastors to provide a reflection of eternal bliss, a celestial panoply on earth. Puritan austerity or Jansenist piety was not for them. Their faith was sensual rather than ethereal. The Madonna almost rated as more important than Jesus Christ himself. James's severe soul found this kind of approach facile. His son Henry, Cardinal York, shared some of these difficulties. The disharmony between Stuart asceticism and Roman *joie-de-vivre* undoubtedly underlay the difficulty Benedict XIV had in communicating with Cardinal York. 'If all the Stuarts are as boring as he,' he remarked, 'no wonder the English drove them out.'

In another way also it can be argued that Rome was bad for James, since it sapped him of what remained of a never full-blooded commitment to Stuart restoration to the British Isles. Eighteenth-century Rome was the most stable society in Europe, suffused with a *dolce far niente* mentality resulting from an inchoate form of clientelism or Welfare State-ism. The basis of the economy of the Papal States was the massive financial subvention throughout Christendom, and especially France (which provided three-quarters of the funds), towards the maintenance of the Vatican as a temporal power. This meant that an enormous amount of unemployment, underemployment and disguised unemployment could be sustained. Nearly all eighteenth-century visitors to Rome commented on the peculiar social situation thus engendered. 'Imagine a populace', wrote Charles de Brosses, the French observer, 'one third of whom are priests, one third doing very little and the other third nothing at all.'

About a third of the population, it is true, were Vatican officials or families of officials: clerks to the Congregations, staff of the papal palaces, the Lateran, Vatican and Quirinale. Some estimates have put the staff of the Congregation as high as 30,000 and the total number of official employees and dependants at 80,000. When Napoleon planned to dismantle the papacy at the end of the century and replace it with his own regime, he found this would mean dispossessing at least half the population of Rome.

Apart from the clergy, their officials, and the handful of aristocratic families, the Romans lived as craftsmen, lackeys or beggars, or simply did nothing. At the end of the century Napoleon's census takers found to their astonishment that there were 70,000 Romans who could not be classified as following any occupation. Needless to say, in such an artificial society the bourgeoisie scarcely existed. There were few entrepreneurial or professional opportunities for them. Neither industry nor commerce flourished in Rome; the only burgeoning activity was that of the artisans. The social cement in eighteenth-century Rome was provided by church patronage. Any social discontent could be diverted at the verbal level by the *pasquinades* and at the economic level by the many fringe benefits of life in the Eternal City – the custom of being able to despoil the palace of any cardinal raised to St Peter's throne, for example.

While political theorists like Montesquieu decried the political system at Rome as 'the worst imaginable', the fact remains that it was the most successful of its time. Without question the most stable society in eighteenth-century Europe was papal Rome. In the absence of an exploiting class extracting a surplus, class conflict in the true sense simply did not exist. Capitalism was able to gain a foothold here only when the impact of external conquerors like the French under Napoleon broke up the old system. As in the Scottish Highlands, war was capitalism's entering wedge.

It is worth reflecting on the fact that Jacobitism's two most congenial homes were the Scottish Highlands and eighteenth-century Rome, both artificial societies out of harmony with the main social currents surrounding them. Had we not the multifarious examples of the Jacobite exiles to ponder, this fact might lead us to posit that Jacobitism was always a hopeless anachronism, thriving in societies that were themselves anachronistic. But the comparison between the Scottish Highlands and eighteenth-century Rome will not stretch any farther than the common factor of Jacobitism. The society of the Highlanders was a truly Machiavellian exemplar: a martial culture, headed by charismatic princes, with no significant division of labour, and exhibiting all the hallmarks of civic *virtù*. As such it was a *locus classicus* for exponents of Country ideology. Eighteenth-century Rome, on the other hand, exemplified all the signs of decadence that so horrified these self-same Country ideologues: the imperial 'bread and circuses' principle was alive and well nearly two thousand years later.

Roman citizens were in thrall to the pleasure principle. The lottery was the dominant subject of conversation. Even popes shared in the general torpor and sybaritism. The much-loved Pope Benedict XIV provides a good example of this relaxed attitude. A fanatical monk once informed him that Antichrist had been born and was already three years old. 'In that case', said Benedict, 'my successor can see to him.' In Gibbon's *Decline and Fall* we can see the Country mentality confronting the perennial hedonism of Rome.

Such was the social milieu in which James Stuart lived for nearly fifty years and in which his two sons were brought up. The impact of this sort of hedonistic, sybaritic society on the young princes has not been fully explored, but the conjecture may be hazarded that it was not really the right kind of environment to prepare them for the harsh realities of life beyond the boundaries of the Papal States.

What sort of picture can we form of the physical environment in which the young Stuarts were reared? Eighteenth-century Rome had a population that rose from 139,000 in 1709 to 165,000 in 1790. Imperial Rome at its apogee had had a population in excess of a million. This reduced population occupied about a fifth of the old city and was clustered together between the Porta del Popolo, the old Forum Boarium, the Trastevere district, the bend of the Tiber, the baths of Diocletian and the slopes of the Quirinal. The roads were not properly paved until the 1770s, sanitation was non-existent, and there was not even a proper street registry until Benedict XIV produced a town map in 1744. Rome was a city of myriad churches and *palazzi*. The classical remains in the Forum and the baths of Caracalla were overgrown with grass, weeds and trees. It was overwhelmingly a city of the clergy. Those who were not priests tried to dress like them or ape their manners. As befitted a society so strongly in the grip of church fathers, it was a highly paternalistic society, where nepotism and primitive notions of honour were endemic. Vendettas and the settling of disputes by the knife were daily facts of life. Casual homicide was therefore common, but the criminal code was lax and even more laxly enforced, undoubtedly because the rights of wealth and property were never threatened. Since there was a high degree of social solidarity and little discontent or class bitterness, the prevalence of murder contrasted with a relative absence of theft or robbery.

The most striking thing about Roman society was its openness, not just in the casual informality between masters and lackeys or in its 'live and let live' attitude (one of the things, incidentally, that made Rome a haven for spies, for in this respect the Eternal City was like Lisbon in the Second World War), but also in the attitude to sex. If the eighteenth century was a permissive age, Rome was the California of the time. It has often been remarked that Catholic societies are harsher on pre-marital sex and Protestant ones on adultery. This generalisation was certainly borne out in Rome in this era. While a woman was allowed no more than a few harmless flirtations before marriage, after marriage she could, if she chose, enter an Elysium of the senses. The cult of cicisbeism was deeply entrenched. A husband was not expected to be able to provide a wife with all the pleasantries and attentions she required, so this role was filled by the *cavaliere servente*. Inevitably, such a relationship frequently spilled over into adultery. But Romans saw nothing shameful in this. Cuckolding carried no stigma; husbands cheerfully discussed their wives' infidelities, and it was jealousy, not adultery, that was the cardinal sin. For all that, Roman culture drew the line at out and out promiscuity, and the coquetry of French women with their trains of admirers was considered indecent. Nevertheless, it is clear that few environments can have been so alien to the sexually timid and puritanically pious James Francis.

On the Stuart princes this society seems to have had quite different effects. The atmosphere of priestcraft seems to have tilted Henry towards religious obsession from an early age. And the atmosphere of casual violence may have communicated itself to Charles Edward. Certainly he learned to shoot when young and was a first-rate marksman. Lord Elcho, who is never reliable where Charles Edward is concerned, has tales of wholesale mayhem carried out by the elder Stuart prince among the blackbirds and thrushes of the Borghese gardens and among the bats at twilight.

There are, too, many contemporary accounts of dinners at the Palazzo Muti which enable us to measure the way of life at the Stuart court against that of Roman society in general. If James gave an audience in the morning, he would invite his visitors to stay for dinner. He had a rule that the table should always be set for eleven. His own courtiers either withdrew or made up the numbers as the occasion required. These dinners were by all accounts grim affairs. Conversation with the doleful Pretender rarely flowed. In any case social lubrication was usually lacking. A decanter of wine for the Chevalier's use was held by a servant during the entire course of a meal, and as it was contrary to etiquette to drink before the 'King' had done so – and he was no drinker – his guests frequently went short of the bottle conjuror. Two English travellers in Rome in 1720 described a meal with James as follows: 'It (the table) is supplied with English and French cookery, French and Italian wines, but I took notice that the Pretender ate only of the English dishes and made his dinner of roast beef and what we call Devonshire pie. He also prefers our March Beer, which he has from Leghorn, to the best wines.'

Part of the problem was that both James and Henry had delicate digestive systems and were excused from rigorous fasts by special papal dispensation. James was even allowed to take a cup of chocolate or cocoa shortly before receiving Communion – quite a concession in the heyday of Catholic protocol, especially when it is considered that a butcher who sold meat in Rome on a Friday was risking being sent to the galleys. James's meals were different from those of the Roman nobility not just in his preference for red meat and in the plainness and lack of seasoning of his dishes but in his indifference to wine. Even at the quotidian level James was always in, but not of, Rome.

The one member of the Stuart household who did go in for conspicuous consumption was, oddly enough, Henry, the most pious of the royal trio. This, however, was something forced on him by his position as cardinal. A Roman cardinal in the eighteenth century enjoyed something of the adulation of a rock star today. Each cardinal had his own claque and group of admirers. Their sumptuous carriages became the outward symbol of their power and status, and a cardinal was immediately recognisable from his 'colours'. Their carriages were driven at great speed through the streets of Rome. On one occasion Cardinal York's driver precipitated a diplomatic incident by wagering with the driver of the senator of Rome's carriage on who would be the first to the French embassy, and then attempting to win his bet by throwing a lighted torch at the horses of his opponent.

It is easy to see how the rhythms of life in such an easy-going city might have sapped the resolve of all but the most stout-hearted. Who would willingly exchange the charm of the Quirinale or the Villa Borghese for the desolation of the Highlands, or the luxurious life of a cardinal for that of an incognito on the run? Yet such was the choice Charles Edward made. In January 1744 he turned his back on Rome for twenty-two years, refusing to accept the comfortable niche in Italian society he might have occupied. Those who condemn him absolutely should remember the society he was raised in, and make the imaginative leap necessary to see how much sheer willpower was involved in the decision to hold out at all cost for the restoration to his family of the three crowns. If the Nietzschean hero is one imbued with the morality of strenuousness and driven by the will to power, Charles Edward surely deserves to rank with Siegfried and the rest. 'Anachronism' is a cant term never far from the lips of the anti-Jacobite Whig supremacists, but the greatest anachronism in the study of the Jacobites is the attempt to see Charles Edward in twentieth-century terms as a disgruntled failed politician.

Chapter 11

Agents and ciphers: the espionage battle

I have always said the first Whig was the devil.

Samuel Johnson

The conformation of his mind was such that whatever was little seemed to him great and whatever was great seemed to him little.

Macaulay (on Horace Walpole)

How can what an Englishman believes be heresy? It's a contradiction in terms.

Shaw, *Saint Joan*

From the very first days of the small exiled court's existence at St-Germain-en-Laye, espionage played an important part in the story of the Jacobites. 'What is proof against the money of Great Britain?' one of Walpole's enemies lamented. The conventional view of historians has been that the Whig intelligence onslaught on the Jacobites was a glittering triumph, underlined by the Walpole emphasis on the venality of man in general and spies in particular. Clearly there is some truth in this view. According to Saint-Simon, even Alberoni, the architect of the '19, was at one stage a British double agent. But the proposition has to be hedged about with caveats. British governments did not enjoy uniform success in the espionage war. William's Dutch favourite, John Simpson, alias Jones, was a Jacobite agent and was thus a 'mole' in Portland's organisation. There were 'sleepers' in the Walpole network of spies as well.

It is impossible to present a complete picture of the extent of espionage and double-dealing in the Jacobite period, though this is not due to any barriers posed by primitive ciphering. Much of the incriminating correspondence from men like Marlborough, who hedged their bets in advance of a possible Stuart restoration by getting pre-dated pardons in return for divulging (medium-level) military intelligence, was destroyed. Jacobites at St-Germain would destroy the originals after deciphering them and translating them for French use. This was because both Paris and St-Germain and their environs were full of spies and there were many leaks from the Jacobite court.

One of the consequences of the Glorious Revolution of 1688 was that the role of the secret service in general and espionage in particular had to be significantly upgraded. It is no exaggeration to say that during the seventy years or so of the Jacobite threat British espionage and counter-espionage were obsessed with the threat from the Jacobites. They seemed a formidable enemy: numerous, well-organised, obstinate, competent in intrigue, and with a tradition of secret organisation dating back to the Stuart exile during the Protectorate. For this reason, the English secret service devoted much of its resources to domestic counter-espionage, and even its role abroad was largely confined to penetrating the inner circles of the Jacobites' exiled court or that of their French supporters.

Yet, paradoxically, intelligence as a professional activity did not thrive. There were in the Jacobite period no significant advances in the art of ciphering or cryptography. The cipher giving details of Monmouth's 1685 rising, which had fallen into government hands that year, had been cracked purely by chance. But although this incident seemed to indicate the need for an efficient cryptographical section in the secret service, nothing was done. Fortunately for the English, the coded messages that went between the Pretender and his English adherents relied on a very simple form of ciphering.

The key to successful espionage in the eighteenth century was overwhelmingly money, and money alone. There are no examples that one can cite of the twentieth-century phenomenon of ideological spying. This provides us with one simple explanation for the failure of espionage to develop into a truly professional activity. The secret service was a by-product of diplomacy, and in the eighteenth century diplomacy itself was conducted almost entirely on a basis of bribery and corruption. Few men paid even lip service to concepts of 'loyalty', 'honour' or 'service'. The cash nexus was all. Foreign offices in every country regularly set aside large sums for routine bribery. The sums spent on the foreign service, both directly and indirectly, were astronomical by the standards of the day. From 1691 to 1700 the average annual cost of the English diplomatic service was about £37,000. By the late 1740s this had risen to an average of £67,000 annually. Salaries ranged from £100 weekly plus £6,800 a year for expenses for the ambassador to France, to £3 daily plus £1,400 for the resident in Venice. Lord Hyndford, the British ambassador to Russia, between 1745 and 1749 spent £1,500 on 'gifts' such as 'wines and liqueurs . . . shaving equipage . . . drinks and snuff . . . a violin for the Chancellor . . . a gold sponge box in the form of an egg at Easter' for important Russian officials. These expenses did not include the huge sums spent on bribery. Men like Sir Robert Murray Keith, English minister in Russia, and Benjamin Franklin, agent for the American colonists, thought nothing of 'losing' £100,000 in their official accounts, really or allegedly on secret service bribery. Nor did the Foreign Office expenses cover the cost of subsidies. These could amount to £5 million a year paid by London to the German principalities. And extra sums were made available for espionage proper. The going rate for a spy in the British service was £400 a year plus expenses.

The entire ethos of diplomacy was suffused with double-dealing and betrayal. Whether we concentrate on the reflex venality of foreign missions or the structural duplicity of Louis XV, with his own secret foreign policy, in flat contradiction to the official policy of his ministers, this proposition can be borne out. A context in which money was the supreme consideration ruled out in advance the possibility of developing a professional system of espionage. Security was simply not good enough to make it worthwhile to devise an elaborate system of codes, when the work of years could be undone in a single night by a destitute noble on the take. And even within these constraints of an amoral, anomic, totally pecuniary system, there was the further drawback that espionage increasingly involved diminishing returns. Spies became greedier and demanded sums of money equivalent to those which in our day only film stars can command. In return they provided information that was often virtually worthless. The result was that it proved difficult to build up a coordinated intelligence system. Counter-espionage against Jacobitism at home was conducted without reference to the *ad hoc* efforts of ambassadors and agents abroad. For this reason many observers have asserted that the quality of the British espionage system in the early eighteenth century actually declined since the great days of Walsingham, even though it never reached the nadir of the last Stuart kings (1660–85).

The other main reason for espionage's relative failure to develop was not unconnected with the first. The eighteenth century was the golden age of the amateur, the adventurer and the eccentric. Casanova, the mysterious 'deathless charlatan' St-Germain, the hermaphrodite Chevalier d'Eon, the astrologer Cagliostro – these were the representative figures of the age. Mountebank qualities can also be discerned in more famous political figures like John Wilkes and Benjamin Franklin, both dabblers in espionage. Those who shone as spies were amateurs like these, possibly because only to people of such individualistic sensibility did real achievement seem of value in itself. For the professionals money was all, and if you could get £2,000 for a real intelligence coup or the same sum for run-of-the-mill stuff, why exert yourself to separate the dross from the gold?

The typical amateur who was drawn into the secret service orbit was the young aristocrat on the Grand Tour, who would be asked to keep his eyes and ears open and report on anything of interest he found on his travels. In this respect he was a close cousin of the twentieth-century Western businessman in Eastern Europe who 'drops into' the embassy afterwards. Particularly successful amateurs, like Sir Francis Dashwood, who had in addition to other talents highly developed skills as lover and seducer, could worm their way into the inmost recesses of a royal court. Dashwood's womanising in Russia enabled him to lay the foundations for an espionage network there, later consolidated by ambassador Sir Charles Hanby Williams. Of course, such success brought its own dangers. Not only was the jealousy of less successful agents aroused – such as that of Sir Horace Mann, the Whig agent in Italy, for Dashwood – but there was the danger that espionage became an end in itself, where the fruits were sold off to the highest bidder. At this point the amateur in effect joined the professionals. Undoubtedly such suspicions lay behind the persistent canard that Dashwood was a Jacobite agent.

One of the striking things about eighteenth-century spies was the close link between espionage and sexuality. Perhaps this has always been a constant in this twilight world, but it was particularly apparent in the 1700s. The four leading members of the secret society 'the Knights of St Francis of Wycombe' (later to achieve notoriety as the Hell-Fire Club) exemplify this clearly. Dashwood, the philanderer; Benjamin Franklin, the cynical and venal sensualist; John Wilkes, the man who boasted that he could seduce any woman in Europe within half an hour, and often succeeded in amatory conquest where Casanova himself had failed; and the Chevalier d'Eon, the epicene degenerate: none of these was exactly *l'homme moyen sensuel*, and all of them engaged in espionage. The pattern is repeated in the case of the other major figures in Jacobite counter-espionage: Defoe, with his notorious weakness for women of easy virtue; Bradstreet, the ponce and pander, with his series of amours, direct and vicarious; and the comte de Bussy, who, as Pitt remarked ironically in the 1760s, was 'scarcely as chaste as Penelope'. Underneath the official Whig humbug and hypocrisy, the eighteenth-century world was, of course, a genuinely 'permissive society'.

Whatever the reasons for the relatively primitive system of espionage in the eighteenth century, Jacobite correspondence, whether written in cipher or in sympathetic ink which became visible when exposed to fire or to the action of certain acids, presented few problems to the code-cracking interceptors of mail. There was a partial injection of expertise into the English secret service after 1688. Charles II had used his agents largely to watch malcontents and Dissenters at home. English ambassadors abroad had no contacts with the government's secret agents. The secret service was neglected to such an extent that in 1699 King William asked Dr John Wallis to train a young man in the art of deciphering 'so that it may not die with him'. The Post Office, a royal monopoly under the control of the Secretary of State, was likewise neglected in this period, though the French ambassador Cominges observed that the London government was more skilful in opening letters than any in the world.

William III reconstructed the diplomatic service and removed the secret service from the control of the Secretaries of State. The slapdash methods of Charles II's reign, when most of the secret service monies had been siphoned off to pay for the royal mistresses, were no longer adequate. In particular a constant watch had to be kept on the exiled Stuarts. This was particularly important, since in the early Jacobite period there were many plots to overthrow the government, of which that of 1694 was perhaps the most serious. There were also schemes to assassinate William III, such as that of 1696, which was betrayed by informers. Fortunately for them, the English found a man with precisely the gifts necessary for such an operation, the poet and diplomat Matthew Prior. Using his position as secretary to the English ambassador in Paris, Prior soon built up an impressive network of agents in France. The Jacobite ranks became infiltrated with spies, and in terms of leaks the Jacobite court at St-Germain-en-Laye became a veritable sieve. In a report to Lord Jersey, to be used by his successor, Prior gave an indication of the kinds of people he used for keeping James II's exiguous court under constant surveillance. There was one Braconnier, a veteran of four years in the Bastille; Brocard, an Irishman who posed as a businessman in return for his £300 a year; Johnson, code-named Baily, a bogus clergyman, 'a cunning fellow and a debauchee'. As ever, women were important in the business of espionage, and Prior mentioned a widow named Langlois and her two daughters as important agents: 'the old woman is as cunning a jade as lives'. Prior was thus able to report accurately on all of the Jacobite initiatives with Louis XIV and the many abortive plans for a descent on England, mainly by using people who had access to the servants and staff at the court. But he spoiled the impact of his undoubted genius for espionage by some rather unworthy gloating over the fate and alleged poverty of James II. 'I faced old James and all his Court the other day at St-Cloud,' he wrote. '*Vive Guillaume.* You never saw such a strange figure as the old bully is, lean, worn and shrivelled, not unlike Neal [i.e. Noll] the protector; the queen looks very melancholy, but otherwise well enough. Their equipages are all very ragged and contemptible.' And again: 'Poor King James is hardly thought on or mentioned. An Italian and a Scotch priest govern him and his whole concern; he is so directly the same way he ever was, persecuting the few Protestants that are about him, though they are ruined and banished for their adhering to him, and rewarding and encouraging any sorry creature that he can make a convert of.'

Prior's successes should not be overestimated. Even he was on occasion let down by his own agents, notably by Mark Lynch. And his bravado concealed a continuing fear of the consequences of James's close relationship with Louis XIV. Moreover, Prior was not above the 'expedient exaggeration' and downright lie when it suited his book. Prior accused James of having approved the Jacobite attempts to assassinate William and claimed that he had said it was exactly the same as if the king had been ambushed when at war in Flanders. And occasionally, when we have independent testimony, we can see that in his reports to his masters Prior invented whole scenes for comic or disparaging effect, as in the following: 'The gentlemen belonging to the Duke d'Orleans and Chartres were embarrassed enough to call him one moment *le roi d'Angleterre* to them, and speak to me the next of *le roi Jacques*. It was, as most things are, a farce ridiculous enough.'

Although Prior left Paris in 1699 and gave up his position as spymaster, being promoted Under-Secretary of State, this was not the end of his association with France and the Jacobites. He played a key role with Bolingbroke and Madame de Maintenon in the secret diplomacy leading to the Treaty of Utrecht, and was a pivotal figure in Jacobite plots for a restoration on the death of Queen Anne. Indeed, it was probably the intelligence he possessed on Bolingbroke's double-dealing that led to the latter's taking flight in 1715 and fleeing to the Pretender's court.

While Prior's espionage in Paris was proving so successful, at home the English were bringing to a fine art the technique of intercepting dispatches. There is no question but that in this period (the last years of the seventeenth century) the groundwork was laid for the continuing supremacy in intelligence and espionage that the Whigs enjoyed over the Jacobites throughout the entire period 1689–1760. Moreover, the Jacobites were rarely free agents in this sphere, unlike their English counterparts. French attitudes towards the Stuarts' supporters were never consistent, and sometimes the undertow of indifference, irritation and suspicion that always adulterated the basic French sympathy changed to decisive action, as in 1703–4 when the Paris police made a clean sweep of all Jacobite agents newly arrived from the British Isles.

Meanwhile counter-espionage in England was bearing spectacular fruit. Many of the French projects to assist the Stuarts up to 1715 never got past first base, as their details were divulged to London as a result of highly competent English intelligence. The so-called 'Lovat affair' of 1703–4 provides a good example of this. In January 1703 the French agent James Murray was sent to

Scotland to foment a rising. In response to his visit Simon Fraser, a scion of the famous Lovat family, brought over to France a scheme for a simultaneous landing of 5,000 French troops and rebellion of 12,000 Scots. He seemed not to have quite the backing and authority the French required so he was sent back by them in company with a *John* Murray. Once in Edinburgh Fraser/Lovat betrayed the plot to the duke of Queensberry. He was commissioned to proceed to the Highlands in order to catch as many clan chiefs as possible in the conspiracy. His principal motive was to entrap the marquis of Atholl, and he seems even to have forged a letter to James III, purporting to come from Atholl, which he passed on to Queensberry. Atholl was an enemy of both Lovat and Queensberry for personal reasons. Although Atholl was able to clear himself, the very fact of accusations being brought against him dealt a death-blow to the conspiracy. Many of James's English supporters were also caught in the net Lovat had woven. However, he then became overconfident and returned to France as a double agent. Learning the truth, Louis XIV had him imprisoned at the château of Angoulême; by the standards of the day he was lucky to get off so lightly.

The mission of French Navy Minister Torcy's agent Colonel Nathaniel Hooke, in August 1705 and April 1707, similarly aborted thanks to good intelligence work. These missions were designed to prepare the ground for a substantial French invasion to restore the Stuarts. Hooke brought back letters from a good number of Highland chiefs plus a memorial signed by several of them, promising an army of 30,000 clansmen if Louis XIV would provide 8,000 regulars and provided prince James came in person to Scotland. In the interception of this intelligence the key figure was Robert Harley, later earl of Oxford. One of his agents, Captain James Ogilvie, had Hooke's measure from a very early stage and betrayed the 1705 mission. He was able to provide even fuller information on the 1707 visit, so that it is no exaggeration to say that the major French effort of 1708 was already doomed by the time it was launched.

Yet another man who played a key role for Harley in the years 1706–7 was none other than Daniel Defoe, author of *Moll Flanders* and *Robinson Crusoe*. Defoe depended heavily on the patronage of Harley in the first decade of the 1700s and sent him many interesting memoranda suggesting how a truly professional secret service could be instituted. In 1704 he toured England to gather intelligence for his patron which he later used as the basis for his famous *Tour through England and Wales*. So impressed was Harley by Defoe's skills that in 1706 he sent him to Edinburgh to promote the negotiations then in progress for an Act of Union between the English and Scottish parliaments. Defoe was given the task of creating a favourable climate of opinion for the merger, and of persuading Scots of all commercial and religious persuasions that Union was best for Scotland.

During the winter of 1706–7 Defoe was engaged in an assiduous propaganda exercise against the Scottish Jacobites, in which his proverbial skill as a liar was much to the fore. At first he pretended he had come to Scotland to start a glass factory or a salt works. Later this story was changed and he said he was a writer, engaged on either a new version of the Psalms or a history of the Union, as the mood took him. 'I act the part of Cardinal Richelieu,' he told Harley. 'I have my spies and pensioners in every place and confess 'tis the easiest thing in the world to hire people here to betray their friends. I have spies in the Commission, in the Parliament and in the Assembly, and under pretence of writing my history I have everything told me.' When the Act of Union was ratified in 1707, Defoe could justifiably claim to have achieved triumphantly the objects of his mission and to have routed the Scottish Jacobites, for whom he had the typical early eighteenth-century English antipathy. He continued to be employed as an anti-Jacobite agent and propagandist, by Godolphin in 1709, and by Townshend in 1716.

Defoe provides an interesting example of the Whig sensibility at work. A Dissenter in the service of the High Tories like Harley, he was a man of contradictions, shot through with duplicity and machiavellianism. Like many other Whig literary figures – Fielding and Sterne are other good examples – he was suffused with hatred for the Jacobites. Defoe was hypocritical and two-faced, and could turn his hand to any kind of journalism or propaganda the particular moment required, but these very qualities made him a superb agent. Technically, he was in a very high class in the field of eighteenth-century espionage. His systematic deviousness enabled him to fulfil the roles of both spy and spymaster with consummate ease. The facility with which he was able to recruit like-minded venal souls to his cause has led some observers to exaggerate and see him as a kind of *de facto* head of British secret service. This is to overstate the case, but it is clear that he continued to be highly regarded by his Whig employers. In the first half of 1714 alone Defoe was paid £500 out of secret service funds.

With Louis XIV's death and the collapse of the Jacobite rising of 1715, the Jacobite spectre seemed to have left the European stage. Walpole's obsession with the Jacobites, however, meant that there was little diminution in the counter-espionage effort in England. His agents successfully bribed or 'turned' most of James Stuart's agents, including, most notoriously Colonel Cecil. Walpole later boasted to the Jacobite scholar Thomas Carte that he had routinely used English Jacobites as spies for years, especially a Mr Avery. To the incredulous Carte he declared with aplomb: 'How else can I learn the Jacobite designs but from the Jacobites themselves? Nobody else could inform on them.'

Meanwhile English espionage followed the Stuarts to their new court in Rome. After 1719 the government in London continued to be well informed about matters in the Pretender's Italian lair. This was regarded as particularly important after James's marriage to Clementina Sobieska and the birth of the two Stuart princes, Charles Edward and Henry. The leading Whig agents in Rome were Philip von Stosch, codenamed John Walton, who reported to Carteret, and Cardinal Alessandro Albani, a powerful pro-Hanoverian force in the Curia. Stosch sent back voluminous material on Jacobite intrigues in Rome, their missions in Russia, the secret support given to the Pretender by the Catholic powers in Rome, and much else. Stosch/Walton was insistent on James's poverty and how this very fact made espionage difficult. He suggested that either his own pay as an agent be increased or that the Jacobites in England be allowed to remit more money to James. Only with money could the wheels of intelligence work be lubricated.

By 1725 Stosch was reporting a growing estrangement between James and his wife. He recounted that Clementina Sobieska had been slighted, scorned and betrayed by James. She had been subjected to mental torture through the knowledge of her husband's many mistresses and frequent infidelities, and had on occasion been beaten. It was from this source also that the personal characteristics of the two Stuart princes were assessed. Two snippets of information on Charles Edward portended the shape of things to come. As a child of four the young prince scandalised the faithful by refusing to kiss the pope's feet during an audience. And in 1733 Stosch reported a ferocious outbreak of temper on the part of the young Charles Edward, who was already beginning to show signs of the later famous coolness towards his father.

Agent Walton was expelled from Rome in 1731, under the new strongly pro-Stuart regime of Pope Clement XII, but continued to send in dispatches from other parts of Italy. His importance decreased in the early 1740s as Horace Mann, the British resident since 1739, began to build up his own network. Meanwhile Cardinal Albani was a continuing tower of strength to the Whigs. His papers contain overtly treasonable correspondence with the English. So fervent was his anti-Jacobitism that Albani did not even try to swap horses when the rebellion of 1745 looked likely to succeed. But the devious, circumspect Horace Mann did not even take the Cardinal completely into his confidence and always possessed a network of agents in Rome in addition to any he contacted through him. Naturally, Albani's position as a prince of the church gave him access to particularly sensitive information, particularly when the younger Stuart prince accepted a cardinal's hat in 1747. By 1752 Alessandri was able to pass on details of the gulf that had by now opened up between James and his second son, in addition to the permanent estrangement from Charles Edward.

Although the twenty-five years from 1715 to 1740 represented something of a lull in the espionage battle between Jacobite and Whig, by the late 1730s it was evident that the war clouds were gathering and that England might soon be at war again with her ancient rival. Against this possibility the Whig elite bent their energies to securing highly placed spies in the French service. Their biggest coup came in 1734 when they procured the services of François de Bussy. Recruited on a down payment of £240, Bussy was soon demanding, and getting, large sums for fairly anodyne information – such as that France did not intend to support the Pretender (this was common knowledge in Europe in the Fleury years). Bussy was 'run' by British ambassador Waldegrave, who frequently complained of the humiliation and inconvenience of the long waits at night on the outskirts of the park at Versailles where he made contact with Bussy. Agent '101' – for such was Bussy's code-name from 1735 on – proved a troublesome and grasping operative. He set his own worth at £2,000 a year and in fact received from the duke of Newcastle an annual sum in excess of this (£2,300). In addition to this 'pension', he received extra amounts for conveying top-secret, high-risk information. Between 1735 and 1740 he received £5,500 for such special assignments.

The investment in Bussy paid off. In 1737 Cardinal Fleury sent him on a mission to England, in effect to negotiate with his own paymasters. And in 1740, in what Newcastle must have considered a stroke of rare good fortune, Bussy was dispatched to London as French plenipotentiary. In August 1740 Agent 101 communicated the text of the treaty between Spain and France, and also the secret order to the French governors in the West Indies. Even so, his greatest service to England was yet to come. On leaving London in 1743 he continued to send valuable intelligence. At the end of that year he learned of the secret French project to land an army under Marshal Saxe in England before a formal declaration of war. This army was to be accompanied by Charles Edward Stuart and its aim was to restore the Stuarts before the Whigs had time to realise what kind of holocaust was upon them. This tip from Bussy was intelligence of the very highest calibre, and in February 1744 Bussy received as his reward from Newcastle a special gratuity of £2,000.

Bussy was not in the decision-making circles in 1745, so could not inform the English of French invasion plans that year. In 1746 he accompanied the duc de Noailles on an important diplomatic mission to Madrid. He used the opportunity to blacken further the character of his nominal boss at the Ministry of Foreign Affairs, the marquis d'Argenson, who was Noailles's deadly enemy. He also wheedled himself into the good graces of Madame de Pompadour, and in 1749 the Pompadour protégé the marquis de Puysieux promoted him to Under-Secretary of State. At this stage, after the peace of 1748, Bussy lost contact with British intelligence. He came to England in 1758 as a protégé of the new Foreign Secretary, Choiseul, but by now he was both wealthy and cautious and would not renew his former relations with the English. In 1767 he retired on 23,000 livres a year (£920) and died in 1780. Bussy was probably the biggest fish British espionage landed in the Jacobite period. He was extremely lucky not to be caught and suffer a traitor's death, but in terms of eighteenth-century espionage he was truly the 'one that got away'. And since France's best-ever chance for a successful invasion of England came in 1743–44, and with it the best chance of a Stuart restoration, Bussy's treachery can be said to have had incalculable consequences for the Jacobites. Thomas Carte had smugly said of the 1743–44 project: 'nothing can hurt the design but want of secrecy'. This 'hurt' Bussy supplied with professional precision.

But though the biggest, Bussy was far from being the only fish netted by British espionage. One estimate for the War of Austrian Succession, during the period when England and France were officially at war (1744–48), states that no less than seventy-two Frenchmen had been in the secret service of England. No such inroads had been made by the French on British security.

The rebellion of 1745 demonstrated how far ahead of their rivals the Whigs were. Externally, one of the factors working against Jacobite success in that rising was that all French attempts to assist or reinforce Charles Edward were known about in England almost as soon as a decision had been taken in Versailles. One Jacobite agent reported from Boulogne in January 1746, when a French invasion fleet was assembling there, that the enemy was so well informed of French intentions that English warships always appeared at the precise point of intended departure. Louis XV's ambassador in Scotland in 1745–46, the marquis d'Eguilles, confirmed this. He reported that the captured correspondence of the duke of Cumberland revealed that the latter knew in great detail all about the Boulogne expedition, which must mean he had spies within the inner circles there. In fact, the evidence for fairly systematic penetration of French military and diplomatic secrets in 1745–46 is very strong, even without Bussy, who was not able to provide much inside information on this occasion, partly because the marquis d'Argenson already suspected him of being a spy.

Within Britain, the Whigs also scored handsomely over the Jacobites. Although Charles Edward's Highland army was otherwise quite impressively organised, one glaring failure was the absence of a system of espionage. Both Lord George Murray, the prince's lieutenant-general, and his quartermaster (and Irish favourite) John O'Sullivan argued strongly that this was indispensable, if only to ascertain the movements and resources of the enemy. But the prince was so little aware of the importance of espionage that he did not even make use of the network of Jacobite spies already in existence. The absurd consequence was that reports from agents in London still went to James Stuart's representatives in Paris. During the prince's sojourn in Edinburgh through October 1745, just one emissary was sent into England to prepare the ground for a rising there. Unfortunately the envoy, John Hickson, was indiscreet and was captured at Newcastle with dispatches from the prince on his person. To save his skin he then turned king's evidence. A second messenger sent south during the advance through the Lowlands to England in November 1745 to report on the dispositions of Marshal Wade also failed to return. In despair, Lord George Murray improvised his own informal system of spying while he was in England.

Perhaps the greatest triumph of the Whigs in the '45 was secured through 'disinformation'. There are reasons for thinking that the famous decision to retreat to Scotland taken on 5 December 1745 at Derby was precipitated by the work of a Whig secret agent called Dudley Bradstreet. On 2 December the duke of Newcastle commissioned him to get accurate intelligence of 'rebel' movements. On arriving in Lichfield from London, Bradstreet was briefed on the grave military situation by the duke of Cumberland, who asked him to find a way to delay the Jacobites 'but twelve hours'. Bradstreet proceeded to Derby, introduced himself to some of the Jacobite military leaders and produced a farrago of nonsense, which was, however, appealing to men who were already disposed to retreat anyway. At this juncture the Highland army was nearer to London than the army (Cumberland's) which was supposed to defend it. But Bradstreet convinced the Jacobite leaders that there was a second army of 9,000 men under General Hawley waiting for them at Northampton. As soon as the Jacobites moved south, they would be caught in a pincer between Cumberland's forces and those of Hawley. As Bradstreet puckishly pointed out: 'Observe that there was not nine men at Northampton to oppose them, much less 9,000.'

The Highland chiefs then withdrew with Charles Edward into the council chamber. Later Bradstreet was called in to repeat his 'intelligence'. The Stuart prince became exasperated. 'That fellow will do me more harm than all the Elector's army,' he cried. Then in desperation he turned to the council members. 'You ruin, abandon and betray me if you don't march on.' But his remonstrations were too late. Bradstreet's disinformation had had its effect on men imbued with defeatism and with a pre-existing will to believe that disaster was just around the corner. Bradstreet accompanied the Highland army on its retreat as far as Preston, where, incredibly, he was then asked to proceed to London as a Jacobite spy. Thus did his dream of becoming a double agent come true.

Despite the failure of the '45, Charles Edward had proved his mettle as a dangerous adversary, and from 1747 onwards it became a prime aim of British espionage to keep track of his whereabouts. The prince for his part hit back. After his arrest and expulsion from France in early 1749, he became the 'elusive Pimpernel' of Europe. Rumours and counter-rumours of his movements proliferated. Whig agents like Philip Yorke in Paris confessed themselves baffled as to his activities and even as to his true identity. For Charles Edward began to use a series of aliases every bit as baffling at the time as those of the twentieth-century Pimpernel B. Traven. At one time he was Mr Williams, at another John Douglas, and even for a time, unbelievably perhaps to us, 'Mr Benn'. The prince's histrionic ability was demonstrated by his genius for disguise. He wore false noses, blackened his eyebrows and beard, wore wigs, rouged his face, and so on. The Whig agents were at their wits' end to know how to conduct a proper surveillance on the man who could at any moment, they thought, return to Scotland and raise another rebellion. At this stage the duke of Newcastle lit upon perhaps his most spectacular anti-Jacobite agent, 'Pickle the Spy'.

Pickle was in fact Aleistair Ruadh MacDonnell, eldest son of John MacDonell, 12th chief of Glengarry. 'Young Glengarry' or Pickle was driven to treachery by financial hardship. Imprisoned after being captured on the high seas on his way from France to Scotland in December 1745, Glengarry languished in the Tower until July 1747. On his release he made his way to France and from Paris wrote to James Stuart in Rome, asking for assistance as he was penniless. James declined on the grounds of his own penury. As Andrew Lang remarked in his work on Pickle: 'It is easy to conceive the feelings and to imagine the florid eloquence of Young Glengarry when he expected a cheque and not a duplicate copy of a warrant (though he had not asked for it) to be a Peer – over the water.'

In August 1749 Glengarry crossed to London, intending to offer his services to the Whigs. Recruited by the Pelhams, Glengarry's intelligence soon proved to be of the finest. He was deeply involved in Jacobite affairs and immediately obtained an interview with James in Rome. The duke of Cumberland marvelled at the accuracy and detail of Glengarry's, code-named Pickle's, advice (Glengarry took the name Pickle from Smollett's 1751 novel *Peregrine Pickle*). But Pickle's greatest coup was to thwart the Elibank plot of November 1752. Alexander Murray, younger brother of the Jacobite Lord Elibank, was to attack St James's Palace and seize George II, aided by a company of French officers and 400 Highlanders. Charles Edward would meanwhile be on the north coast of France, awaiting developments and ready to cross over at a given signal. From the very beginning Pickle was at the heart of the plot. He met the conspirators with Charles Edward at Boulogne and discussed the project in detail. Having immediately betrayed the plotters to the English government in his very next dispatch, Pickle had the audacity to argue against any delay in implementing the coup when some of the intriguers considered postponing it. Pickle's kinsman Donald of Lochgarry and Dr Archibald Cameron, brother of the 'gentle Lochiel' of the '45, had been sent to coordinate activities in Scotland. Cameron was apprehended at the border, tried for treason and executed in 1754. Significantly, though, he was hanged, not for the treason of the Elibank plot, to have produced evidence for which would have revealed the Whig channel of communication, but for the old crime of having been 'out' in the '45.

It was Glengarry's information too which thwarted the 1753 Prussian plot. Frederick the Great had decided to hit back at England, from which he had received no satisfaction when his merchant ships had been seized by privateers, by backing the Jacobites in Scotland in a plan for an armed uprising. In 1754 Pickle's career as a spy came to an end. When his father died, young Glengarry had to return to Scotland as head of his clan, and so could no longer be at Charles Edward's elbow, reporting his every movement. But by 1754 Charles Edward had alienated nearly all his followers and was no longer a serious threat to the English government.

The history of the Highlands in the decade or so after Culloden was itself a saga of espionage and counter-espionage, with chiefs and tacksmen reporting on each other, some to London, others to the now splintered Jacobite movement in London. On the Whig side there were accomplished liars like Glengarry, Barisdale and James Mohr MacGregor. The Jacobites could muster but a few unfortunate survivors of the post-Culloden pogroms like Fassifern, brother of 'gentle Lochiel' of the '45. Treachery and mistrust were endemic, and it is this atmosphere of disintegration in the Highland ethos that Stevenson captures so well in *Kidnapped* and *Catriona*.

Meanwhile in Europe itself, after the activities of Pickle, the Whigs gradually tightened their grip. Bransbury Williams in Russia, Horace Mann in Rome and Philip Yorke in Paris ran an increasingly competent network of agents. By 1755 there was confidence that the Young Pretender would not strike again on his own account and would need massive assistance from France, such as the duc de Choiseul in fact proposed to give him during the Seven Years' War. The espionage drive against the Jacobites could then be subsumed in that against France. During the Seven Years' War Pitt completely outclassed the French secret service in espionage matters, even though Choiseul made a valiant effort to even the score by a new deployment of agents in England.

But Jacobitism as a bugbear never really lost its power until well into the 1770s, and as long as Charles Edward lived the English ministers felt that the file on the Jacobites could never be closed. Their final recruit in the espionage battle against the Jacobites was the infamous Chevalier d'Eon de Beaumont, whose sexual identity was always in doubt and who would seem to have been that rare bird, a genuine hermaphrodite. The significance of d'Eon was that he had been sent to Russia in 1755 as Louis XV's personal representative in the 'King's Secret' – Louis's parallel but clandestine foreign policy that he conducted by secret correspondence with Europe's rulers. D'Eon carried out this entire mission dressed as a woman. When all French representatives were expelled by the Czarina in 1756 following a scandal involving the ambassador of France, d'Eon was sent to London as secretary to the French ambassador there. But court intrigue at Versailles led to his humiliation as minister plenipotentiary. In fury d'Eon offered to defect to the British. Realising his value, they took him in and used him to penetrate many secret societies such as the 'Knights of St Francis of Wycombe' in search of closet Jacobitism. It is perhaps not surprising that, in the company of fellow knights like Dashwood, Wilkes and Franklin, d'Eon found not a trace of Jacobite sentiment. By this time the House of Stuart was discredited even among devotees of obscure causes.

Chapter 12

'Jamie the Rover and bonnie Prince Charlie': the last Stuarts

There's some wha say he's no the thing
And some wha say he's no our king.
But to their teeth we'll rant and sing
'Success to Jamie the Rover!'

Hogg, *Jacobite Relics*

The adventurous Prince, as is well known, proved to be one
of those personages who distinguish themselves during some
single and extraordinarily brilliant period of their lives, like
the course of a shooting star, at which men wonder, as well
on account of the briefness as the brilliancy of its splendour.
A long trace of darkness overshadowed the subsequent life of
a man who, in his youth, showed himself so capable of great
undertakings . . . the latter pursuits and habits of this unhappy
Prince are those painfully evincing a broken heart, which
seeks refuge from its own thoughts in sordid enjoyments.

Scott, Introduction to *Redgauntlet*

Then let your schemes alone,
Adore the rising sun
And leave a man undone to his fate.

Burns

James Francis Edward Stuart – the 'Old Pretender' to the Whigs
and Hanoverians, 'James III' to the Jacobites, and 'Jamie the
Rover' to the balladeers – was cursed with more than his fair
share of ill luck. He lacked charisma and any of the qualities the

leader of a dissident movement needs. He had many fine attributes but they were the wrong ones for the leader of the Jacobites. In *Henry Esmond* Thackeray caricatured James as a bird–brained, drunken Lothario. The truth was otherwise: he had little inclination towards women or the bottle and was certainly a good deal more intelligent than his father. If literary parallels are in order, it is probably true, as Lees-Milne says, that Mr Kennedy in *Phineas Finn* and Mr Casaubon in *Middlemarch* are better models than the perfervid constructions of Thackeray's imagination.

The legendary bad luck attaching to the Stuarts assumed gigantic proportions in the case of James. Serious historians notoriously dislike categories like 'luck' or 'fate', preferring to consign the imponderables of history to that vast limbo called 'contingency'. But the run of random, adventitious circumstances attaching to each individual is surely not enough to explain James. Every time he set foot on board ship for an attempted restoration in Britain, the elements would take a hand, almost as though by a kind of pre-established harmony. Storms, tempests, contrary winds, winter snows: these were the lot of 'Jamie the Rover'. Every Jacobite rising except the disastrously bungled '19 came to its climax in the dead of winter, in an epoch when the winters were far more formidable than those today. The Jacobite era came at the end of a 200-year phase of exceptionally cold winters, beginning some time around 1550. The winter of 1708, the year of the first Jacobite enterprise in Scotland (the '08) reached new extremes of cold even within the mini ice age itself. In France peasant children froze to death in their beds; cattle became blocks of ice as they stood in their byres; the Seine became a solid lake of ice; and the sea was frozen over along the Atlantic coast.

James's pattern of bad luck was repeated in almost every area of his life. True, his judgment of people was poor, but simply by the laws of probability he ought to have found *some* people to serve him with devotion. The long list of Jacobite Secretaries of State tells its own story. It was James's fate to be let down or betrayed by the people he cared for most; his half-brother Berwick during the '15, his wife Clementina Sobieska, and his beloved elder son. Few things mattered more to James than his adored 'Carluccio', yet when he said goodbye to Charles Edward at the beginning of 1744, he saw him for the last time, even though he lived another twenty-two years.

There is something very poignant about the constant appeals James made to Charles Edward after the '45 to return to him in Rome. This quotation, from a letter of 1764, may be described as pathetic or heartbreaking according to taste:

> Will you not run straight to your father? . . . here is no question of the past but only of saving you from utter destruction in the future. Is it possible you would rather be a vagabond on the face of the earth than return to a father who is all love and tenderness for you?

The story was the same in James's relations with women. The one woman he seems genuinely to have fallen in love with, Benedicta, eldest daughter of the duke of Modena, turned him down. Or rather, her father the duke turned down her suitor, for fear of offending England. James himself rejected a woman who later became Czarina of Russia and would have been a mighty ally in the Stuart cause. The woman he did marry, Clementina Sobieska, turned out to be a disastrous choice who suffered from religious mania and paranoia.

His continuing and sustained ill-fortune might have turned James himself towards paranoia. Instead it induced a form of nervous depression, whose most common symptom was illness at the point where momentous events were in train and difficult decisions had to be made. Like Louis XV, James had a neurasthenic's dislike of having to make decisions, and the strain of having to make them perforce brought on many maladies of undoubted psychosomatic origin. Like his son Henry, James had a delicate digestive system and was excused from rigorous fasts by papal dispensation. He was undoubtedly one of the century's great valetudinarians, and there was no shortage of this species in the eighteenth century. We hear of attacks of quartan ague in 1704–1708 (when the descent on Scotland was being planned), 1710, 1713, 1715 (both in France when he was waiting to cross the Channel and in Scotland at the end of the rising), 1717 (when the Swedish plot to restore him collapsed), two separate bouts in 1719 (the year of the third Jacobite rebellion), and almost continually from 1759 on. After 1731 he was rarely in good health and had to give up his favourite sport of hunting. In addition he suffered a severe attack of pneumonia in 1704, measles in 1708, smallpox in 1712 and was operated on for an anal fistula in 1716. The last rites were administered on three occasions, before the final Extreme Unction of 1766.

Yet for all this James, like many valetudinarians, lived to a ripe old age, being the longest-lived *de jure* or *de facto* monarch in English history, with sixty-four years as 'James III' to his credit (Queen Victoria reigned sixty-three years, and George III a mere sixty). Apart from the obviously 'organic' illnesses, it is clear that the aetiology of James's ailments was psychological. Quartan ague, his perennial malady, was a form of malaria characterised by a recurrent fever over four days with consequent debility and depression, and was responsive to treatment by quinine. Any form of personal or political crisis could trigger the condition. Apparently chronic malaria sufferers can reactivate the disease by overreaction to stress. The regularity of the quartan ague syndrome in James at times of crisis makes him almost a textbook case for psychosomatic medicine.

In fairness to James, it should be pointed out that *the maladie imaginaire* was a cultural constant of the eighteenth century. Just as Victorian ladies were apt to produce fainting fits at will to evade sexual demands or chafe against the second-class status of their sex, so did Jacobite dignitaries use illness, real or feigned, to put off the terrors of making a definite decision. Whenever a Jacobite emissary came to England or Scotland to plan a new rising, at least some of the principals involved would claim to be too ill to see the envoy. So it was with the dukes of Hamilton and Atholl and the Earl Marischal when Colonel Nathaniel Hooke visited Scotland in 1707. So it was when Louis XV's emissary James Butler came to England in 1743 to canvass support. And so too when Berwick wanted to keep out of the 1715 enterprise: he alleged he could not travel from Paris to Lorraine to meet James because of a bad cough! In this connection one is tempted to point to hypochondria as a symptom of a deeper malaise. The contradiction between the naturally circumspect temperament of the nostalgic conservative and the very different personality required by the revolutionary was never better illustrated than in the case of the Jacobites, in whom the two had perforce to be united. This cautious conservatism, amounting at times almost to apathy and defeatism, can be detected in many of the Jacobite luminaries: Mar, John Hynde Cotton, Barrymore, Watkin Williams Wynn, Lord George Murray, the Earl Marischal and most of the Scottish clan leaders.

But although James was not physically robust like his elder son, he did not lack physical courage, and he served with distinction during the military campaigns of 1708–10 in Flanders, at Oudenarde, Malplaquet and elsewhere. The problem was not one of courage but of temperament. The same fundamental self-doubt that triggered the quartan ague attacks made James's at times admirable caution and sobriety tip over into a kind of defeatism. James carried the saying 'what can't be cured must be endured' to the point of anticipating that every problem would turn out to be one that had to be endured rather than cured.

Whether this was cause or consequence of his embrace of the philosophy of quietism or whether ideology and temperament were mutually reinforcing is unclear. Certainly James was deeply influenced by Archbishop Fénelon of Cambrai, whose *Explication des maximes des saints*, published in 1697, set out the basic doctrine. The true saint, Fénelon maintained, laid emphasis on Christ as the universal redeemer rather than his or her personal saviour. Quietism, in other words, sought to obliterate the self as a principal actor in theology. A good deed consciously aimed at was the sign of a corrupt mind; the truly good deed proceeded from a spiritual state of passivity, receptive to direct inspiration from God.

Innocent XII had sided with Bossuet in his quarrel with Fénelon over the *Maximes*. Louis XIV had followed the papacy's line and exiled Fénelon to Cambrai. James met Fénelon there in 1709 and was deeply impressed by him. He took over much of the doctrine of quietism to evolve his own version of Christian stoicism. But whatever the virtues of quietism, they did not provide the right kind of ideological fuel for the leader of a revolutionary movement, which in a political sense was what James was.

Nevertheless, quietism bred in James a spirit of toleration, especially in religious matters, which contrasted sharply with his father's. Declarations of religious tolerance were to feature largely in all James's manifestos to the people of England. His openness in this area made James particularly irritated with his wife's religious mania and with sects like the Jesuits. As he told an English visitor in 1721:

I have been told by several of the most eminent prelates of the Church of Rome, particularly my friend the late Archbishop of Cambrai, that it should never be my business to study how to be an apostle, but how to become a good king to all my people without distinction, which shall be found true if ever it please God to restore me.

A letter to Abbé Gaillard in 1718 is also revealing:

Alas, all Catholics are not saints and there are only too many among them who have still more ambition than true zeal. With such people the solid foundations are little regarded . . . I am a Catholic but I am a king, and subjects of whatever religion they may be have an equal right to be protected. I am a king, but as the Pope himself told me, I am not an Apostle. I am not bound to convert my people otherwise than by my example, nor to show apparent partiality to Catholics, which would only serve to injure them later.

In James's philosophical attitudes, to some extent shared by his second son Henry, we see the origin of the fatal rift between James and Charles Edward after the '45. Quietism bade fair to become mere resignation as far as James's temporal interests were concerned. If the Divine Will did not choose to place the sceptre in his hands, so be it. Hence his offer to abdicate in favour of Charles Edward in 1745 if the latter succeeded in regaining the throne. But if there was one attitude Charles Edward could not stand, it was resignation of this kind. After the failure of the '45, both James and Henry concluded that the restoration game was up, almost glad, it seemed, to be rid of the burden. For Charles Edward, on the other hand, life had no meaning if he did not come into his own. Hence the paradox that James, the official leader of the Jacobite movement, was after 1746 no longer in any real sense a Jacobite. Charles Edward, by contrast, could be nothing if not a Jacobite. There are even grounds for suspecting that James was glad to have male heirs principally so that he could slough off the problems of a Stuart restoration onto them while he retired into a life of contemplation. Whatever the truth, James certainly needed all the formidable spiritual strength quietism provided in order to deal with the heartbreaking disappointment caused him by a reckless and dissolute elder son. He derived from quietism, in a word, the strength to endure problems he might not have had in the first place without his embrace of the doctrine.

James's views on the nature of kingship are difficult to pin down. There is little reference in his letters to Divine Right, and much more to the need not to 'disquiet' his subjects. 'A king cannot be happy if his subjects are not at ease' was one of the maxims he cherished. Certainly by eighteenth-century standards he was a deeply humane man. Mar's scorched-earth policy in Scotland in early 1716, which he witnessed in person, caused him deep distress. On the other hand, he also showed himself to be a traditionalist in many areas. In Bologna in 1722 he revived the ancient practice of touching for the king's evil. In pre-Enlightenment days it was widely held that a king of the legitimate line had a God-given power of curing sufferers from scrofula by the laying on of hands. The king would read the gospel text 'You shall lay hands on the sick and they shall recover' and then proceed to touch the scrofulous, usually children. Needless to say, faith-healing often did the trick in this context as in others.

His habit of attracting misfortune apart, and judged by personal qualities alone, James would have made a well-above-average monarch. His greater intelligence, stoicism and breadth of vision made him incomparably an improvement on his father. Even the arch-curmudgeon on matters Jacobite, Bruce Lenman, admits: 'Though not an inspiring leader, James Edward might have made rather a good constitutional monarch had he reached the throne.' Very occasionally the mulish obstinacy inherited from his father would come to the fore, as in his wrangle with Pope Clement XI over James's insistence that he be allowed to reside at Castelgandolfo. Occasionally, too, Fénelon's philosophy failed him, as when he lost his temper and raged over his half-brother Berwick's quite reasonable refusal to go to Scotland to head the rising in 1715. 'I shall write to him no more and must suffer the humiliation of courting a disobedient subject and a bastard too, rather than risk everything in the main point', was his intemperate reaction.

Such an outpouring of malice and bitterness against a man whom until then he had trusted completely and loved dearly is significant. What was it in James that caused him, whenever he snapped out of his habitual indecisiveness, to make the wrong decision? That made him unable to choose good advisers or servants? That led him into bitter rifts with his wife, beloved elder son, and Berwick, the three people for whom he had cared most in his life? Part of it was undoubtedly the same lack of self-confidence that brought on the attacks of ague at moments of stress. This was the area where he was most unlike Charles Edward. James was a man of thought, not action, and manifestly lacked the common touch. His meeting with the clansmen in Perth in 1716 was a classic instance of failure to communicate. Where his son Charles would have won the Highlanders over in a trice, as he demonstrated when he came to Scotland in 1745, James's awkwardness and aloofness left the clans alienated and disenchanted.

On the credit side James was almost always a humane, generous leader with considerable gifts of statesmanship and diplomacy. Few Jacobite émigrés went to him in vain with hard luck stories. He solved difficult problems with tact, especially those involving Highland clans who, while owing a common allegiance to the Stuarts, were at each other's throat. The deadly struggle of the Macphersons and the Gordons in the 1720s was a case in point. Here James had to conciliate two Jacobite clans with diametrically opposed interests. He constantly managed to keep Jacobite plotters and intriguers at arm's length without alienating or making enemies of them – something Charles Edward signally failed to do. And if there were any doubts about his humane impulses, his comments to his son in 1750 – when Charles Edward had asked for renewal of the powers of regency – would dispel them:

> You must be sensible that you have acted towards me for these five years past in a manner which no ways deserves so great a mark of trust and kindness; but far be it from me to act towards you from pique or resentment. It is true the treatment you give me is continual heartbreak to me, but it excites my compassion more than my anger because I will always be persuaded that you are deluded. If you seem to forget that you are my son, I can never forget that I am your father and whatever you may think I can have no other interest than yours and therefore I send you . . . the commission you want in hopes it may soon be use to you and that so great a mark of my goodness at this time may touch your heart and open your eyes . . . But let me recommend it to you not to use other people as you do me by expecting friendship and favours from them, while you do all that is necessary to

disgust them, for you must not expect that anybody else will make you the return I do.

When we turn to Charles Edward, it becomes clear how difficult it was for a Stuart to find the equilibrium point between inertia and rash adventure, that elusive optimum between excessive circumspection and hypertrophied willpower. If James was a 'loser', he was to some extent in a situation where he could not win. As Berwick shrewdly pointed out during the 1715 rising: 'the same people who now accuse him [James] of timidity would call him rash and ill-advised when he had failed'. 'Rash' and 'ill-advised' – exactly the reach-me-down adjectives which are habitually used to describe the career of Charles Edward Stuart. Nor is this all. For some Jacobites, such as Earl Marischal Keith, Charles Edward was the epitome of all that was despicable. Tight-fisted, woman-beating, alcoholic, mindless skinflint – can this really be the 'bonnie Prince Charlie', the hero of the '45? With Charles Edward the problems of biographical interpretation become acute. How difficult this matter is to resolve can be seen from the character portraits which present the conflict of evidence at its most acute. Here is Lord Balmerino speaking just before his execution in 1746:

> I must beg leave to tell you the incomparable sweetness of his nature, his affability, his compassion, his justice, his temperance, his patience, and his courage are virtues seldom to be found in the person. In short he wants no qualifications requisite to make a great man.

There could scarcely be a greater contrast between this and the portrait painted by the former English Jacobite Dr William King, who saw the prince as the repository of all the vices including 'love of money, the certain index of a base and little mind'. How do we reconcile these two accounts? The penny-in-the-slot answer would be to say that Balmerino wrote his assessment before the rot in Charles Edward had set in, while King wrote his in the light of the prince's forty years of drunken decline. But there is more to it than that. King was an apostate, a convert to Whiggery who wanted to expunge his past and chose denigration of the Jacobites as the way to do it. He met Charles Edward only once, in England in 1750 when the prince was still at the height of his powers. For his portrait he relied on the hearsay evidence of hostile witnesses. The real truth about the 'bonnie Prince' is far, far more complex.

Charles Edward's personality remains an enigma. Few historical figures have been fated to shine so brightly for a brief period, only to be totally eclipsed thereafter. It is almost as though Charles Edward crammed the whole of his life into those fourteen months between July 1745 and September 1746, that stupendous period of high adventure and romantic flight that is the basis of his legend. As Scott expressed it in the introduction to *Waverley*: 'On the whole, if Prince Charles had concluded his life soon after his miraculous escape [from Scotland], his character in history must have stood very high. As it was, his station is amongst those, a certain brilliant portion of whose life forms a remarkable contrast to all which precedes, and all which follows it.'

The received opinion is that after the '45 Charles Edward should have bowed to the inevitable and accepted that the House of Stuart could never be restored. His failure to do so is variously ascribed to immaturity, lack of intelligence, mulishness, or a mean spirit. His increasing fondness for the bottle is seen as proof of weakness rather than a quite understandable reaction to a lifetime of being spurned and underestimated. Throughout such assessments lies the ludicrous, unspoken premise that failure to win a crown is to be regarded as the same kind of thing as failure to gain a seat on the board, win an academic chair or captain the cricket eleven. Few brickbats are hurled at the defeatism of his father and brother after the '45. This is taken to be sensible, mature and statesmanlike.

It is true that there are many glaring contradictions in Charles Edward's personality. He was inconsistent. He could switch from intransigence to abject retreat at bewildering speed. He was a poor negotiator. He would take an obstinate, uncompromising stand on an issue but would climb down at the last minute and so obtain worse terms than if he had been conciliatory right at the beginning. In the '45 we can perceive a revolutionary flair of the first order side by side with very poor political *nous*. Charles Edward correctly intuited the possibilities within his grasp at Derby but had not, as a good politician would have done, won the Scottish leaders over to his side before ever the Council met on 5 December 1745. Again, only an extremely poor politician would have delayed the return to Rome until after his father had died. James was already recognised as *de jure* king of England by the pope. Had Charles Edward wished to inherit this papal recognition, he should have returned to Rome while his father was still alive, and obtained formal credentials as Prince of Wales from Clement XIII. It would then have been impossible for the pope to refuse him the title of Charles III *de jure*. As it was, all he got from Clement was the useless title 'count of Albany'.

In Charles Edward we can perceive a coldness towards well-wishers, especially his women friends, that contrasts oddly with a humane, chivalrous and generous spirit. During the '45 campaign many obvious traitors whom the clan leaders wanted to execute owed their lives to the prince's merciful intervention. When, on the afternoon after Culloden, Lochgarry wanted to waylay Cumberland and assassinate him, it was Charles who vetoed the proposal. Ever afterwards he opposed all plots to kidnap George II or murder the Hanoverian royal family. It is only fair to point out that such magnanimous behaviour was not reciprocated by the Hanoverians.

The real peculiarity of Charles Edward's personality has usually been overlooked, however. This was his relationship with his father. Even the superficial observer might conclude that there was something odd about someone who avoided his father for the last twenty-two years of his life. When Charles departed from Rome early in 1744 he was never to see James again. This was his choice, not his father's.

In the case of the two Pretenders we surely encounter a mutual disharmony of rare vintage. There were signs of the future rift early in Charles Edward's life, in the correspondence between father and son when the young prince was at the siege of Gaeta in 1734. On James's part there is affection and patience. On Charles's side there is curtness and distaste for the parental authority. Even at this early stage, it seems, Charles Edward might have perceived his father's weakness. In his letter to James announcing the launching of the '45, it is not hard to see whom the prince has in mind when he writes:

> I cannot but mention a parable here which is this. A horse that is to be sold, if when spurred it does not skip or show some signs of life, nobody would care to have him even for nothing; just so, my friends would care very little to have me if after such usage which all the world is sensible of, I should not show them that I had life in me.

Charles's dissatisfaction with his father was reinforced by his unfortunate experiences with other father-figures during the '45 campaign. As he saw it, both Lochiel and Lord George Murray, born within a few years of his father, exhibited the same depressing 'realistic' (i.e. defeatist) tendencies. To Charles Edward they were the villains of the Derby decision, the men who, above all others, had betrayed him. The prince never liked Lord George and grew to hate him. The antipathy was probably not assuaged by the fact that Charles Edward, strategic genius notwithstanding, proved a poor field commander, in his own right, at Culloden, easily the inferior of Lord George. The prince never forgave Lord George for his 'treachery' and refused to be reconciled with him in later years.

All other father surrogates turned out the same way. He made desperate attempts to conciliate Earl Marischal Keith, doyen of the 'old Jacobites', but Marischal, usually so humane and friendly, had a blind spot where Charles Edward was concerned and regarded him with loathing and disgust. There is no question but that Marischal was at fault here.

The failure of his actual father and all possible father figures to throw up someone he could truly respect came to seem particularly acute when these same men appeared to him to connive at those who harassed and persecuted him. The failure of the '45, attributable to the human weakness of the men of his father's generation, was only the first in a series of incidents in which this crop of men abetted his other betrayers. First came Derby, then the retreat into the Highlands after Falkirk which led to the débâcle of Culloden. But on his return to France things got even worse. At first his father would not help him put pressure on Louis XV to mount another expedition. Then he concealed from him his brother Henry's intention to become a cardinal and compounded the deceit by defending Henry's treachery (as Charles Edward saw it).

France's desertion of him in 1748, when the Treaty of Aix-la-Chapelle contained a provision for the expulsion of the 'Young Pretender' from French territory, was the last straw. In the view of some biographers the events of 1748 were the really crucial ones in the life of the prince, more so even than those of 1745–46. They argue that he could have recovered from the blow of the '45 but not from the Treaty of Aix-la-Chapelle. Charles Edward's alleged obstinacy in refusing to leave France after the treaty –

which led eventually to his arrest and imprisonment in the Bastille – can be read as simple incredulity at Louis XV's perfidy.

By the time of the years of exile and incognito, beginning in 1749, the stage was set for a fairly wholesale mental disintegration. As he saw it, his father, his brother, Louis XV, Lord George Murray, Lochiel and the Earl Marischal had all betrayed him. In his mind the old Jacobite party had turned on him because of his failure in the '45 – a failure they themselves had compassed by their defeatism! Moreover, their idea of 'maturity' was to return to the exiled court in Rome and to accept the values of his father and brother, who had lost hope in a Stuart restoration and to all intents and purposes were no longer 'Jacobites'. People spoke of 'Hamlet without the prince'. Here now, in Charles Edward's view, was the Jacobite movement without a king.

The prince struck back. His betrayers expected him to toe a line they had drawn. Very well, he would hit back where it hurt. Hence his decision to preserve an incognito and to become a rover across the length and breadth of Europe. The 'old Jacobites', such as Marischal and Bulkeley, shared James's horrified reaction to this. To the modern sensibility there is something very prim and prissy about the disapproval of the 'old Jacobites' for Charles Edward's incognito. But perhaps nothing better illustrates the gap between the sensibilities of the eighteenth-century aristocrat and our own than this business of the incognito. James's point, of course, was that Charles Edward could not marry and produce heirs to secure the Stuart succession if he remained incognito. Charles's response to this was that James's concern for heirs for his royal house had not been very much in evidence when he permitted Henry to become a cardinal.

Everything his father did grated on him and increased his feelings of resentment or hatred. James made a tactless intervention to minimise unfavourable publicity over Clementina Walkinshaw's desertion in 1760, which infuriated Charles Edward even more. Once again, he reasoned, his father had taken the side of his enemies. James had helped his brother become a cardinal, had abetted the king of France when Louis XV wanted him to leave France in 1748, and finally had helped Clementina Walkinshaw keep his child from him.

All the things that happened to Charles Edward fuelled his sense of being singled out for especially discriminatory treatment. Most of all he blamed his father for this and punished him by depriving him of his presence. But, as so often with paranoia, this feeling of being persecuted was accompanied by a deep sense of guilt. It was almost certainly this deep-seated 'guilt complex' about his father that was the key factor in his plummeting into semi-alcoholism, not, as is usually alleged, some childlike or 'immature' feelings of pique. An eye-witness in Rome offered support for this view, speaking of the prince as drinking 'like one absent in mind when he met with things that vexed him, as too often was the case'. In any case, the political significance of Charles Edward's drinking has been overplayed by hostile critics. It is quite clear from a close study of the evidence that the French were not unduly perturbed when the prince arrived drunk for his 1759 meeting with Choiseul to discuss a French descent on Britain.

Charles was no intellectual, but he had a certain aesthetic sense, which he indulged in the years of incognito travel by becoming a collector of antiques. In his youth it was his prowess as a cellist that was most noted. We even know something of the prince's taste in music. One of his favourite pieces was Corelli's *Notte di Natale* or Christmas Concerto (Concerto Grosso No. 8 in G. Minor).

Charles Edward was too rough-hewn a character to fit easily into polite society. He was fluent in French, Italian and English – the last of which he spoke with a slight foreign accent – but by no stretch of the imagination could he be considered an educated man, especially by the stiff standards of the eighteenth century. For all that, he was, two centuries of adverse propaganda notwithstanding, an intelligent man with a quick understanding. His weaknesses were not primarily ones of intellect but of temperament and character.

He seems to have been largely uninterested in women. The best efforts of novelists and popular biographers have been unable to turn the famous meeting with Flora MacDonald into a romantic encounter. Nor did Whig propaganda manage to pin an unsavoury liaison on him despite the valiant fabrications of Fielding and others. Mistresses he had, certainly. There was Madame de Guémené on his return to France in 1747, the Princesse de Talmond from 1748 to 1750, and Clementina Walkinshaw, who bore him his only child, a daughter, from 1753 to 1760. But if he spent any considerable time with a woman he would row with her and end by beating her. The scenes with

Madame de Talmond were frightful; those with Clementina Walkinshaw less so, as she took her beatings in silence. No doubt reasoning that if she could not beat *him*, she had better join him, she assuaged her sorrow by taking to the bottle. But eventually even she could take no more and deserted him, as his wife Louise was to do twenty years later.

Charles was no ladies' man; the last Stuart with such tastes seems to have been Charles II. He was a man of action and, until he succumbed to drink, something of a 'macho'. His cold dismissal of Madame de Talmond is instructive. He wrote to her that if she did not love him that was a great deal, but if she *did* love him that did not amount to much. When Clementina Walkinshaw signed a formal denial that she and the prince had ever married in secret, he thanked her as follows: 'His Majesty begs you will always remain in a monastery.'

The misfortunes of the Stuarts tended to repeat themselves and nowhere more so than in the experience of the Old and the Young Pretender with their wives. Both the exiled Stuarts had to suffer the humiliation of having their spouses desert them and seek sanctuary in a convent, Clementina Sobieska in 1725, Louise of Stolberg in 1780. This was not so much a question of history occurring twice, the first time as tragedy, the second as farce, as of a single farce being replicated. At least here James fared better than his son, since his wife was persuaded to return to him from the convent. Moreover, she had already provided the Chevalier with two sons, whereas Louise was not able to provide a single heir for Charles Edward. In James's case, too, less provocation was offered by the husband.

Charles's marriage to Louise of Stolberg was the most notorious disaster in the long story of his fiascos with women. Married in 1772, when he was fifty-one and the bride just twenty, the couple did not long remain in marital bliss. Charles undertook the marriage in the first place solely to receive a pension of 40,000 crowns from the French. The irony was that this was never paid. Soon there were drunken scenes, recriminations, beatings. The royal pair seem to have been incompatible in every sphere: temperamental, intellectual, sexual. In 1780 Louise ran off with Vittorio Alfieri, the Italian poet and playwright. Although the royal couple's childlessness was almost certainly due to Louise's barrenness, this juicy scandal was too good for the Hanoverians to miss. When Louise went to live in Cardinal

Henry Stuart's palace (at this time Henry was unaware of her liaison with Alfieri) Horace Walpole, constant gadfly of the Jacobites, tried to work up his greatest propaganda triumph to date. 'Are they', he wrote, 'Jews enough, if the Count [Charles] should die, to uncanonise the cardinal and make him raise up issue to his brother, which the brother could not do for himself?'

If Charles Edward's bad luck or bad judgment with women was a common feature of the later Stuarts, his attitude to religion was very much his own, distinguishing him clearly from his father, mother, grandfather and brother, all to varying degrees deeply pious people. As Lord Elcho remarked during the '45, Charles Edward's religion was 'to seek'. He took an extremely cavalier attitude to religious belief. The best creed for him was the one that enabled him to gain the throne of the United Kingdom. If this turned out to be Protestantism rather than Catholicism, so be it. In 1750, during a secret visit to London, he entered the Church of England, purely for reasons of expediency. His principal motive was to make himself more acceptable to the ferociously anti-Catholic English people, to increase his credibility as a would-be king, and to dispel the miasma of 'Polish Pretender' that clung about him. He had another motive too. To turn Protestant would be the surest way to spite those who had failed to support him or had betrayed him – his father, the pope, and his brother the cardinal.

James reacted in horror to his son's apostasy. The realisation that Charles Edward had forsaken the faith of his fathers seems not to have dawned on him until 1759, when he wrote in some anguish:

> I am far from dissuading you to seek a temporal kingdom
> which will be one day your own, and it is also manifestly for
> the good of our country . . . But you must remember it is not
> lawful to pursue the most just ends by unjust and unlawful
> means, and what will avail to you all the kingdoms of the
> world for all eternity, if you lose your soul . . . For his Divine
> Majesty seldom fails punishing even in this world the sins of
> great princes who abandon him.

By this time Charles Edward was not answering his father's letters anyway.

In general, Charles seems to have had a contempt for clerics of all descriptions, a contempt not assuaged by the pope's refusal to accept him as King Charles III in 1766. Convents seemed to excite a particular rage in him. On one drunken occasion in the town of Bouillon he amused himself by firing through the convent windows. But these monastic retreats were destined to pay him back with interest. When Clementina Walkinshaw deserted him, she took refuge in a nunnery. Charles replied by raging that he would sack every convent in Europe until he found her and his child. And when Louise of Stolberg eloped with Alfieri in 1780, a convent was once again the key to the escape. Charles Edward, who watched his wife like a hawk, agreed to accompany her to the convent of the Biachette, ostensibly to inspect the nuns' needlework. At the threshold of the nunnery Charles was detained in conversation with one of Louise's accomplices while she went inside. A few minutes later Charles found that the door had been closed behind his wife. Knocking impatiently for it to be opened, he was informed by the abbess that his wife had sought sanctuary in the convent and had been granted it. The situation was as ludicrous as that of the abbess's sheltering Antipholus and Dromio in the *Comedy of Errors*, except that this time there was no happy resolution.

No greater contrast can be imagined than between Charles Edward's religious attitudes and those of his pious brother Henry. If Charles Edward was in many respects, save for the Merry Monarch's penchant for women, a throwback to Charles II, Henry was undoubtedly in many ways an epigone of James II. The religious mania of Henry Stuart, duke of York, and after 1788 the 'cardinal king', was in evidence from an early age. In 1742 his Protestant tutor Lord Dunbar expressed concern to James about him, pointing out that he was living the life of a neurotic at seventeen. He rose at six each morning, prayed for an hour, spent another hour with his confessor after breakfast and passed most of the rest of the day in chapel, praying or hearing mass. On Sundays and holy days he would hear as many as four masses. This religiosity profoundly irritated the libertine duc de Richelieu when Henry was with him in Boulogne early in 1746, waiting to cross the Channel with the French expeditionary force. Richelieu remarked bitterly that that sort of piety might win the kingdom of God but would never win the kingdom of England.

In some ways, then, Henry's decision to accept a cardinal's hat in 1746 ought to have come as no surprise. But to his brother it came both as a sensation and as a signal act of treachery, especially since his father and brother had planned the move behind his back. As Charles said to his father: 'Had I got a dagger through my heart, it would not have been more sensible to me than at the contents of your first [letter].' The reasons for Charles Edward's rage were threefold. Collusion between his father and brother over the cardinalate meant that both had effectively despaired forever of a Stuart restoration. And there were two further implications of Henry's choice of career. As a cardinal he would be a prince of the very church so profoundly hated in England. It was often said that the association between the Stuarts and Catholicism had always been the principal barrier to their restoration, and here was Henry reinforcing that barrier. Moreover, as a celibate Henry could have no legitimate issue to maintain the line of succession. If Charles himself failed to beget heirs, there was no second line of defence. Henry's cardinalate, in fact, was regarded by Charles Edward as his father's most blatant act of betrayal. It was the last straw in their already badly damaged relationship. And it was a long time before the prince consented to be reconciled with his brother.

To the modern mind there is something ridiculous and almost grotesque about a young man of twenty-one ascending to the purple before he had even been ordained a priest. But in the eighteenth century such an elevation was not unprecedented. It was not until Pius XI's papacy in the following century that one could no longer become a cardinal without having first been a priest. Yet there can be no doubt that Henry made a success of his career. He was an imperious, high-handed and hot-tempered individual who clashed violently with his father in the 1750s, when the old man was becoming more cantankerous, over his association with musicians and good-looking young male admirers. Towards his brother, to whom he was reconciled in 1765, Henry was always deferential, though he continued to wring his hands in despair over his drinking. The usual judgment on Henry is that he was proud, level-headed, realistic, pious but dull. Benedict XIV is said to have exclaimed after an audience with him in the 1750s: 'If all the Stuarts are as boring as he, no wonder the English drove them out.' The most controversial aspect of his personality was his alleged homosexuality, towards which there are many convincing circumstantial pointers. His most solid achievements were as cardinal-bishop of his beloved

Frascati and as a patron of arts and learning. He became the elder statesman of the Curia and in his old age supported Pius VI and Pius VII in their desperate struggle against Napoleon.

Yet Henry's life is properly a subject for biographers and historians of the Catholic church rather than for the analyst of the Jacobite movement. In any case, he lived twenty years beyond the 'Jacobite century' and into the turbulent years of the French Revolution and after. His main significance for the Jacobite world was that, throughout the post-1745 period and until financial ruin in the last years of his life as a result of Napoleon's attempt to destroy the papacy, he was the principal source of financial patronage for needy Jacobites, towards whom he invariably responded with great generosity. His revenues from ecclesiastical preferments were enormous. His income from abbeys and other religious institutions in Flanders, Spain, Naples and France amounted to some £40,000 a year. He also held sinecure benefices in Spanish America and owned land in Mexico, all of which generated substantial income. The most flattering estimate of Henry would see him as combining the stoicism of his father with the worldliness of his brother. Certainly he was the only one of the three later Stuarts who died reasonably content.

One final controversial coda must be added to the story of Henry's later years, since it touches on many of the themes central to Jacobitism. In 1799 the French Revolution succeeded in reducing Henry to penury. All his French income and all his South American benefices were wiped out by the Revolution, and he had sold off all his family jewels to help pay Napoleon's exorbitant fine on Pope Pius VI. By a roundabout route, involving Cardinal Borgia and William Pitt, news of Henry's destitution reached George III. The king responded with a show of magnanimity. In January 1800 a pension for life of £4,000 was settled on Henry at George's express request.

However, the Hanoverian monarch's gesture was not quite so generous as it seemed. The arrears on Mary of Modena's jointure, to which Henry was legally entitled by the 1685 Act of Parliament, had amounted to £2½ million by the time of her death in 1718, and to a much vaster sum by 1799. All in all, then, it seems less sentimental and more hard-headed to see George III's action less as an example of *noblesse oblige* and more as a calculated piece of *Realpolitik* from which the Hanoverian dynasty could extract maximum propaganda advantage. Perhaps it is not fanciful to see the 1800 pension payment as the long arm of Walpole stretching out from beyond the grave and coopting the stricken Stuarts into his infamous system of Hanoverian jobbery and clientelism.

Chapter 13

Jacobite epilogue

Que les hommes privés, qui se plaignent de leurs petites
infortunes, jettent les yeux sur ce prince et sur ses ancêtres.

Voltaire, *Précis du siecle de Louis XV*

Ye northern chiefs, whose rage, unbroke
Has still repell'd the tyrants shock
Who ne'er have bowed beneath his yoke
With servile base prostration;
Let each now train his trusty band,
'Gainst foreign foes alone to stand
With undivided heart and hand,
For freedom, king and nation.

(Verses composed on the restoration of the forfeited estates, 1784)

Hogg, *Jacobite Relics*

After the refusal of the pope to recognise him as king of England,
Scotland and Ireland in 1766, Charles Edward commenced a steep
decline into drunken incompetence. There followed the disastrous
marriage with Louise of Stolberg, her eventual flight with Alfieri,
and the prince's death in 1788. His brother Henry lived through
the turmoil of the Napoleonic era, dying in 1807. After 1766 only
Charles III of Spain remained as a nominal supporter of the
Stuarts. France was too crushed after her disastrous defeat in the
Seven Years' War to have any time for Charles Edward. There
were to be more attempts at a descent on England, notably by
Choiseul in 1768–70 and by the French in partnership with Spain
in 1779, but the Stuarts did not feature in these plans. Ironically,

it was only after the Jacobite period proper that France bestowed a backward glance or two on the Stuarts. When Wolf Tone was intriguing for a French invasion of Ireland in 1796, the Directory ministers mentioned Cardinal York as a possible king of Ireland. Wolf Tone replied dismissively: 'Who the devil is this pretender *in petto*? It is all one to us, however, for we will have nothing to do with him.' Later, when Napoleon summoned Louise of Stolberg (countess of Albany) to his presence in 1809 to answer for her subversive activities, he asked her whether she had ever had a son by Charles Edward. On being told no, Napoleon replied that it was a pity, since he could have used a Stuart prince as a puppet monarch on the English throne.

The only political event that seems to have impinged on Charles Edward's consciousness in his later years was the American War of Independence, which some Jacobites welcomed as a blow against Hanoverian England. Indeed, according to Sir Charles Petrie, there was at one time a vague plan to set Charles Edward up as 'king of America', *pour épater les Anglais*. Charles Edward did not live long enough, unlike his brother, to span the gap between Jacobites and Jacobins, and by the 1770s he was in another world in more senses than one.

Thirty years only separate the Jacobite rising of 1745 from the American Revolution, but already we are in a different dimension. The tables are now turned. Those who supported the '45 now vehemently oppose the American independence movement and *vice versa*. Samuel Johnson said with scorn of the revolutionaries: 'How is it that we hear the loudest yelps for liberty among the drivers of negroes?' And even more strongly: 'I am willing to love all mankind except an American.' On the other hand, Pitt, staunch opponent of the '45, welcomed the American Revolution and spoke warmly in favour of the colonists' cause. Edmund Burke, who was to the political theory of the last quarter of the eighteenth century what Hume was to the third sector, upheld the rights of the Americans to rebel, because they sought to return to the *status quo ante* the 1760s. Benjamin Franklin, as outspoken as any in his condemnation of the 'unnatural' rebellion of 1745, now stood forth as an apostle of the new liberty.

Theorists of the Hume/Burke persuasion regarded the '45 as a more serious threat to the established order than the American Revolution, because the latter was a logical step in the process inaugurated in 1688, whereas the Jacobite risings appeared to seek to dismantle the work of the Glorious Revolution. In truth, the exact opposite was the case. The creation of a rival mercantile capitalist power was, long-term, a far greater threat to British economic interests than the Jacobites could ever have been.

In one way contemporaries *did* lump the two rebellions together. The American affair was thought to be, in military terms, a rerun of the '45. Provided sufficient military force was brought to bear on the rebels in North America, they would collapse as the Highlanders had. There is a lesson here for those historians who work from hindsight and tell us that such and such an outcome was 'inevitable'. The rising of the 1745 had as a matter of fact been suppressed; therefore, the argument runs, its suppression was 'inevitable'. According to the same logic of inevitability the defeat of the Americans was only a matter of time. When, contrary to expectations, the colonists went on to victory, the pendulum swung the other way. Historians writing in the late 1860s and 1870s often found it impossible to explain how the North had prevailed in the American Civil War. On paper the task of defeating the South was far more formidable than that faced by the British in 1775. Therefore the triumph of a secessionary South ought to have been 'inevitable' too.

The truth of the matter, which we in the twentieth century can appreciate better, having seen many successful revolutions in Latin America and the Third World inspired by the so-called 'subjective conditions', is that arguments from 'objective conditions' and inevitability are fraught with risk. Even Lenin, early in 1917, did not think he would see the Revolution in his lifetime. Once again we can appreciate that the Jacobite risings are respectable counterfactual candidates, that they did not represent a hopeless and anachronistic fantasy of counter-revolution. Perhaps this explains the intense interest Charles Edward took in the progress of the American war, almost as if the colonists were proving the truth of the points he argued at Derby thirty years before.

In the fury of the revolutionary last decade of the eighteenth century the Jacobites faded quietly out of history. Yet at the precise moment of their disappearance, with the death of Henry Stuart in the first decade of the new century, they began to re-enter men's consciousness through the portals of legend. In 1805 Sir Walter Scott began work on *Waverley* or ' 'Tis Sixty Years

Since', thus launching the nineteenth-century craze for all things Jacobite and Scottish.

Waverley marked the first fully fledged appearance of the Jacobite *legend*, but the Jacobites had made earlier appearances in literature. *Tom Jones*, published in 1749, was set four years earlier during the rising which Fielding did so much to combat at the propaganda level in the *True Patriot*. Such is the fidelity of *Tom Jones* to the calendar that the details of its plot can be checked almost day by day against Charles Edward's advance into England. Another classic from the same period, Laurence Sterne's *Tristram Shandy*, is consistently and violently anti-Jacobite in tone. Dr John Burton, one of the prince's supporters in the '45, reappears in caricatured form as Dr Slop. The only English literary figure of moment in the thirty-year period after the '45 who is at all sympathetic to Jacobitism is Tobias Smollett. In *Humphrey Clinker* he produced a devastating attack on the intellectual competence of the duke of Newcastle, of which the following extract gives the flavour:

'What, is Cape Breton an island?' said the Duke.

'Certainly.'

'Ha. Are you sure of that?'

When I pointed it out in the map, he examined it earnestly with his spectacles; then, taking me in his arm, 'My dear C——!' (cried he) 'you always bring us good news – egad! I'll go directly and tell the king that Cape Breton is an island!'

Perhaps the first genuine literary commitment to the Jacobite cause was that of Robert Burns. It does seem paradoxical that Burns, devotee of *Jacobinism*, should also have attached himself to the aristocratic cause of the Stuarts. But already by the late eighteenth century we are in an era when Jacobitism has passed out of the gates of history and into legend. Burns's Jacobite attachment was of the sentimental variety, as he himself admitted. Like many people of imagination, he was drawn to the dramatic and romantic aspects of the House of Stuart and its misfortunes. Politically he was a democrat and egalitarian and, in contemporary terms, a revolutionary. His desire that Charlie should enjoy his own again was an expression of poetic licence. Yet Burns's Jacobitism was important, for it was through his verses that Jacobite songs entered the mainstream repertory.

There is another aspect of Burns's sentimental Jacobite

attachment that is important, since it underlines once again the power of the 'consoling legend' of Jacobitism as part of the ideological superstructure of Scottish nationalism. This is undoubtedly the explanation of the attraction of the Jacobite story for literary Scots of the most varied persuasions. Whether members of the squirearchy like Scott, anti-aristocratic egalitarians like Burns, Victorian writers like Robert Louis Stevenson – who acknowledged Henry James as 'the master' – or a dour, abstemious, Calvinistic son of the manse like John Buchan, all the leading writers from north of the border have revealed their fascination with the Jacobite era.

It was Scott with *Waverley* and later with *Redgauntlet* and *Rob Roy* who launched the Jacobite boom. The rosy Jacobitism of legend fitted well into the general context of the Romantic movement and the Gothic Revival. Sentimental Jacobitism became the rage. Scott made many powerful converts, among them George IV himself, who came to Scotland and set the royal imprimatur on an interest in all things Highland. At Holyrood Palace he dressed himself in a uniform of scarlet kilt, plaid, bonnet, eagle feathers, broadsword, dirk and *skean dhu*. Tartans, most of them invented and then ascribed anachronistically to the various clans, became the Victorian fetish. The entire Balmoral ethos of Queen Victoria and Prince Albert was suffused with this sort of nostalgic regard for Highland society and, by extension, for Jacobitism.

Yet it is a mistake to lay the responsibility for the more crazed manifestations of Victorian Jacobitism at Scott's door. Both *Waverley* and *Redgauntlet* present highly nuanced pictures of Charles Edward and his supporters, portraying them 'warts and all'. One of the bases for a claim to literary greatness for *Waverley* is precisely its ability to chart the turbid waters between illusion and reality. In its suggestion that there was something about the 'illusion' of Jacobitism that transcends its 'reality', *Waverley* links with the greatest works in the appearance/reality mode, worthy to be mentioned in the same breath as Flaubert's *Sentimental Education*, if not quite with an eternal masterpiece like *Don Quixote*.

Inevitably there was a reaction to all this. We have already had occasion to mention Thackeray's anti-Jacobite broadside in *Henry Esmond*. Even more violent was the anti-Jacobitism of George Borrow. Borrow was a Protestant zealot of almost paranoid dimensions. He linked the rise of sentimental Jacobitism with Catholic Emancipation in England and saw the vogue for Scott and his creations as a Trojan horse for the spread of an aggressive and proselytising Catholicism. In his mind Catholicism, Scottishness and Jacobitism were three heads of a single monster. Hence the vehemence with which he assails all three in *Lavengro* and *The Romany Rye*. Scott is accused of having turned the nineteenth-century fashion for 'cant' and 'gentility' into a corrupted passion for all things Jacobite. Borrow even asserts that Scott's novels are the provenance of the Oxford Movement. Charles Edward Stuart is showered with a barrage of rebarbative epithets: 'worthless', 'ignorant', 'illiterate', 'profligate', 'loathsome', 'contemptible', 'not a vice or crime of which he was not guilty'. In his totally fictitious comic description of the Highlanders' fording of the river Esk in December 1745 Borrow outdoes Defoe and Fielding in scurrilous anti-Jacobite propaganda:

> They commenced dancing Highland reels and strathspeys on the bank of the river, for joy at their escape, whilst a number of wretched girls, paramours of some of them, were perishing in the waters of the swollen river in an attempt to follow them; they themselves passed over by eighties and by hundreds, arm in arm, for mutual safety, without the loss of a man, but they left the poor paramours to shift for themselves, nor did any of these canny people after passing the stream dash back to rescue a single female life – no, they were too well employed upon the bank in dancing strathspeys to the tune of 'Charlie o'er the water'. It was indeed Charlie o'er the water, and canny Highlanders o'er the water, but where were the poor prostitutes meantime? *In the water.*

After such intemperate polemics the pendulum was bound to swing back. It founds its equilibrium in the works of Robert Louis Stevenson, whose attitude to Jacobitism is sympathetic and insightful without being starry-eyed. The moral ambivalence of the Master of Ballantrae and his brother Henry (is there, one wonders, a distant echo of the difficulties between the Stuart brothers, in this choice of name for the Master's younger brother?) well expresses Stevenson's subtly modulated stance towards the Jacobites. Jacobitism – in the form of the famous 'Appin murder' of Campbell of Glenure – also formed the backcloth for Stevenson's masterpeice *Kidnapped* and its sequel *Catriona*.

That the Jacobite legacy had already been absorbed into the bloodstream of Victorian novelists can be demonstrated by a number of odd little pointers. To take one example, in George Eliot's *Adam Bede*, where the action takes place in the Derbyshire of 1799, 'Feyther Taft' is described thus by Old Martin: 'I remember Jacob Taft walking fifty mile after the Scotch raybels when they turned back from Stoniton.'

The Stevenson tradition of a broadly sympathetic, though not fanatical view of the Jacobites was taken up by John Buchan in his novels *Midwinter* and *A Lost Lady of Years*, concentrating on the 'old fox' Lord Lovat of the '45, as also in his biography of Montrose. The subject is also the motif for some of his short stories, notably 'The Company of the Majolaine' in the collection *The Moon Endureth*.

The rest is history, in more senses than one. In a recent book Professor Speck remarked ruefully: 'Hardly a year goes by without the appearance of a new life of Bonnie Prince Charlie or a Jacobite saga.' The reason is not hard to find. The saga of the Jacobites is one of the great stories, as perennially fascinating as the *Iliad*, the *Odyssey* or the *Morte d'Arthur*, with the added piquancy of being located firmly within history. One of the great Jacobite scholars, R.C. Jarvis, remarked on this as follows: 'Many sober devotees of history have approached this particular field with an honest intention to truthful inquiry and impartial investigation only to be lured away to fall victim to the well-known magic spell. He has been seduced from history to romance: he has, perhaps all unwillingly or possibly quite unwittingly, been converted – corrupted – from historian to romancer.'

This is a danger every historian of the Jacobites must guard against. But every historian who believes that the truth about the past cannot be totally retrieved from documents and archives must be open to the dimension of the imagination. The honest historian of Jacobitism, recognising how powerful is the sway of the irrational over human beings, will always leave the door slightly ajar to myth.

Select bibliography

Place of publication London unless otherwise indicated.

Abbey, C.J., and J.H. Overton, *The English Church in the Eighteenth Century* (1878).

Anderson, M.S., *Eighteenth-Century Europe 1713–89* (Oxford 1966).

Andrieux, Maurice, *Daily Life in Papal Rome in the Eighteenth Century* (1968).

Ashley, M., *The Stuarts in Love* (1963).

Atholl, 7th duke of (ed.), *Chronicles of the Families of Atholl and Tullibardine*, 4 vols (Edinburgh 1908).

Aubrey, P., *The Defeat of James Stuart's Armada 1692* (Leicester 1979).

Baines, J., *The Jacobite Rising of 1715* (1970).

Barrow, G.W.S., *The Kingdom of the Scots* (1973).

Beaumont W. (ed.), *The Jacobite Trials in Manchester in 1694* (Manchester 1853).

Bell. R. Fitzroy (ed.), *Memorials of John Murray of Broughton* (Edinburgh 1898).

Bennett, G.V., *The Tory Crisis in Church and State 1688–1730: The Career of Francis Atterbury, Bishop of Rochester* (Oxford 1975).

Berwick, James Fitzjames, duke of, *Mémoires écrits par lui-meme*, 2 vols (Paris 1778).

Blaikie, W.B., *Itinerary of Prince Charles Edward Stuart from His Landing in Scotland July 1745 to His Departure in September 1746* (Edinburgh 1897).

Blaikie, W.B., *Origins of the Forty-Five* (Edinburgh 1916).

Boswell, James, *The Journal of a Tour to the Hebrides with Samuel Johnson* (1786).

Bradstreet, D., *The Adventures of Captain Dudley Bradstreet* (1755).

Brewer, J., *Party Ideology and Popular Politics at the Accession of George III* (Cambridge 1976).

Brooke, J. *George III* (1974).

Brosses, Charles, de, *L'Italie il y a cent ans, ou lettres écrites d'Italie à quelques amis en 1939 et 1740*, 2 vols, ed. M.R. Columb (Paris 1826).

Browne, J., *A History of the Highlands and of the Highland Clans*, 4 vols (Glasgow 1832–3).

Broxap, Henry, *A Biography of Thomas Deacon* (Manchester 1911).

Broxap, Henry, *The Later Non-Jurors* (Cambridge 1924).

Buchan, John, *The Massacre of Glencoe* (1933).

Bulloch, J.M., *The Gordons of Invergordon* (Dingwall 1906).

Bulloch, J.M., *The House of Gordon* (Aberdeen 1912).

Burt, Edward, *Letters from a Gentleman in the North of Scotland* (1818).

Campana de Cavelli, *Les Derniers Stuarts à Saint-Germain-en-Laye*, 2 vols (Paris 1871).

Campbell, R.H., *Scotland since 1707* (Oxford 1971).

Carpio, M.J., *España y los ultimos Estuardos* (Madrid 1952).

Carswell, J., *The South Sea Bubble* (1961).

Chambers, R., *Jacobite Memoirs of the Rebellion of 1745* (1834).

Chambers, R., *History of the Rebellion of 1745–46* (1869).

Charteris, E., *William Augustus, Duke of Cumberland, His Early Life and Times* (1913).

Chesterfield, Philip Stanhope, 4th earl of, *Letters of Lord Chesterfield*, ed. B. Dobree, 6 vols. (1932).

Christie, I.R., *Myth and Reality in Late Eighteenth-Century British Politics* (1970).

Churchill, W.S., *Marlborough, His Life and Times*, 2 vols. (1947).

Clark, Manning, *A Short History of Australia* (Sydney 1963).

Clement XI, *Opera Omnia* (Frankfurt 1729).

Colin, J.L.A., *Louis XV et les Jacobites: Le projet de débarquement en Angleterre en 1743–44* (Paris 1901).

Colley, Linda, *In Defiance of Oligarchy: The Tory Party 1727–1760* (Cambridge 1981).

Coxe, W., *Memoirs of the Life and Administration of Sir Robert Walpole, Earl of Orford*, 3 vols (1798).

Coxe, W., *Memoirs of the Administration of Rt. Hon. Henry Pelham* (1829).

Cruickshanks, Eveline, *Political Untouchables: The Tories and the '45* (1979).

Cruickshanks, Eveline, *Ideology and Conspiracy: Aspects of Jacobitism 1688–1759* (Edinburgh 1982).

Cunningham, Audrey, *The Loyal Clans* (Cambridge 1932).

Cuthell, Edith, *The Scottish Friend of Frederick the Great: The Last Earl Marischal* (1915).

Daiches, D., *Robert Burns* (1966).

Daiches, D., *Charles Edward Stuart* (1975).

Dickinson, H.T., *Bolingbroke* (1970).

Dickinson, H.T., *Walpole and the Whig Supremacy* (1973).

Dickinson, H.T., *Liberty and Property: Political Ideology in the Eighteenth Century* (1977).

Dickson, W.K., *The Jacobite Attempt of 1719* (Edinburgh 1896).

Duff, H.R., (ed.), *Culloden Papers* (1815).

Dunn, J., *The Political Thought of John Locke* (Cambridge 1969).

Elcho, Lord, *A Short Account of the Affairs of Scotland in 1744, 1745 and 1746* (Edinburgh 1973).

Ellis, K., *The Post Office in the Eighteenth Century* (1958).

Erskine-Hill, Howard, *The Social Milieu of Alexander Pope* (1975).

Ettinger, A.A., *James Edward Oglethorpe* (Oxford 1936).

Ewald, A.C., *The Life and Times of Prince Charles Stuart*, 2 vols (1875).

Fay, C.R., *Adam Smith and the Scotland of His Day* (Cambridge 1956).

Feiling, K.G., *A History of the Tory Party 1640–1714* (Oxford 1924).

Feiling, K.G., *The Second Tory Party 1714–1832* (1938).

Fergusson, Sir James, *Lowland Lairds* (1949).

Fergusson, Sir James, *Argyll in the '45* (1952).

Figgis, J.N., *The Divine Right of Kings* (Cambridge 1914).

Findlay, J.T., *Wolfe in Scotland in the '45 and from 1949 to 1753* (1928).

Flood, J.M., *The Life of Chevalier Charles Wogan* (Dublin 1922).

Foord, A.S., *His Majesty's Opposition 1714–1830* (Oxford 1964).

Forbes, Duncan, *Hume's Philosophical Politics* (Cambridge 1975).

Forbes, R., *The Lyon in Mourning*, 3 vols (Edinburgh 1896).

Fothergill, A.B., *The Cardinal King: Henry Stuart, Duke of York* (1959).

Fraser, Sir W., *The Chiefs of Colquhoun* (Edinburgh 1869).

Fraser, Sir W., *The Earls of Cromartie* (Edinburgh 1876).

Fraser, Sir W., *The Chiefs of Grant*, 3 vols (Edinburgh 1883).

Fritz, Paul S., *The English Ministers and Jacobitism between the Rebellions of 1715 and 1745* (Toronto 1975).

Garrett, Jane, *The Triumphs of Providence* (Cambridge 1980).

Gibbon, Edward, *Memoirs of My Own Life*, ed. G.A. Bonnard (1966).

Gibson, J.S., *Ships of the '45* (1967).

Grant, I.F., *Everyday Life on an Old Highland Farm* (1924).

Grant, I.F., *The Macleods* (1933).

Grant, I.F., *Highland Folkways* (1961).

Greene, D.J. *The Politics of Samuel Johnson* (New Haven 1960).

Hamilton, H., *The Industrial Revolution in Scotland* (Oxford 1932).

Hamilton, H. *An Economic History of Scotland in the Eighteenth Century* (Oxford 1963).

Hart, J., *Viscount Bolingbroke, Tory Humanist* (1965).

Hartmann, C., *The Quest Forlorn* (1952).

Haynes, Renée, *Philosopher King: Pope Benedict XIV* (1970).

Henderson, G.D., *Mystics of the North-East* (Aberdeen 1934).

Henderson, G.D., *Chevalier Ramsay* (1952).

Hill, Bridget, *Eighteenth-Century Women* (1984).

Hill, Patricia K., *The Oglethorpe Ladies and the Jacobite Conspiracies* (Atlanta 1977).

Hogg, James, *The Jacobite Relics of Scotland* (1819).

Holmes, G., *British Politics in the Age of Anne* (1967).

Holmes, G., *The Trial of Dr. Sacheverell* (1973).

Home, J., *History of the Rebellion in the Year 1745* (1802).

Hooke, Nathaniel, *Secret History of Colonel Hooke's Negotiations in Scotland in 1707* (Edinburgh 1760).

Horn, D.B., *Great Britain and Europe in the Eighteenth Century* (Oxford 1965).

Horwitz, H., *Parliament, Policy and Politics in the Reign of William III* (Manchester 1977).

Howell, T.B., *A Complete Collection of State Trials*, 34 vols (1828).

Hughes, E.W., *North Country Life in the Eighteenth Century*, 2 vols (1952).

Irish, G.P., *The Scottish Jacobite Movement* (1952).

Jackman, S.W., *Man of Mercury* (1965).

James, F.G., *Ireland in the Empire 1688–1770* (Cambridge, Mass., 1973).

Jarvis, R.C., *The Jacobite Risings of 1715 and 1745* (Cumberland 1954).

Jarvis, R.C., *Collected Papers on the Jacobite Risings* (Manchester 1972).

Johnstone, Chevalier de, *A Memoir of the '45* (1820).

Jones, G.H., *The Mainstream of Jacobitism* (Cambridge, Mass., 1954).

Jones, J.R., *The Revolution of 1688 in England* (1972).

Kenyon, J.P., *Revolution Principles: The Politics of Party 1689–1720* (Cambridge 1977).

Kettler, D., *The Social and Political Thought of Adam Ferguson* (Columbus, Ohio, 1965).

King, William, *Political and Literary Anecdotes of His Own Time* (1819).

Kramnick, Isaac, *Bolingbroke and His Circle* (1968).

Lacour-Gayet, G., *La Marine militaire de la France sous le règne de Louis XV* (Paris 1910).

Lang, Andrew, *Pickle the Spy* (1897).

Lang, Andrew, *The Companions of Pickle* (1898).

Lang, Andrew, *The Highlands of Scotland in 1750* (1898).

Lang, Andrew, *Prince Charles Edward Stuart* (1903).

Langford, P., *The Excise Crisis* (1975).

Lart, C.E. (ed.), *The Parochial Registers of Saint-Germain-en-Laye*, 2 vols (1912).

Lecky, W.E.H., *Ireland in the Eighteenth Century*, 5 vols (1892).

Lees-Milne, J., *The Last Stuarts* (1983).

Lehman, W.C., *Henry, Lord Kames, and the Scottish Enlightenment* (The Hague 1971).

Lenman, B., *The Jacobite Risings in Britain 1689–1746* (1980).

Levron, Jacques, *Daily Life at Versailles in the Seventeenth and*

Eighteenth Centuries (1962).

Lewis, Lesley, *Connoisseurs and Secret Agents in Eighteenth-Century Rome* (1961).

Linklater, Eric, *The Prince in the Heather* (1965).

Lodge, Sir Richard, *Studies in Eighteenth Century Diplomacy 1740–1748* (1930).

Macaulay, T.B., *History of England*, 6 vols (1914).

MacDonald, Rev. A., *The Clan Donald* (Inverness 1904).

Mackay, Angus, *The Book of Mackay* (Edinburgh 1900).

Mackay, W., *Urquhart and Glenmoriston* (Inverness 1893).

McKendrick, Neil (ed.), *Historical Perspectives* (1974).

Mackenzie, Alexander, *A History of the Mackenzies* (Inverness 1894).

Mackenzie, Sir Compton, *Prince Charlie and his Ladies* (1934).

Mackenzie, W.C., *Simon Fraser, Lord Lovat* (1908).

Macky, John, *Memoirs of the Secret Services of John Macky during the Reigns of King William, Queen Anne and King George I* (1733).

McLaren, M., *Lord Lovat of the '45* (1957).

Macleod, R.C., *The Macleods* (Edinburgh 1929).

McLynn, F.J., *France and the Jacobite Rising of 1745* (Edinburgh 1981).

McLynn, F.J., *The Jacobite Army in England 1745: The Final Campaign* (Edinburgh 1983).

MacPherson, C.B., *The Political Theory of Possessive Individualism* (Oxford 1962).

Mahan, A.T., *The Influence of Sea Power in History 1660–1783* (1890).

Mahon, Lord, *History of England from the Peace of Utrecht*, 7 vols (1858).

Maxwell of Kirkconnell, James, *Narrative of Charles, Prince of Wales's Expedition to Scotland in the Year 1745* (Edinburgh 1841).

Menary, G., *The Life and Letters of Duncan Forbes of Culloden* (1936).

Miller, David, *Philosophy and Ideology in Hume's Political Thought* (Oxford 1981).

Miller, Peggy, *A Wife for the Pretender* (1965).

Miller, Peggy, *James* (1972).

Mitchison, R., (ed.), *Essays in Eighteenth-Century History* (1966).

Mitchison, R., *A History of Scotland* (1970).

Mitchison, R., and N. Phillipson (eds.), *Scotland in the Age of Improvement* (Edinburgh 1970).

Mitford, Nancy, *The Sun King* (1966).

Moncreiffe, Sir Iain, and D. Hicks, *The Highland Clans* (1967).

Montesquieu, *Voyages*, ed. Baron de Montesquieu (Bordeaux 1894).

Mossner, E.C., *The Life of David Hume* (1954).

Murdoch, A., *The People Above: Politics and Administration in Mid-Eighteenth Century Scotland* (1980).

Namier, Sir Lewis, *The Structure of Politics at the Accession of George III* (1957).

Nicholas, D., *Intercepted Post* (1956).

Nordmann, Claude, *La Crise du nord* (Paris 1956).

O'Callaghan, J.C., *History of the Irish Brigade in the Service of France* (Glasgow 1870).

Oliphant, T.L.K., *The Jacobite Lairds of Gask* (1870).

Oman, Carola, *Mary of Modena* (1962).

Overton, J.H., *The Non-Jurors* (1902).

Owen, J.B., *The Rise of the Pelhams* (1957).

Owen, J.B., *The Eighteenth Century 1714–1815* (1974).

Owen, J.H., *War at Sea under Queen Anne 1702–1708* (1901).

Petrie, Sir Charles, *The Marshal Duke of Berwick* (1953).

Petrie, Sir Charles, *The Jacobite Movement* (1959).

Pitsligo, Lord, *Moral and Philosophical Essays* (1762).

Pitsligo, Lord, *Thoughts Concerning Man's Condition* (Edinburgh 1854).

Plumb, J.H., *The Growth of Political Stability in England 1675–1725* (1967).

Pocock, J.G.A., *Politics, Language and Time* (1971).

Pocock, J.G.A., *The Machiavellian Moment* (Princeton 1975).

Polnay, Peter de, *Death of a Legend* (1952).

Prebble, John, *Culloden* (1961).

Prebble, John, *The Highland Clearances* (1963).

Prebble, John, *Glencoe* (1966).

Prebble, John, *The Darien Disaster* (1968).

Prebble, John, *Mutiny* (1975).

Pryde, G.S., *The Treaty of Union between Scotland and England 1707* (Edinburgh 1950).

Ramsay, J., of Ochertyre, *Scotland and Scotsmen in the Eighteenth Century* (Edinburgh 1881).

Remond, A., *John Holker* (1946).

Richmond, Sir H.W., *The Navy in the War of 1739–48*, 3 vols (Cambridge 1920).

Robbins, Caroline, *The Eighteenth-Century Commonwealthman* (Cambridge, Mass., 1959).

Robson, R.J., *The Oxfordshire Election of 1754* (Oxford 1949).

Ross, I.S., *Lord Kames and the Scotland of His Day* (Oxford 1972).

Rousseau, J.-J., *Confessions*, Pléiade edn. (Paris 1964).

Rude, G., *Paris and London in the Eighteenth Century* (1970).

Rude, G., *Hanoverian London* (1971).

Rude, G., *Europe in the Eighteenth Century* (1972).

Ruvigny, Marquis of, *The Jacobite Peerage, Baronetage, Knightage and Grants of Honour* (Edinburgh 1904).

Saint-Simon, Louis de Rouvroy, duc de, *Memoires complètes* ed. A. de Boilisle, 41 vols (Paris 1930).

Salmond, J.B., *Wade in Scotland* (1938).

Sareil, Jean, *Les Tencin* (Geneva 1969).

Sedgwick, Romney (ed.), *The History of Parliament: The House of*

Commons 1715–1754, 2 vols (1970).

Seliger, M., *The Liberal Politics of John Locke* (1968).

Seton, Sir Bruce, and J.G. Arnot, *The Prisoners of the '45*, 3 vols (Edinburgh 1929).

Shield, A., *Henry Stuart, Cardinal of York* (1908).

Shield, A., and Andrew Lang, *The King over the Water* (1907).

Simpson, Llewellyn Eardley, *Derby and the Forty-Five* (1933).

Sims, J.G., *The Williamite Confiscations in Ireland 1690–1703* (1956).

Sims, J.G., *The Treaty of Limerick* (Dublin 1961).

Sims, J.G., *Jacobite Ireland 1685–91* (1969).

Sinclair-Stevenson, Christopher, *Inglorious Rebellion: the Jacobite Risings of 1708, 1715, 1719* (1971).

Smith, Annette M., *Jacobite Estates of the Forty-Five* (Edinburgh 1982).

Smollett, T., *A History of England* (1760).

Smout, T.C., *A History of the Scottish People 1560–1830* (1969).

Speck, W.A., *Tory and Whig: The Struggle in the Constituencies 1701–15* (1970).

Speck, W.A., *The Butcher: the Duke of Cumberland and the Suppression of the Forty-Five* (Oxford 1981).

Stephen, L., *English Literature and Society in the Eighteenth Century* (1963).

Straka, G.M., *Anglican Reaction to the Revolution of 1688* (Madison, Wisconsin, 1962).

Sykes, N., *Church and State in the Eighteenth Century* (1930).

Tayler, A. and H., *Jacobites of Aberdeenshire and Banffshire in the '45* (1928).

Tayler, A. and H., *Jacobite Letters to Lord Pitsligo* (1930).

Tayler, A. and H., *The Old Chevalier* (1934).

Tayler, A. and H., *1715: The Story of the Rising* (1936).

Tayler, A. and H., *A Jacobite Exile* (1937).

Tayler, A. and H., *1745 and After* (1938).

Tayler, A. and H., *The Stuart Papers at Windsor* (1939).

Tayler, Henrietta, *The Jacobite Court at Rome in 1719* (Edinburgh 1938).

Tayler, Henrietta, *A Jacobite Miscellany* (Edinburgh 1938).

Tayler, Henrietta, *The Jacobite Epilogue* (1941).

Tayler, Henrietta, *The History of the Rebellion in the years 1745 and 1746* (Oxford 1944).

Tayler, Henrietta, *Prince Charlie's Daughter* (1950).

Terry, C.S., *The Chevalier St. George* (1901).

Terry C.S., *The Albemarle Papers* (Aberdeen 1902).

Terry, C.S., *The Jacobites and the Union* (1922).

Terry, C.S., *The Forty-Five: A Narrative of the Last Jacobite Rising by Several Contemporary Hands* (Cambridge 1922).

Thompson, E.P., *Whigs and Hunters: The Origin of the Black Act* (1975).

Thompson, E.P., with D. Hay and P. Linebaugh (eds), *Albion's Fatal Tree* (1975).

Tomasson, Katherine, *The Jacobite General* (Edinburgh 1958).

Tomasson, Katherine, with F. Buist, *Battles of the '45* (1962).

Vaughan, H.M., *The Last Stuart Queen* (1910).

Vaussard, Maurice, *Daily Life in Italy in the Eighteenth Century* (1968).

Vitelleschi, Marchesa Nobili, *A Court in Exile*, 2 vols (1902).

Voltaire, *Oeuvres Complètes*, ed. Moland (Paris 1885).

Voltaire, *Correspondance*, ed. Besterman (Geneva 1970).

Voltaire, *Précis du siècle de Louis XV*, ed. Beuchot (Paris 1888).

Wall, Maureen, *The Penal Laws 1691–1760* (Dublin 1961).

Walpole, Horace, *Memoirs of the Reign of George II*, ed. Lord Holland, 3 vols (1846).

Walpole, Horace, *Correspondence* (Yale edition), ed. W.S. Lewis, 39 vols (New Haven 1974).

Ward, W.R., *Georgian Oxford* (Oxford 1958).

Warrand, Duncan (ed.), *More Culloden Papers*, 5 vols (Inverness 1930).

Waugh, W.T., *James Wolfe, Man and Soldier* (Montreal 1928).

Weber, Max, *The Theory of Social and Economic Organisation* (1947).

Western, J.R., *The English Militia* (1965).

Western, J.R., *Monarchy and Revolution* (1972).

Wilson, A.M., *French Foreign Policy during the Administration of Cardinal Fleury 1726–43* (Cambridge, Mass., 1936).

Yorke, Philip C., *The Life and Correspondence of Philip Yorke, Earl of Hardwicke*, 3 vols (Cambridge 1913).

Youlton, J.W. (ed.), *John Locke: Problems and Perspectives* (Cambridge 1969).

Youngson, A.J., *After the Forty-Five: The Economic Impact on the Scottish Highlands* (Edinburgh 1973).

Index